RAMBO

RAMBO

THE TRUE ACCOUNT OF SPECIAL FORCES OFFICER
MAJOR SUDHIR WALIA

Col Ashutosh Kale

An imprint of
Srishti Publishers & Distributors

Srishti Publishers & Distributors
A unit of AJR Publishing LLP
212A, Peacock Lane
Shahpur Jat, New Delhi – 110 049

editorial@srishtipublishers.com

First Published by Bold
an imprint of Srishti Publishers & Distributors in 2024

Dedicated to the men of 9 Para (Special Forces)
and everything that they live by,

&

To the spirit called INDIA.

Contents

FOREWORD

Major Sudhir Kumar was posted as my ADC (Security) soon after I took over as Chief of Indian Army. By then, he had already made a name for himself as a thorough professional, dedicated and exceptionally brave officer in his unit 9 PARA (Special Forces) and others who knew him. He had considerable combat experience and had been awarded the Sena Medal for gallantry twice. In his last action in Jammu and Kashmir, he had been wounded, but was physically fit now. After he reported to me, I also learnt that he had topped a Special Forces course in the USA. While his colleagues in India fondly called him Rambo, his course-mates on the Special Forces Course called him 'Captain Coomer'. Towards the end of his course, out of respect for his professional competence, they started calling him 'Colonel'.

Gradually, like other ADCs, he became a member of our family and a mentor for the two other ADCs.

In the performance of his duties, I found Sudhir always very alert, responsible and mature. He was well read and took interest in all types of books. Off parade, he was sober; but on occasion, he would be full of life. He had a good sense of humour and enjoyed the company of his male and female friends. During a Lohri function in the Army House, he sang many Hindi, Punjabi and Himachali songs. He spoke less to me, but would chat more easily with my wife and travelled with us very often, within India and abroad. One day, he told my wife that he would buy a house in Panchkula, where we also planned to settle after retirement.

When the Kargil war was mid-way, Sudhir's tenure with me was almost over. He asked to be sent back to his unit fighting the war. That, he told me, was the tradition of his battalion. In a war or war-like situation, 9 Para officers, wherever posted, would find a way to re-join their battalion. Not wanting to break such a norm, or his spirit, I let him go. Before his return to the unit, the Army House gave him a very affectionate send-off, which he richly deserved.

Sudhir was a brave and over-enthusiastic soldier who would volunteer for every challenging mission. Within ten days of his departure, he led his 'A' Team to capture Zulu Top, over 5200 metres high in the Mashkoh sector. That was just one day before we declared successful achievement of the political mission given to the armed forces during Kargil war. In this action, thirteen Pakistani soldiers belonging to the 19 Frontier Force were killed.

Few days later, when I questioned him on going for this action without acclimatization, he said, 'Sir, you know that I am a Pahari (from the mountains). I don't need acclimatization.' With a smile, I told him not to break the laid-down rules again.

After the Kargil war, Sudhir re-joined the rest of his unit engaged in anti-terrorist operations in the Kashmir Valley. Exactly a month later, Sudhir volunteered for a mission tasked to search and destroy a terrorists' hideout in the dense Haphruda forest near Kupwara. He and his buddy Naik Kheem Singh had spotted and surprised the terrorists deep in the jungle. In the ensuing fire fight, they killed nine terrorists. It was a daring action. Sudhir led all the way from the front, but was fatally wounded, and died before he could be evacuated to the hospital. He was recommended for, and received, Ashok Chakra, the highest gallantry award during peacetime.

As I wrote somewhere else, the nation lost a gallant and a specially gifted soldier on 29th August 1999. My loss was personal. In a short period, he had become an affectionate and responsible member of our family.

Writing a biography of a born combat leader who unfortunately lived for only 30 years cannot be easy. Colonel Ashutosh Kale has done immense research on the subject and admirably utilised his military experience and literary talent in writing this book. His narration of combat situations wherein Sudhir and his colleagues were involved is most realistic and gripping. Also, having already authored two books – one involving national progress from a humane perspective and the other related to a historical and mythical episode in a foreign country – he has developed a very strong sense of dramatic storytelling and writing style.

Rambo is an insightful, engaging and thrilling book.

Gen V.P. Malik, PVSM, AVSM
19th Chief of Army Staff of the Indian Army

Praise for the book

"I knew Maj Walia well. We were both posted in Army HQ together. Rambo is a gripping, intriguing, and a must read book on the brave heart. I found the book extremely enjoyable."

- Brig Khushal Thakur

War veteran, Social activist,
Defence analyst, Ex CO 18 Grenadiers

PREFACE

Writing is always a release. Writing this story has been a catharsis. This story had to be told.

Not because Maj Sudhir Walia was brave, not because his tales of daredevilry and courage are beyond the beliefs of ordinary men, swayed by consuming ambition, rivalries and personal gains.

Stories such as these, men such as these, deeds such as these, awaken our conscience. How else can we transcend politics, regionalism, faith, caste and greed?

How else will a man sleeping in his warm bed realise the immense sacrifice that goes into providing him that security? When will our hearts beat in sync as a nation? How else will Rabindranath Tagore's cry ring true?

Where the mind is without fear
and the head is held high,
Into that heaven of freedom, my Father,
let my country awake.

If his story inspires one boy from a nation of around 150 crores to grow up into another Sudhir Walia, his sacrifice will pursue redemption. One boy.

In the narrative, I have mentioned the family of Maj. Sudhir Walia only in passing. Not because their sacrifice can be disregarded, but because the story focuses on the military nature of operations. In fact, I found the family incredibly proud of the hero, Sudhir Walia. They just mourn their son, whose tragic death has left open a raw wound. They keep his memory alive, ensuring that his legacy lives. But is it only their sole responsibility? Honouring the memory and legacy of a fallen hero is the collective responsibility of the nation and the society at large.

To my uniformed brethren and everyone who knows this story personally, cut me some slack. Built word by word, I have endeavoured to stay close to the truth. At places I did dramatise, unapologetically, using my creative licence as an author only to emphasise a story that was bereft of detail after nearly twenty-five years. Brickbats and bouquets I shall accept equally, as is bound to be, given the emotional nature of such a project.

Jai Hind.
Col. Ashutosh Kale

ACKNOWLEDGEMENTS

I wish to thank my literary agent, Suhail Mathur and The Book Bakers literary agency, for bringing me this assignment. By convincing me, he has done me more than a favour. I cannot thank him enough.

Arup Bose, Publisher, Srishti Publishers – thank you for believing in me. Thank you for all the guidance, encouragement and patience. You gave me a renewed sense of purpose when I was losing mine. The untiring, Stuti Sharma Gupta, Chief Editor, who indomitably took up my unending corrections and the tech snafus that I launched. I am in awe of your patience and perseverance.

Thank you ADG PI for sanctioning this project. The endless coordination, my needless calls and for going out of your way. And for slicing through red tape, if it existed.

I want to thank Gen. Ved Malik and Mrs. Malik, for graciously indulging me. They set the pen rolling and put me in context.

Anirban, I want to express my deep gratitude to you. Your careful study, meticulous ability and skillful artistry with the sketches have inspired imagination to a complex story line.

The gallant Commanding Officer and men of 9 Para (Special Forces), I cannot thank you enough. The extent of your help is only surpassed by the loftiness of your deeds. You have been spontaneous, willing and spot on. Despite the punishing schedule of your responsibilities, you stood steadfast in your commitment.

To the nameless few, the soul brothers, the band of Maj. Sudir Walia, who breathed fire and emotion in this story. You brought alive a hero. Your reverence, sinewed by emotion, laced with unbridled loyalty infused this story with his spirit. You owed him that, in this life or the next. You have stood in heroic silence, cherishing his memories long after the bugles calls, and the drums rolls stopped. You helped me piece the mosaic of his life. In your homage, I have found my salvation.

Abbreviations and Acronyms

ADC	Aide de Camp
Air OP	Air Observation Post
APHC	All Parties Hurriyat Conference
AC	Ashok Chakra
Bde. HQ	Brigade Headquarters
Brig.	Brigadier
Capt.	Captain
Chief/ COAS	Chief of Army Staff
CI	Counter Insurgency
Col.	Colonel
Corps Cdr.	Corps Commander
Div HQ	Division Headquarters
DGMO	Director General of Military Operations
DGMI	Director General of Military Intelligence
DGISI	Director General ISI
FCNA	Forces Command Northern Areas
Gen.	General
GHQ	General Headquarters, Pakistan
GOC	General Officer Commanding
GR	Gorkha Rifles
Gren	Grenadiers
HAWS	High Altitude Warfare School
Heptr	Helicopter
Hav.	Havaldar
HQ	Headquarters
HuA	Harkat-ul-Ansar

HuM	Harkat-ul- Mujahideen
HuJI	Harkat-ul-Jehad-al-Islami
HM	Hizbul Mujahideen
Int	Intelligence
IED	Improvised Explosive Device
Inf Div	Infantry Division
ISI	Inter-Services Intelligence
J&K	Jammu and Kashmir
JCO	Junior Commissioned Officer
JKLF	Jammu and Kashmir Liberation Front
JeM	Jaish-e-Mohamad
JeI	Jaamat-e-Islami
LoC	Line of Control
LTTE	Liberation Tigers of Tamil Elam
Lt.	Lieutenant
Lt. Col.	Lieutenant Colonel
Lt. Gen.	Lieutenant General
Maj.	Major
Maj. Gen.	Major General
MI	Military Intelligence
Mtn Div	Mountain Division
Mtn Bde	Mountain Brigade
MVC	Maha Vir Chakra
NLI	Northern Light Infantry
Nk.	Naik
Op(s)	Operations(s)
Pak/Paki	Pakistan
PARA	The Parachute Regiment

PIKA	Pulemyot Kalashnikova Machine Gun
PM	Prime Minister
POK	Pakistan Occupied Kashmir
PVC	Param Vir Chakra
R&AW	Research and Analysis Wing
Regt	Regiment
RR	Rashtriya Rifles
RV	Rendezvous
SM	Sena Medal
SF	Special Forces
SLR	7.62 Self Loading Rifle, replaced by the 5.56 INSAS Rif in Kargil
Sig Int	Signal Intelligence
US	United States
UN	United Nations
VHF	Very High Frequency
VrC	Vir Chakra

LIST OF ILLUSTRATIONS

THE MAKING OF JIHAD

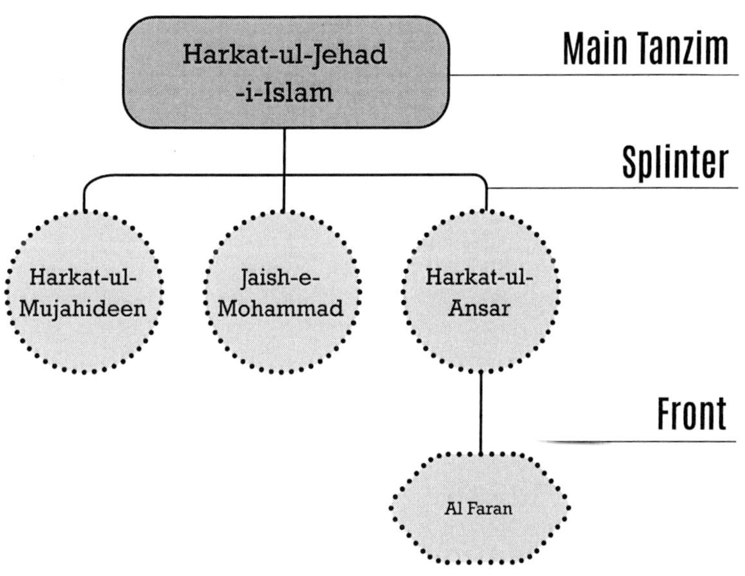

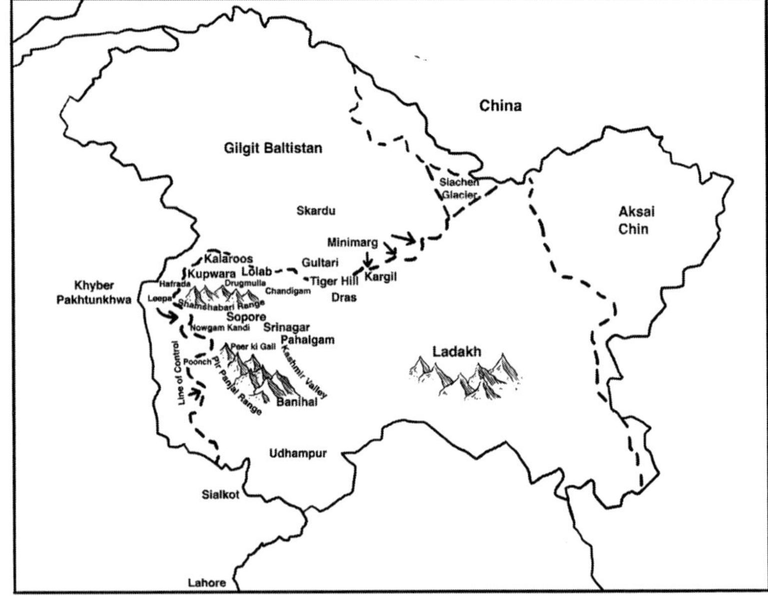

Jammu & Kashmir

KARGIL

Cliffs, Courage & Glory
Operation Vijay

> *I won't die in an accident or of any disease.*
>
> *I will die in glory.*

Mushkoh Valley
24th July 1999

He sniffed the air like a predator on a hunt. The unmistakable pungency of kerosene, urine and…fear. Leering, he wet his cracked sore lips. He would get his kill and his glory. Clinging on to the rock, he heaved himself up, just an inch.

Dried mucus caked his nostrils, constricting the already rarefied oxygen. The wind stung his face and eyes. His fingertips were raw. The skin peeling off from the sub-zero temperatures of the rough rock surface. He only felt a thrill surging through his veins, unmindful of the screaming muscles. They did not matter.

Squeezing his eyes, he forced out the tears blurring his vision. He focused on the ghostlike figure, silhouetted by the blizzard beyond the rocky sangar wall. India sweltered in the summer heat. But here in the Mushkoh valley, at 5200 metres above sea level, the harsh winter was still clinging on, refusing to leave. Like the Pakistani intruders who had infiltrated into the ridgelines of Kargil.

Men sweated here to pluck out the enemy violating the sanctity of their country. Hanging next to him, Naik Vinod nudged Sudhir, pointing down at the small band of brave men – Anchal, Bijli, Kheem Singh, Darpan – balanced precariously on the narrow ledge. It ended in a dark, bottomless abyss.

It had taken the Alpha team all night, in pitch darkness, to clamber up through the minefield, fixing the ropes. Defying gravity on the vertigo rock face. A free climb was only possible without cumbersome gloves. Sudhir had attempted the climb, barely 10 days after leaving Delhi. Without any acclimatisation.

Huddled against the howling icy wind, they shielded their freezing bodies against an outcrop. Thawing their frozen trigger fingers against warm breaths, the Alpha team savoured what could be their last moments. Bravery aside, it could go either way. A hollow pull in the stomach, the bladder pain from frozen tubes refusing to piss out, lungs heaving from exhaustion and the nagging fear were familiar sensations. They knew how to overcome fear. The panic that could blow an untrained mind apart. That's why they had risked it, again and again. And had survived. Till now.

They trusted him. More than their own beliefs, more than their own gods. In this moment, they wanted no one else. Fused with their souls, he felt bonded with each of them; a mysterious feeling that connects men, willing to die together… for each other.

In the breaking light of the false dawn, he quickly pointed out the positions as best as he could. Outnumbered, they always operated at odds, in small teams. Surprise and the violence of their attack would give them the edge.

The Zulu ridge comprised of three distinct complexes – the Tri Junction, the Spur and the Top. The 3/3 Gurkha Rifles had captured the Tri Junction and Spur. The escaping enemy soldiers had gathered at the Top.

It was now the mission of the 9 Para (Special Forces) to capture the Top.

Looming ominously beyond was the dark, craggy escarpment, marking the end of the Zulu Top. Between them and the gigantic rock was a narrow strip of land, a mere 75 metres long. They knew they would have to fight for every metre of that ledge. Step by bloody step.

* * *

Vinod
Palampur

The spectacular Dhauladhar range has nestled Palampur in its lap since eternity. The thin mountain air here smells different. Besides the oxygenated purity, it also carries an essence of something inexplicable. It infuses young men with something profound. Vikram Batra, Saurabh Kalia, Sudhir Walia and a score of other young men. Nothing like this exists in any other part of the country.

I stood on the steps of the proud house, my eyes transfixed on the picture on the wall and the framed citation. It was the first thing you saw.

Holding on to a pillar to dam the flood of emotions that swept through me, I bowed in reverence. The memories came rushing back, as they always did, when I made this pilgrimage.

I am Vinod. I served in the 9 Para (SF). Sudhir sir was my mentor, my confidant, my soul brother. We had spent years together deciphering life and death.

This is his story.

* * *

Batalik
3rd May, 1999

Tashi Namgyal, a 56-year-old shepherd, had gone up to the mountains above his village, near Batalik, about 60 Kms from Kargil. Breathing in the crisp fresh air, he searched for his yak that had gone missing. It had probably wandered off towards the lush meadows in the upper reaches, which had come alive after the thawing of the winter frost.

As he scanned the mountains with his binoculars, he saw something that sent a tingle down his spine. He stumbled, crushing the yellow wildflowers, splashing through the streams and scraping his shins. He burst through to the nearest army post. Blabbering, he stuttered, frightened.

> *"Groups of men in Pathani suits and…soldiers in camouflaged uniforms. digging… digging bunkers. Some of them are armed…*
>
> *…not possible to tell their numbers…but one thing I am sure of, they have come from the other side of the LoC."*

* * *

Bajrang Post, Kaskar, 13,000 feet.
15th May 1999

Lieutenant Saurabh Kalia and five soldiers of 4 Jat, were out on a routine patrol. They got engaged in a firefight with the intruders. When they ran out of ammunition, they were encircled and captured before reinforcements could reach them. Radio Skardu[1] boasted of their capture, a confirmation of their being alive.

* * *

Force Command Northern Area (FCNA) Headquarters, Gilgit, POK.
October 1998

The tenure as the military attaché in Washington had not softened the hawkish attitude of Major General Javed Hasan, Commander of FCNA. FCNA was a division-sized force. The notorious battle plans had been devised by the hard-nosed general. He planned to employ the locally recruited Northern Light Infantry units under him to maintain secrecy. Only officers were posted from the regular Pakistan army, the men were Pashtun and Balti.

The new appointee, the Rawalpindi based 10 Corps Commander Lieutenant General Mahmud Ahmed, had gleefully codenamed it OP

---

[1] A radio channel in Pakistan.

Koh Paima (KP), the Mountain Climber.

So secretive were the plans that even the prime minister, Nawaz Sharif, was unaware of its existence. Not only was the sinister plan hidden from the naval and air force chiefs, but the GHQ[2], the DGMO, DGMI, DGISI, and principal staff officers were all kept in the dark.

Only four people were privy to the hushed plan. The infamous Kargil clique of Pakistan.

Commanders of FCNA and 10 Corps, Chief of General Staff, General Aziz Khan and the Army Chief, himself. All hand-picked by General Pervez Musharraf.

Like a seasoned chess player, Musharraf had placed his men in key positions within hours of being appointed as Chief of the Pakistan Army on 7th October 1998.

The clique conducted planning and meetings in small rooms, their secretive maps spread across dinner tables. Even the troops were told that this was a mere tactical exercise.

Bristling from the loss of Siachen to India, the Pakistan GHQ had tossed the draft plan around within the Pakistan army echelons since 1984. They reviewed, debated and stored the plan in secret files at the Military Operations directorate.

The implications and impracticability of the plan ruled out its feasibility.

Taking advantage of the Indian Army vacating posts because of extreme weather, the FCNA sent in the NLI[3]. The incursion was initially planned in only one sector; through the Pakistani 80th Infantry Brigade in Minimarg, opposite Dras.

Finding gaps, the creep forward by the FCNA resulted in the occupation of an unprecedented 140 posts across five sectors in a frontage of 150 kilometres.

---

[2] *General Headquarters equivalent to India's Army Headquarters*
[3] *Northern Light Infantry Battalions*

Pakistan had about 700 troops deployed on the ridge lines on the Indian side. However, with troop rotations and other factors, nearly 4,000 troops finally took part in the operations.

They occupied the heights in October, within the same month of Musharraf's takeover. A man in a hurry, he had not wasted any time after assuming command.

It took seven months for their discovery by the grazers and the summer patrols of the Indian Army, after the snows melted.

It was a huge intelligence failure for India. The Srinagar based XV Corps and Leh based 3 Mountain Division had paid little heed to ground inputs of heightened activity across the Line of Control (LoC).

Interestingly, Nawaz Sharif and the rest of the Pakistani establishment got to know about the operation only when all hell broke loose. Around the time India got to know. India was embarrassed, but Nawaz Sharif faced an even greater humiliation.

The Pakistani government's ignorance of what its own army had carried out in Kargil matched the Indian government's ignorance of the extent to which the Pakistani army had walked into India.

* * *

Ojhari Camp, Rawalpindi
17th May, 1999

Deceived, fed with half-truths and briefed on maps without LoC markings, Nawaz Sharif's ignorance grew like a mushroom in the dark.

The intrusions had already been discovered 14 days ago by Tashi Namgyal. Lt. Saurabh Kalia's patrol had been captured two days back. When the truth could no longer be hidden, a meeting was held at ISI's Ojhari Camp in the Rawalpindi military district on the 17th of May.

Maj. Gen. Javed Hasan started briefing on the large map.

"I... we cannot go ahead with all this." His hand shook. A hesitant Nawaz Sharif was unconvinced. "It's not right." His neck felt hot.

This would kill the recent upswing in the India-Pak relations, the Bus diplomacy, the Indian PM's friendly overtures. Most importantly, he was against deceiving Atal Bihari Vajpayee.

Javed Hasan exchanged a glance with Gen. Musharraf.

"*Fatah-e-Kashmir.*" The words were deliberate, "*The Liberator of Kashmir.*"

Peeling his eyes from the map, Nawaz Sharif craned his neck to look at Gen. Aziz sitting on his left.

"Miyan Sahib, you would be equal only to *Quaid-e-Azam.*"

Nawaz Sharif sat up, squaring his shoulders. He picked up a *chilgoza* (pine nuts) from a silver bowl and chewed on it. His eyes lit up. He nodded and turned his attention back to the map.

"Go ahead… continue your briefing."

Gen. Aziz watched Nawaz Sharif. A sly smile touched his lips. Seduced with a grandiose image, Nawaz Sharif had succumbed to the general.

By then, unknown to Nawaz Sharif, the die had already been cast.

* * *

May 1999

Peace was in the air. Indian Prime Minister Atal Bihari Vajpayee and his Pakistani counterpart Nawaz Sharif had signed the Lahore Declaration just four months back. Vajpayee's Lahore bus trip in February 1999 had stirred hopes of bonhomie between two distrustful neighbours.

However, all this bonhomie crumbled to dust.

* * *

9th June, 1999

Lt. Saurabh Kalia and the five soldiers were kept alive till 7th June. In the 23 days of captivity, they were subjected to barbaric torture; cigarette burns, crushed skulls, ear drums pierced with rods, broken teeth, eyes punctured before being removed, chipped noses and amputated limbs and genitalia.

They were shot on 7th June. The mutilated bodies were handed over on 9th June.

* * *

June 1999

What had looked like a small intrusion by some ill-trained militants turned out to be a full-fledged military operation of the Pakistani army. The infantry patrols confirmed multiple infiltrations across the LoC.

The intrusions spread from the lower Mushkoh Valley in Dras to Kargil, the Batalik sector, Chorbat La and the Turtuk Sector, south of Siachen.

Additional troops were quickly inducted into Kargil from Jammu and Kashmir. The 9 Para (SF), also called the Ghost Battalion[4], was one of them.

As the fighting intensified, casualties mounted.

Prime time television beamed video grabs of young officers leading attacks fearlessly; capturing peak after peak with the Bofors guns booming in the background.

* * *

Horrifyingly, India discovered, in stages, the scale of operation, the number of peaks occupied and finally, who had occupied them.

Intercepts of the Pashtun and Balti transmissions led India to believe that these were the mujahideen. This was also widely reported in the Indian media initially.

Pakistan brilliantly fed this misconception and used it to strengthen India's belief through deception. Pakistan ordered its troops to shed its uniforms and wear Pathani suits. It kept up the intercepts in the dialects and parroted the story internationally too, till their bluff was called out.

---

[4] 9 Para (Special Forces) was nicknamed the Ghost Battalion because they appeared silently, struck terror and melted away like ghosts. It was the secretive nature of their operations.

Misjudging the military situation in May, India's hesitant response strikingly improved by June.

India pressed in the Air Force. Precision-guided munitions, gunships and Mirages shredded the invaders. Amassed Bofors and artillery in direct fire pulverised the interlopers and the mountains.

India now unleashed a military and diplomatic blitzkrieg.

* * *

Raisina Hill, New Delhi
5th July, 1998

A young captain sitting in his plush office on Raisina Hill, flanking the Rashtrapati Bhawan, studied the battle reports as they passed his desk. His boss, the Chief of the Army Staff sat next door. Enraged, the captain felt chained to his desk, almost claustrophobic. Trained for action, he couldn't wait much longer.

Gen. Ved Malik, the Chief of the Army Staff, reviewed the request for immediate transfer with swelling pride, tinged with sadness. Posted to the Army HQ from his unit 9 Para (SF), the application had been submitted by his own aide-de-camp, Captain Sudhir Kumar Walia, requesting for permission to rejoin his unit in Kargil to fight the Pakis.

It was his right as a soldier.

* * *

"Why can't he just stay here in Delhi…safely?" the clerk in the MS[5] branch, was puzzled. "He's got a glamorous job."

Not everybody became the ADC to the Chief of Army Staff, after all. The young soldier, carrying the sanctioned application, met the clerk's bewildered gaze with a smirk.

"That's why we call him Rambo," said the soldier sitting next to him, with a quiver in his voice that made the clerk pause and stare at the receding back of the paratrooper.

---

[5] *Military Secretary Branch – responsible for postings of officers.*

* * *

The distant ringing of the phone reminded Sudhir how far away his home was from the bustle of Delhi, tucked away in an obscure narrow lane with the fragrance of eucalyptus and geraniums wafting in the air. He pictured his mother, sitting on the veranda, winnowing grain in the mellow afternoon sun.

Closing his eyes, he listened to the ringing, knowing she would be rushing back in, panting from the effort. Four rings before she picked up.

"Sudhir? Hello… Hello… Sudhir? Where…how are you, beta?" Her voice was thick, hesitant.

The sadness in her voice tugged at his heart. A lump in his throat made him gulp painfully.

Her aging face and wrinkled hands belied her personality. He recollected her picture from his childhood, with her vibrant red bindi and the prominent Dogri nose ring. Her once thick, dark hair was now thin and grey.

He swivelled his chair, the leather creaking, to face the office wall. "*Ija*[6], how do you know it's me?"

"The ringing…it's different. I can tell."

He could tell she was struggling to keep her voice steady, her words tight and controlled.

"It's always the same, Ma!" He pretended to tease her.

"No, yours…it's different." Exasperation crept into her voice. "Aren't you coming home?"

"I can't, Ija. That's why…" He swallowed his words with his pain. "They have cancelled all leaves."

"Yes… Munni heard in college." Her voice was something like a sigh. Asha—Sudhir called her Munni—and Arun were his younger siblings. They looked up to him. He always carried that weight. Rajeswari Devi

---

6   Mother in Pahari language

refrained from adding that their TV set had stopped functioning. Sudhir had planned to replace the old set during his next leave.

"I am leaving Delhi, Ma. I'm going back to my unit." He tried to sound steady.

"Oh, and the General? He won't…?"

"My unit needs me more, Ma." The resolute tenor was unmistakable. "My men...too."

"We… we need you too, Sudhir," she said, her tone gentle yet urgent.

Drawing in his breath sharply, Sudhir's fingers clutched the handset, turning his knuckles white.

"It will be cold, Sudhir." Her gentle concern cleaved his heart, driving another wedge of pain.

"I have the sweater, Ma," he chuckled, "and some of your pickle. All packed and ready." His hollow laugh didn't quite sound right. It was a war; this time might turn out to be very different.

He never told her, but every time he missed her, he would snuggle up in the familiar softness of the sweater. He could feel her love in each stitch, her warmth in each knot.

There was silence at the other end of the line.

He could hear her heavy breathing. He knew, she was holding back her tears.

"Ma?" he said, grimacing as the painful lump reappeared. "Look after yourself, Ma. I'll be home soon." Disconnecting the call abruptly, he gulped down a glass of water. Waiting for his bloody nerves to quieten.

The guilt of not spending enough time with her often gnawed at him. Growing up away from home, when he went away to Sainik School and then the Army service had kept him further away.

She had always been his safety net. And yet, he hadn't done enough for her. He promised himself, he would. Soon.

* * * *

Dras
June, 1999

The 8 Mtn Div HQ[7] was in Matayin, a village twenty-one kilometres from Dras.

They studied the map in silence. The crackling static of the radio set reminding them that the battle was far from over. Difficult choices and heavy sacrifices weighed on them, yet they were determined to succeed.

By now, it was confirmed that these were enemy troops from the elite Special Service Group and four to seven battalions of the NLI.

"So, what do you think?" posed the general, his brows furrowed in concentration. The clipped voice did not falter. The sleepless nights marked by the puffed eyes and saddlebags below them. He eyed the packet of India Kings next to him, but controlled his instincts.

Grappling with the uncertain situation, they had pumped 8 Mtn Div,[8] into Kargil.

As General Officer Commanding, 8 Mtn Div, Maj. Gen. Mohinder Puri had the moral responsibility to ensure that his men succeeded in the mission assigned by the COAS[9] Gen. Ved Malik – 'Evict the intruders and recapture the heights'.

The staff officer tiptoed in. His presence marked only by the rustle of the papers he held. Glancing over at the trio before handing the situation report, his eyes flickered in awe and reverence. Since Kargil began, between them, the three officers had delivered the most spectacular victories to a grateful nation.

The first was Tololing, India's inaugural victory. Taking eleven hours to climb up the 16,000-foot peak in the Dras sector, the enemy had occupied the formidable Tololing, reigning over the Srinagar-Kargil-Leh highway.

---

[7] *Mountain Division Headquarters*
[8] 8 Mountain Division, specializing in mountain warfare.
[9] *Chief of Army Staff*

56 Mountain Brigade led by Brig. Amar Aul, captured Tololing after three weeks of intense fighting. The final assault on 13th June was a hand-to-hand fight between 6 NLI and 2 Rajputana Rifles. The capture of Tololing was a turning point in the conflict.

In the other sectors, the Indian Army reclaimed 140 vantage points, the sound of their guns echoing over 150 kilometres. Such was the heroism, that the tales of grit and spunk seemed to eclipse the impressive heights re-captured. No mission was too difficult. No peak unscalable. No sacrifice extreme. No victory unachievable.

As the nation sat spellbound, the valour of its sons beamed through TV sets, brought tears to a billion eyes. Never had India experienced such frenzy up close, such raw emotion or such disregard to personal life for the sanctity of the country by an entire generation of young men.

Vikram Batra, Manoj Kumar Pandey, Anuj Nayyar, Rajesh Adhikari, Gurinder Suri, Balwan Singh, Yogendra Singh Yadav, Keishing C. Nongrum, Sonam Wangchuk, Padmapani Acharya, Digendra Kumar, Sanjay Kumar – just a few of these heroes; each a legend, infused with a spirit that became the singular war cry of the nation.

* * *

And then came Tiger Hill.

The highest feature in the Dras sector, Tiger Hill was the pinnacle of the conflict. It not only dominated the highway, but allowed the Pakistani intruders to direct artillery fire across a wide area. Tasked for the capture of Tiger Hill, Brigadier MPS Bajwa commanding 192 Mtn Bde, planned to launch the 18 Grenadiers and the 8 Sikh.

Along with the Tiger Hill attack, they planned another attack. The recapturing of Sando Top – a peak close to Tiger Hill.

"We need to starve them … cut off their tails," said Maj. Gen. Puri.

The Brigadier, his eyes fixed on the map, suggested that they create a foothold on Sando Top as well. "We must destroy the Pakistani dump at Gultar."

"That's behind Sando. So, we capture Sando first and then move to Gultar," said the general, tracing the ridgeline on the map.

This would also cut off the Pakistani reinforcements, while Tiger Hill was under attack.

The approach had vertical ice walls. The Brigadier considered the problem.

"We need paratroopers, sir." They were trained for such assaults.

"I'll request the Corps Cdr[10]," said the general. "No promises."

Waiting for the call, Maj. Gen. Puri paced his office, deep in thought. A hundred things flashed through his head. The fights so far had been treacherous. Only the determination of the junior leadership and the overwhelming firepower had brought in the victories.

A vein throbbed in his temple.

Opening the drawer, he ran his fingers over the sealed envelope from his daughter, Ayesha, that had been sitting there for two days. The shrill ringing of the phone cut through the silence. "Sir, the Corps Commander." The operator announced briskly.

His gaze held the letter for a moment longer, then pushing the drawer in, he sighed, "Perhaps after Tiger Hill."

"Mohinder, request accepted," said the Corps Cdr. firmly.

"About time, sir," said Maj. Gen. Puri, stiffening. "We are losing precious time."

The staff officer jumped to his feet, as the general strode into his office.

"Get me the CO 9 Para." He was impatient, "and fast."

"Yes, sir." The staff officer, scrambled for the telephone.

Colonel John de Britto, CO 9 Para, heard the deep rumble of the Bofors guns as he arrived to meet to meet Gen. Puri.

* * * *

---

[10] *Commander 15 Corps, based in Srinagar*

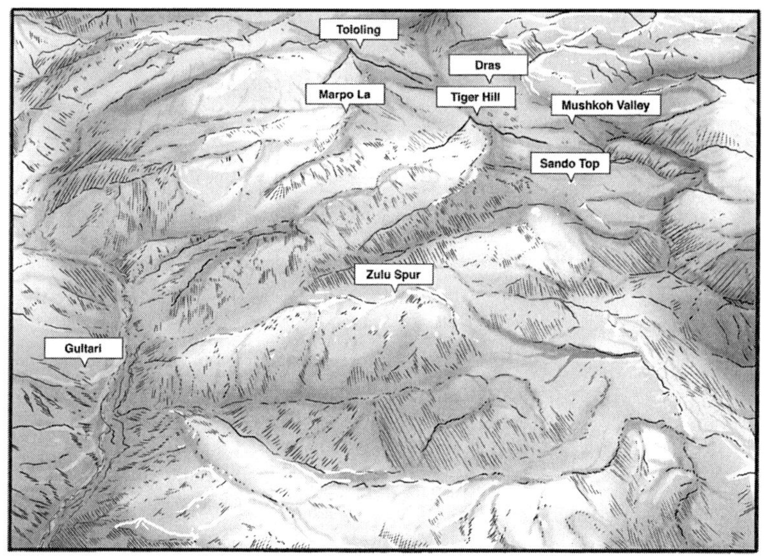

Dras, Tololing, Tiger Hill, Zulu Spur, Kargil.

Sando Top
30th June, 1999

Enemy positions along the ridge lines were unknown, but they could risk a chance. Maj. Gen. Puri gave the go ahead to 9 Para. This was their first mission in Kargil, and Sudhir was yet to join the unit.

Maj. Nirmal Dhaliwal led the 70-odd men of Bravo Team on this daredevil mission. Unaware of what was to come, they did not realise that this mission would leave a lingering dread that would haunt them for a long time.

Accompanying him were two more officers, Maj. Gaurav Rishi and Capt. Milan Nalawade and two young lieutenants. The team fixed the ropes and started the climb.

All night long, they battled the freezing temperatures and snow, while the near-precipitous slopes challenged them all the way. Every step on the ropes was a struggle.

Muscles in agony, their legs felt rubbery from the strain of the rigorous climb. Their hands had gone raw from gripping the rugged rocks and ropes. When the night faded, they were still short of the peak.

With a team of experienced climbers, Lt. Prince Jose and Lt. Ashish Hooda moved ahead to make the final push towards the Top.

Already decorated with a Sena Medal before Kargil, the twenty-six-year-old Lt. Prince Jose had led a raid on a militant stronghold in Tilpatra forest, Kupwara. Vinod was in his troop that day. They had eliminated six militants.

The rest of the team, with Nirmal Dhaliwal was following behind. After another hour of climbing, the squad gazed up at a tall seventy-degree ice wall, the sheerness of it causing them to take a breath. With a sense of urgency, they quickly affixed the ropes to climb the ice face. They had to make it to the Top before daylight.

As the ropes were being secured, a paratrooper noticed some movement. His hair bristled, *"Sir!"* he cried out, alerting Jose.

Jose's voice was barely audible, "My god."

Close to 30 enemy soldiers were moving towards Sando Top from a connecting ridge line. Frantic, he bellowed through the radio set, "Artillery… Covering fire… Sando Top."

The artillery already had the grid designations for the objectives. They promptly poured fire on Sando Top, the adjoining saddle and a nallah close by. But the Indian troops were close by, and they had to be careful.

Soon the Indian artillery had to stop its punishing barrage as they could not differentiate between their own and the enemy positions.

Wanting to close in quickly, the 9 Para squad continued to scale the ice wall and reached a ledge. The enemy's mortars now pelted Sando Top with a ruthless fury, the explosions echoing in the air. The Indian artillery started a retaliatory bombardment to suppress the enemy fire.

The air, thick with black smoke, clung to their throats, as shells whistled overhead. The explosions sent shrapnel flying through the air. Each boom caused a sharp pain in their eardrums, the pressure wave hitting their faces.

Stuck on the ledge, they clung on for life, hugging the wall. An artillery shell landed ten metres away. A chill ran down their spines. The man closest to the shell licked his lips, hugging his weapon tightly. The one next to him pressed his back into the wall, desperately trying to shield himself. The soldier standing next to him gritted his teeth, the veins standing on his neck. Jose felt his heart thump.

Every moment seemed to last an eternity. They watched the shell with a macabre fascination, a growing dread in the pit of their stomachs, every man wondering if this would be his last breath. With their feet dangerously close to the edge of the narrow ledge, the men huddled, the smell of sweat and fear heavy in the air.

Luckily for them, it did not go off, possibly because of a faulty fuse. Jose smiled, recalling Sudhir once telling him, "Fear...it affects everyone. It's how you handle it, that's important."

The relief was however short-lived.

A second shell landed close by. This time, it exploded. The pressure wave blew Jose away. Thrown off the ledge, he landed a hundred meters below, unmoving.

"Is… he alive?" screamed a soldier, watching his immobile body. Two soldiers climbed down unfazed by the detonations.

"Yes, a pulse… he's breathing."

"Pull him up!" yelled someone. They dragged a bleeding, unconscious Jose precariously up.

A small red trickle flowed out from his ears. Mucus and blood blew out of his nostrils in darkish bubbles, tinged by the soot on his face.

He sputtered awake some thirty minutes later, breathing in spasms. Spitting out the dirt from his mouth, he looked around, glazed and disoriented. Bloodied, his tongue hurt. His buddy held him down, as a numbed Jose made feeble attempts to stand up.

Realisation slowly broke through his groggy brain, speared by the piercing pain jamming his thinking. He closed his eyes again, as explosions rattled the ground he slept on. His memory crept back gradually. Rudely shaken by the shoulders, he opened his eyes. The memory lapse and head injury would affect him later in life, causing a stroke. For the moment, he just thanked god that he was alive. Springing to his feet, he barked orders.

It was almost 0730 hrs. The early morning sun broke through the haze and smoke. Suddenly, the sharp crack of fire echoed around them. Accurate machine gun fire rained down from Sando Top, pinning them. The enemy fire was incessant.

Nk Brijmohan Singh got a foothold near the top. Crawling ahead, he lobbed a grenade and fired, killing one Pakistani soldier. Completely surprised, the enemy fired back at him. He crouched below a rock and again lobbed a grenade. This time he charged the nearest enemy position, shooting down two soldiers.

Brijmohan's fearless actions baffled the enemy. He drew fire on himself, helping his pinned down colleagues.

Lobbying yet another grenade, he again dared death by fearlessly charging, killing two more Pakistani soldiers. Retaliatory fire was now intense, forcing him to retreat.

Losing his foothold, he slithered down, rolling, falling, protecting himself as the artillery airbursts blew up rock and ground around him. Miraculously, he tumbled into the team a few hundred metres below.

Awaiting below, exposed completely on the rock slope, the rest of the team had shell after shell exploding around them, ripping bone and muscle. Breaking up into smaller groups, they sought refuge under low overhangs and rocks, just enough to protect their heads or torsos.

Suddenly, two shells collided and imploded. The explosion sent a shower of debris in all directions. Shredded out of a shoulder, an arm flew past.

A broad-shouldered burly Sikh, Nk. Mukhtiar Singh ran, ripping open the field dressing in his medical satchel. Trained in battlefield nursing, he doubled up as a nursing assistant. The red fountain gushing out of the young soldier's shoulder socket felt warm. Another colleague helped him drag the screaming soldier under a rock.

A paratrooper had his legs blown away. The thighs ended in exposed bone and muscle leaving a horrifying trail in the soft snow. Tearing up the soldier's now useless trousers, they wrapped him up tightly. Mukhtiar shot in an injection and covered the wound as best as he could.

Machine gun fire now tore into the ground, as the artillery barrage echoed in their ears. The enemy had taken up positions on U-Cut and the Saddle, two features above them, and were raining fire on their exposed position.

"Over here!" hollered Maj. Rishi pointing to Brijmohan.

Mukhtiar crawled up to see intestines hanging out, covering a gaping hole where his genitalia should have been. "Wahe Guru!" muttered Mukhtiar under his breath, recoiling at the sight of Brijmohan's gaping stomach wound.

Tearing the packet open with his teeth, his shaky hands spilled the bleed-stop powder. Cursing under his breath, he wiped the sweat off his brow, smearing his forehead red from the blood of multiple men.

It did not matter.

In this treacherous desolation, what mattered was survival. Survival brought out the purity of brotherhood. In such primal times, it even stood above god and religion.

Controlling his nerves, Mukhtiar covered the wounds with a field dressing. He could feel the soldiers' ragged breath on his neck. He forced a smile, eyes staring into the soldier's pain-stricken face, "We are… getting you down."

The darkness in his eyes revealed his intention. Alarmed, Mukhtiar turned to see Brijmohan's hand wrapped tightly around his weapon, his face a mask of determination. Mukhtiar swiftly snatched the weapon, flinging it away.

"Don't!" admonished Mukhtiar, shaking his head, but it took him a moment to find his voice. "Live… don't weaken."

Grinding his teeth, Brijmohan lifted his palm, gesturing at his battered body, the words stuck in his throat.

"Let me die…" he pleaded; his voice thick. "Shoot me… just let me die."

The burly Sikh held Brijmohan, shielding him as another shell exploded nearby. He whispered a few lines of a *Shabad*[11] in the din of the exploding artillery, hoping it would comfort his brave colleague.

Nalawade tried to lead an assault through the rocks to force the enemy back and divert the pressure. Stonewalled by the accurate fire and the sheer rockface, he found the going impossible. The firefight and the artillery pounding seemed never-ending.

Nirmal glanced at his wrist. Almost 1500 hrs in the afternoon; the air still thick with acrid smoke. And yet the firing just wouldn't stop. Nirmal ordered some men to move down. Despite his protests, he ordered his buddy Lance Nk. Anil Rawat, "Climb down!"

As Anil got up, a bullet ricocheted and hit him. He stumbled.

The squad, sitting below the ledge, felt a chill as they watched Anil come bumping down. Shot in the chest, he rolled down the 70-degree slopes from the Saddle, gathering momentum. Frozen at the sight of their colleague falling, they watched in horror as his rucksack strap snagged on a rock.

Jerked up from the sudden impact, he oscillated precariously in mid-air, probably alive. Unable to just watch any longer, Nk. Hem Singh and Nk. Anand Bisht struggled up the slope, even as artillery shells rained death around them. Cutting the strap with a bayonet, they lowered him down between them. Mukhtiar struggled to give Anil first aid.

Another shell burst overhead.

---

[11] *In Sikhism, a shabad is a sacred song selected from the scripture, Guru Granth Sahib.*

Having cheated death minutes earlier, Nk. Hem Singh's luck ran out. An exploding shell blew him and Nk. Mangal Singh to death. Six others were badly wounded.

The young Mukhtiar had witnessed sights so gruesome that they would haunt him for a lifetime. Numbed, all he could smell was his own breath, his own body and the faint metallic odour of blood and death.

Jose and his squad had slipped down almost six hundred feet because of the enemy fire. They finally re-established contact with the rest of the Bravo Team.

Appraised of the situation, Maj. Gen. Puri ordered the team back. It would be futile to press on. 3/3 GR[12], which was to be launched on the Tri-junction in simultaneity was also held back.

Nirmal gathered the wounded soldiers and extricated the team under heavy artillery fire. Seeing the sullen faces of the team, he spoke up. "We live to fight another day… the war is not over yet."

Carrying their wounded colleagues down the ropes was precarious. Already tired, the men pushed themselves beyond their endurance. Unfortunately, the wounded soldiers died one by one, breathing their last on the bruised shoulders of their brothers. They would have wanted it no other way.

"Some men are lost in their fires. Others are forged in them," said Rishi, as he watched the last of the bodies being lowered down over the ropes.

"Not for kings…not for glory, but for the one next to me," said Nirmal, looking on. "That's what it boils down to, Rishi."

Rishi nodded silently in agreement.

* * * *

The failure to capture Sando Top did not deter the attack on Tiger Hill.

18 Grenadiers, commanded by Col. Khushal Thakur, scaled a 1,000-

---

[12] *Gurkha Rifles*

foot vertical cliff on the rear side of the mountain to surprise the enemy at Tiger Hill. The spectacular victory of Tiger Hill on 8th July, broke the spirit of the intruders. The Indian Army also captured point 4875, another dominating feature.

This marked the beginning of the end.

The Pakistani army accepted the ceasefire and withdrawal on India's terms.

* * * *

Broken Promises
14th July,1999

The Pakistani intruders however reneged on their promise of going back after the fall of Tiger Hill and point 4875. Curiously, they had forsaken their civilian clothes, donned their uniforms and were now deployed on Zulu Spur, a prominent feature two kilometres south of the LoC.

"We need your boys to scale the Zulu Top," said Gen. Puri, getting straight to the point.

Col. Britto wasn't too happy with the mission. "These are typical infantry attacks, sir." The Para Commandoes, being specialised troops, were meant for strategic tasking and hence were not being optimally utilised here.

"Your boys have the experience, Britto."

"But sir…"

"Your small teams are perfectly suited for this." His eyes held the colonel's gaze. Overriding the colonel's objections, the general drew him to the map, outlining his plan. "Secure a lodgement on Zulu Top."

Britto just tightened his jaw.

The general directed. "Let's secure the other tactical features as well; we need a better view beyond." Britto's gaze rested on the map.

"When can I expect a plan, Britto?" Britto eyed the general's fingers tapping the table.

"After my recce, sir." Britto held his ground. The general agreed reluctantly.

True to his word, Britto drew up the plan after a detailed reconnaissance.

Brig. Bajwa outlined the plan. "We attack Tri Junction with 3/3 GR. In simultaneity, 9 Para will then scale the Zulu Top with two teams and evict the enemy."

Gen. Puri and Britto listened attentively.

"And when will the attacks begin, Bajwa?"

"2030 Hrs, 22nd July, sir," said Brig. Bajwa, twirling his moustache.

* * *

Army House, New Delhi
12th July, 1999

Mrs. Malik had organised a small farewell for Sudhir before he left Delhi. The manicured back lawns of the Chief of Army Staff's official residence on Rajaji Marg had an elaborate tea laid out.

A doctor herself, she had served in the army for five years as a captain. Married in 1968 to Capt. Ved Malik, after they met at a party, Ranjana Malik looked upon the ADCs dotingly. They were almost her son Sachin's age.

"It won't be the same without your singing, Sudhir," she said, her voice full of tenderness. Sudhir had the remarkable ability to sing in multiple languages. The previous year, on Lohri, his voice had filled the celebrations with a vibrant medley of Hindi, Punjabi and Himachali songs.

"Let's not forget the dancing," the cook said quietly, his voice full of admiration. Sudhir could fluidly break into a jig with grace.

"Ma'am, he still hasn't completed the handover yet," said one ADC with a smirk, the corners of his mouth twitching.

"What handover?" asked Mrs. Malik, arching her eyebrows. Sudhir glowered at the captain; the air thick with anticipation.

Mrs. Malik's eyes crinkled as she witnessed the exchange between the young men.

"He hasn't yet handed over the list of phone numbers, ma'am." The captain grumbled.

Her lips breaking into a mischievous smile, Mrs. Malik's eyes widened in mock surprise.

"Ma'am, these rogues! Please don't listen to them." Sudhir groaned averting her gaze, stuffing a sandwich in his mouth.

Her eyes twinkled. "I agree with them."

"… and that incident, ma'am?" recalled a captain laughing.

Gen. Malik had received an invitation to address the students at Miranda House, an all-girls college. She recalled the sound of her husband's voice, confused as he spoke to the vice chancellor. Perplexed, the general could not comprehend how he had received the call out of the blue.

"Sudhir was behind that," the other ADC chuckled. "He wanted to show off to the girls. And he ended up getting so many phone numbers…"

Sudhir's ears flushed red.

"When are you getting married, Sudhir?" He shook his head. "Not so soon, ma'am." The eyes gave him away.

"Is there…?" Piqued, she searched his face.

"No…no, ma'am." He kept a stone face, but his eyes lit up with a memory as his thumb caressed a nail scratch on his wrist. Her flying schedules and his demanding job threw up infrequent moments, which they clutched hungrily. He knew she was perfect.

Sudhir looked away, embarrassed, concealing his emotions.

An ADC, his subordinate, quickly came to Sudhir's rescue.

"What's your favourite food, sir?"

"My mother's rajma-chawal," he said nostalgically, without blinking an eye. The very aroma of the dish triggered childhood memories.

Mrs. Malik embraced him, her voice thick with emotion as she said, "We will miss you, son."

"Me too, ma'am." Sudhir saluted her, as he fought to keep his composure.

Inexplicably, a feeling of unease washed over her as he walked away.

* * * *

Lucky to get a day off, Sudhir went home on a quick day trip before reporting to his battalion. He drove down in his gleaming new Maruti car, showing it off with pride. The entire family joined in and visited the Chamunda temple on that sunny day. After a long time apart, they finally had a chance to spend a lovely day together. Sudhir did not want to tell them he was going to war. They were just aware that he was re-joining his battalion.

The weight of the dusky evening pressed upon him as the shadows gathered. The sounds of laughter and chatter grew distant. His head swam with a gnawing guilt. Torn between the need to say a heartfelt goodbye and yet not wanting to confess his mission, which could be his last, he felt dreadful.

She had made his favourite rajma-chawal. Sudhir gazed at his ageing mother, taking in the way her eyes crinkled at the corners as she beamed a warm loving smile at him. She looked pretty as the years melted away.

The sight broke Sudhir's heart.

No longer able to contain himself, he blurted. "I don't want to die in an accident or disease, Ma, I want to go down in glory."

Taken aback, Rajeswari Devi swayed and clutched the door, her mouth set in a hard line. Her flashing eyes shimmered through her gathering tears. "Nonsense. Stop!" she shouted, her voice shrill.

Sudhir, caught up in the moment, did not stop there. "I want to come back wrapped in a tricolour, Ma."

She sat down in a huff. "You are not going anywhere."

Her voice was breaking. A raised finger admonished Sudhir. No words emerged. About to strike him, she clutched him, pressing him to her bosom in maternal protection, rocking back and forth. "You are not going anywhere," she continued to mutter, squeezing her eyes shut.

A bewildering silence clung to the house.

Munni's eyes darted outside. The flickering streetlight cast an eerie glow on the road outside. The cold evening breeze sent a shiver down her spine.

Little did they know that this would be Sudhir's last trip home.

* * * *

Zulu Spur
22nd July, 1999

16 Frontier Force, a regular Pakistani army unit, was occupying Zulu Spur.

Brig. Bajwa had planned the attacks at 2030 hrs. Sudhir reported to 9 Para after his short leave and immediately volunteered to be part of the attack.

They woke up to an overcast sky. By mid-morning, the weather had completely packed up. Taking advantage of the worsening weather, Brig. Bajwa, a brilliant tactician, executed a daring plan and caught the enemy off guard. At 1315 hrs, he ordered a company of 3/3 GR, to attack the Tri Junction. Curiously Capt. Amit Aul, who led the attack was the son of Brig. Amar Aul, commander of the neighbouring 56 Mtn. Bde.

Expecting a night attack, the Pakistani soldiers of Bravo Company, 16 Frontier Force, under their Company Commander Maj. Malik, were taking a nap on the reverse slope. The Gurkha troops virtually walked over and captured the Tri junction without firing a shot.

The next night, 3/3 Gurkhas, wielding their assault rifles and *khukris*[13] with equal ferocity, captured the next peak. The enemy, now on the run, concentrated on Zulu Top, leaving the approaches mined

---

[13] *Nepali long-curved knife*

and booby trapped.

Working tirelessly, the sound of their efforts echoing off the cliffs, the engineer teams removed 550 mines from the area. Yet, many more remained, and the limited time to clear them was a source of stress. The enemy had to be evicted quickly, before they dug in and made their positions impenetrable.

* * *

Vinod

They had tasked Alpha Team to head to the *Safed Nallah*[14] by encircling Tiger Hill through the U-Cut and attempt to cut off enemy reinforcements. This additional mission was to be completed before the Zulu Top attack.

They had promoted me to a Naik. I was fixing the ropes to climb the ice wall when an exploding artillery shell unhinged the embedded picket supporting the climbing rope. I fell on my back, injuring my spine. My colleague fell on a rock, splitting his stomach open.

Brig. Bajwa wanted 9 Para to attack Zulu Top early, so he preponed the launch time to the afternoon.

Nirmal Dhaliwal sir and Sudhir sir led the Bravo and Alpha teams. Bravo team were to attack Zulu Top from the east, Alpha under Sudhir sir, from the south-east.

As the time for the Zulu assault was preponed, they ordered the team back. My back was in acute pain. They administered morphine that numbed the pain.

* * *

---

[14] white stream

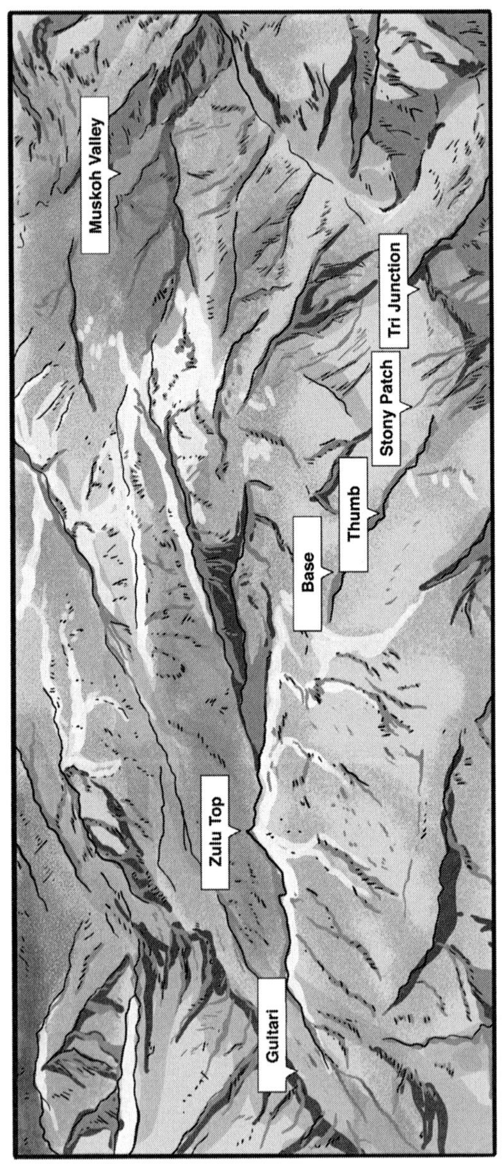

Zulu Spur, Tri-Junction, Mushkoh

Vinod
Zulu Base
1500Hrs, 24th July, 1999

Both teams reached Zulu Base. The air was damp and chilly, the ground slick with mud. Sudhir sir and Nirmal sir shook hands firmly.

"See you on the Top," said Sudhir sir. Nirmal sir nodded, placing his hand on Sudhir's shoulder.

"This is it, boys," said Nirmal sir, looking over his men, "Let's go fuck them." Gripping the rope firmly, he turned his back and started the climb.

Yet to extract their vengeance of Sando Top, the men watched him climb, knowing what he meant. There is no greater motivation than revenge.

Sudhir sir led our team towards the other side. We had a difficult route. It would, however, ensure complete surprise, essential for the operation. "Let's go, team," he whispered.

He had heard the eyewitness account of what had transpired at Sando Top. He had clenched his fists, recalling the faces of the eight men who had perished, two of whom he had served with in operations.

Sudhir sir saw the grimace on my face.

"Go back," he ordered. "You are injured."

I was adamant. "I am climbing. Just give me more morphine."

They gave me another morphine injection. Digging into his rucksack, Sudhir sir fished out some biscuits and a juice pack.

"You're spiked with morphine." He forced me to eat. "We don't want you hallucinating…having a raving time," he winked, giving me a charming smile and turned away to give some instructions to the others.

I envied him through my pain. He was cool and had not lost his sense of humour, even here.

* * *

Waiting for the ropes to be fixed, Sudhir allowed his thoughts to drift.

For a task that could demand so much, it was a minor extravagance.

He recalled her face and the memory of her radiant smile made his heart flutter. The good-bye in Delhi had been brief, but painful. He had always been careful to seal his vulnerabilities and plug his chinks. The turmoil inside had left him unsteady. An alien emotion, he was still grappling with feelings that he never knew existed.

"Don't over plan your life, Sudhir," she had said indulgently, when he went to pick her up at the airport. Conscious of her cabin crew uniform, he sat stiffly in the car. She ruffled his nape playfully, "Let life happen, Captain."

He realised he liked her more than he would care to admit. He had just beamed with joy like a puppy. "The vastness of life is so great," she had whispered, pulling at his ear, "that it's impossible to plan it all."

He wondered in amazement where she had gained such wisdom.

* * *

Vinod

"Done!" I shouted. It broke his reverie. Indulgence over, he went back to thinking of our mission.

At 0200 hrs, B team reached the RV, 100 metres short of their objective. Our Alpha team had not yet fetched up. B team crept forward. A small two-man tent came into view. Meant for lookouts, the tent appeared to be vacant.

Creeping ahead, Bravo team found belted ammunition boxes, rucksacks and a radio set inside.

Nirmal sir moved ahead and deployed the team cautiously.

Sudhir sir and I took the lead. We had instructed the team to wait on the ledge. We both reached the top and signalled. "Let's go…let's go!" I shouted down. On the ropes, the Alpha team was climbing steadily.

A shot whizzed past.

A second shot skipped off the cliff, ricocheting off a rock, creating a shrill, whistling sound as it flew into the void. The sky came alive with a relentless hail of fire.

"Don't stop…keep climbing!" yelled Sudhir sir.

He could feel the heat of the bullets whizzing past. The only way to stay alive was to get out of the firing line.

"It's Bravo firing," protested someone as a shot nicked his arm.

"Keep moving!" I yelled, holding the rope, "Don't bloody stop!"

Close to the south-west spur, Mukhtiar could see two enemy soldiers firing at the Alpha team from a *sangar*. He fired back, killing one of them.

"Don't fire on us!" shouted Sudhir sir on the radio set. The Alpha team thought Bravo was firing on them erroneously.

* * *

"It's the enemy," clarified Mukhtiar to his squad commander, who came running to stop him from firing. "See, I killed one." The squad commander nodded and radioed back to the Alpha team.

In close combat firefights, the decisive factors were the recognition of friend and foe, the adherence to fire discipline, a coordinated effort, and a swift response. It took consistent practice and hard training to get it right. The line between living and dying was sometimes so faint, it was like a wisp of gun smoke, barely there.

* * *

Zulu Top, The Assault

Just two months older than 30, Sudhir sir signalled the men. The men climbed up furtively. Holding their breaths, they sprinted across the rubble.

I was still at the ropes.

A young soldier Bijli, like a snow leopard, was already stalking his prey, silently. The mist obscured further vision.

"Uggghhh…" He slit the Pakistani lookout's throat silently.

Clearing the south-east end, the Alpha team joined with Bravo on top. They had cleared the immediate Top of the enemy for the time being.

"Redeploy quickly." Sudhir sir knew we needed to be prepared for a counterattack.

"Check the ammunition," ordered Nirmal sir. We carefully divided the ammunition between ourselves, considering the balance left with each.

"Take up position on… that outcrop," ordered Sudhir sir pointing out an elevated rock. Hav. Girish and Nk. Kamlesh Yadav sprinted, setting up the dependable 7.62 mm PIKA[15]machine gun, its muzzle pointed towards the direction of the likely counter-attack.

For a brief minute, all we could feel was the stillness of the air. Then a crackling shot echoed through the brief lull.

Hav. Girish lay sprawled on the barrel, shot through the head. Nk. Kamlesh ducked behind a rock, its jagged edges poking against his cheeks as he peered cautiously. He could hear the muffled sound of Pakistani soldiers creeping up towards him.

Kamlesh leapt behind the PIKA gun, trying to align the machine gun towards the enemy. Unknown to him, a Paki sniper perched on an escarpment shot him through his chest. Driven, a visibly wounded Kamlesh struggled feebly to shift the machine gun. Unfortunately, another two rounds pierced his chest in quick succession, spinning him around. He fell in a heap.

The men zigzagged through bursts of automatic fire, that raked up earth and pebbles. They fired from instinct, from muscle memory.

The enemy was firing from the bunkers, shielding themselves against the rough sangars. Sudhir sir led three men towards the nearest bunker. Another team took the next one. Lobbing in a grenade, they waited and charged in, daring death. Moments later, they emerged having cleared

---

[15] *PIKA-Pulemyot Kalashnikova, is a belt fed general purpose machine gun, chambered for the 7.62 mm rimmed cartridge.*

the fortification.

Anchal's arm was bleeding.

Sudhir sir looked at the wound, "You okay?"

Anchal smiled, "Can't feel a thing, sir."

"That's cause it's only a flesh wound, idiot," Sudhir sir nudged him with his elbow. "At least get shot properly."

White teeth glinted, contrasting with Anchal's face, which was smeared in red. The intruder he had bayoneted had spouted like a fountain.

Cleaning the bloody bayonet against his thigh, Anchal chuckled. "Sir ji…" The rest of the sentence drowned in a grenade blast. He dived, pulling Sudhir sir with him.

Thrown from up close, the grenade almost blew them up. Gritting his teeth, regretting his stupid joke, Sudhir sir shot back, screaming profanities.

He charged in firing, regardless of the lurking danger. He continued to fire until he emptied the magazine, putting the last bullet through the invader's forehead. Stopping for a moment, he looked down at the bodies of the two intruders he had killed. Vaulting over them, he then emerged out of the dugout, jaw set, teeth on an edge.

He had no time to mourn Hav. Girish or the other dead comrades. He had to take care of the men who were alive. They trusted him with their lives.

Sprouting sparks and incendiary tracer rounds, an enemy heavy machine gun opened fire from the southwest. The spectacular parabolic belt of fire spewed death. It cut down one paratrooper.

Mukhtiar, with a team of two men, crawled up to silence it. Adjusting the rocket launcher on his shoulder, he kneeled on the jagged rock, impervious to the sharp stone pricking his knee. Mukhtiar yelled out the order, "HE bhar."[16] His buddy loaded a high explosive rocket projectile

---

[16] *High Explosive (HE)*

into the tube, locking the venturi.

"Ready!" he yelled, tapping Mukhtiar on the shoulder.

Calmly aiming for the machine gun, Mukhtiar looked through the sights, steeling his jaw. He pulled the thick trigger.

The pressure wave from the shoulder-fired rocket projectile compressed the air, numbing ear drums. The blast blew the stone wall over and whatever was behind it.

More heavy fire came down from a rocky outcrop. An RPG[17] blasted the rock in front of them. Ears bleeding from the blast, Nk. Ashwini fell on his stomach. Disoriented, he felt a sharp pain in his back, that was probably shrapnel. His legs were numb. Saliva laced with blood dripped from his bleeding tongue. It caked his mouth with mud. He knew the second rocket would bodily lift him and blow him to smithereens.

Strategically in position, the 9 Para sniper tore his eyes away from his fallen colleague and scanned the area through his telescopic sight looking out for the RPG firer. The Pakistani soldier stood up confidently with the rocket launcher on his shoulder. His number two, the loader stood next to him, feeding in the rocket projectile.

Catching them in his sight, the sniper let go of two precise shots in rapid succession.

The first shot caught the RPG firer in the head. Shifting his aim, the sniper shot the loader through his chest.

Ashwini closed his eyes as a spasm shook his body. He sputtered blood and stopped breathing.

Nk. Sunil Dutt, his buddy, fired back, trying to pull Ashwini's body back. Reeling from a shot in the shoulder, he gritted his teeth but continued to fire with his good arm, finally succumbing to the automatic fire. He died with one arm protectively thrown over Ashwini, the other clutching his weapon, finger still on the trigger, eyes beholding the sky above.

---

[17] *Rocket Propelled Grenade*

A hand-to-hand fight had ensued by the trenches. A cornered duo in khaki uniforms of the Frontier Force fought back ferociously. Ripped through the middle, a Pakistani soldier with his entrails trailing, fired his AK-47 unsteadily. Echoes from the automatic fire reverberated as they bounced off the rocks.

The bloody fight was soon over. The ferocity of the retaliation unnerved the remaining Pakistani soldiers. They fell back, quickly slithering down the ropes attached on the reverse slope. Sudhir sir ran behind them. The enemy cut off the ropes as they slithered down, making it impossible to follow them.

Stationed at Gultar to interdict the Pakistani administrative base, Maj. Gaurav Rishi with the Charlie team had a clear view of the leeward side of the Zulu Spur. Training his binoculars, he saw the enemy scrambling down the ropes. "Enemy escaping. North rear slopes," radioed Maj. Rishi. "… struggling… with the wounded."

Interestingly, we caught a Pakistani soldier, Mohd Ashraf.

Sudhir sir yelled, "Mukhtiar, deploy and reposition the machine guns!"

The men organised the defence, bracing themselves yet again. Dawn finally broke and sun rays streamed down through the rising clouds, mist and gore.

"What's the head count, Mukhtiar?"

"We lost five men, sir."

Sudhir gritted his teeth. After a moment, "… And the kills?"

Mukhtiar glanced at him, a glint in his eyes. "Thirteen. 16 Frontier Force, sir."

I showed Sudhir sir the Pakistan army identity cards and letters we had recovered from the bodies. There was a nominal roll with names of the enemy platoon in a partially burnt diary.

"Keep them properly. They are soldiers." He pointed towards the bodies.

Mukhtiar pulled out a folded flag from his backpack. He yelled at a young soldier, "Unfurl the tricolour!" He had carried it from the base, at the cost of personal rations.

A playful smile touched Sudhir sir's cracked lips. Innocence dripped from his voice, "Who will see this, Mukhtiar?"

"The spirits of these dead Pakistanis," Mukhtiar's eyes blazed with fire. "Let them carry this last memory to their jannat."

By 1000 hrs, 25th July, 3/3 GR had reached Zulu Top and relieved our two teams of para commandos.

Sudhir sir and I were the last people to climb down.

We heard that evening that the Pakistani Commander, Col. Mustafa, CO of 16 Frontier Force, had requested Brig. Bajwa for the dead bodies of his soldiers. The request was graciously accepted and the bodies handed over with full military honours.

Though angry at having lost my brothers, I was proud of the ethos of our army. We honour the dead, irrespective of nationality. Friend or foe.

The capture of Zulu Top by Maj. Sudhir Walia and our Alpha Team along with Maj. Nirmal Dhaliwal and his Bravo team, marked one of the last fights for Kargil on the 25th of July 1999.

Recommended for a Vir Chakra, India's third highest award for gallantry in battle, they finally awarded Sudhir sir a Sena Medal. The battalion was now to be called the Bravest of the Brave.

* * *

The Kargil war ultimately led to Nawaz Sharif's ouster through a coup by Gen. Musharraf.

* * *

The COAS Gen. Malik flew to Srinagar on a situation assessment mission after the Kargil war. Sudhir drove down specially to meet his old boss. They shook hands formally.

Fumbling with their emotions, they were unsure of what to say, acutely conscious of others present. Their body language was wooden. Struggling with their awkwardness, constrained by their gender and rank, their eyes nevertheless, spoke more.

Gen. Malik's gaze flickered over the young man who had been part of his family while in Delhi.

The General scowled at Sudhir, in stark disbelief. "You went for the assault?" Running his hand through his hair in bewilderment, "Without acclimatisation?"

Sudhir smirked, his eyes twinkled with the arrogance of youth. He waved away the infringement. "Sir, you know I am a Pahari. I do not need acclimatisation."

The air around Gen. Malik was thick with annoyance, but his voice tremored with concern. He pointed an accusing finger at Sudhir, like a father confronting his son. "You will not break rules again."

The cap on Sudhir's head arrested the General's gaze. The cap, a gift during the visit to Vietnam was symbolic of the time they had spent in travels together and the relationship they shared.

They had travelled to Vietnam on a diplomatic visit to strengthen relations. The Vietnamese officers had challenged the other staff officers and Sudhir. The challenge was to drink them under the table and run through the war-era Cu Chi labyrinthine tunnels. Alarmed when Sudhir gleefully accepted the challenge, Gen. Malik had grudgingly trusted the young man.

True to his word, Sudhir had shown remarkable ability in both. He had also kept an eye on the other Indian staff who had been willingly armtwisted in the drinking bout, too.

Sudhir removed the cap. He ran his hand through his tousled hair, eyes avoiding the General. A grin forced itself on his lips. Sudhir's irresistible charm broke through the stoic stance of the General. A wry smile touched Gen. Malik's lips. He carried Sudhir's infectious grin in his heart on the long flight out of Srinagar.

Three days later, while having breakfast with his wife, Gen. Malik on impulse asked for a call to the GOC 15 Corps Lt. Gen. Krishan Pal, responsible for the Valley.

The operator put the Corps Commander on line, from Srinagar.

"Krishan, be careful in employing Sudhir… and his team."

"Yes, sir!"

"Sudhir is… brave and …. overenthusiastic."

"Sir…"

"He will stupidly volunteer for every challenging mission."

"I understand, sir."

"We should not allow him to take risks day after day."

The call surprised Mrs. Ranjana Malik. She had never seen her husband do anything like this in thirty years.

She gaped at him, trying to read his mind. Gen. Malik just looked away, deliberately ignoring the warm flush on his neck from an ominous apprehension.

* * *

SRI LANKA

Sea, Sacrifice & Blunders: Operation Pawan
Vavuniya
October 1988

The humid, balmy weather lulled the young subaltern to sleep. They had left the brilliant blue of the Indian Ocean, the powder soft sands and the idyllic palms two hours back.

The road meandered through deep jungles now. Perched in the truck, Sudhir could see his senior, the captain in the Jeep leading the convoy. Jolted out of his wistful thoughts by the sounds of automatic fire and the thump of mortars from just across the lagoon, Lt. Sudhir heard the deafening crescendo of 57-mm rockets fired in a shallow dive.

Black smoke bellowed over the treetops as an acrid smell hung in the air.

Peering out of the army truck, he noticed the Mi-8 gunships circling like vultures. The Indian Air Force gunships were hunting the LTTE[18] in the tropical jungles.

Suddenly, exploding glass shards cut his face. The staccato sound of machine gun fire accompanied the rush of air through the shattered windshield. He eyed flashes from the deep undergrowth across. Holding up his arm to protect his face, he saw the driver's head jerked back, split open. The truck wheeled sharply, hitting a tree.

Sudhir tumbled out, dazed, seeking protection against the truck tyre. "Fire!" the captain's voice barked, "Fire!"

Cocking the rifle, Sudhir fired randomly. The first shots hit a tree.

"Shoot those fucking bastards, not the fucking trees!" the captain yelled.

Steadying his arm, Sudhir tried to aim for the flashes. Before he

---

¹⁸ *LTTE - Liberation Tigers of Tamil Eelam*

could fire effectively, the fight was over. The LTTE Tigers[19] had silently melted away in the deep forests after the ambush, leaving a carnage. The air smelt of burnt tyres, brakes and spilled gasoline.

The captain walked up and looked down at Sudhir, tapping him on the shoulder.

"This is bandit country. Think like a bandit, always be ready to hunt. And stop gaping like a tourist."

Sudhir nodded. A lesson he would never forget in his life.

Removing the cork with his mouth, the captain took a swig from the hip flask and held it out to Sudhir. "Welcome to Vavuniya."

Holding the Army issue flask encased in canvas, Sudhir wrinkled his nose as he took a sip of the sour-smelling water.

"Worry about staying alive first, then worry about how to live, you bugger."

Sudhir learnt his second lesson of life. That too from someone who was barely a few years older than him. This is what war did to boys. It made them men much before their time.

* * *

Less than a kilometre away, men were still fighting and dying. The LTTE had ambushed a company of Gurkhas on patrol. In the hand-to-hand fight that ensued, heavy casualties had occurred.

IAF's lethal Mi-25 Heptr[20] gunships unleashed 23-mm cannon fire, 57-mm rockets and 500 kg HE[21] bombs against the Tigers. A lone army Cheetah Heptr[22] circled above, an Air OP[23] picking targets and directing fire.

Reinforcements were required to be flown in before dusk, so some

---

[19] *Tigers- Cadres*

[20] *Helicopter*

[21] *High Explosive*

[22] *The Hindustan Aeronautics Ltd-built SA Lama*

[23] *Airborne observation post*

Mi-8 gunships were diverted in for a quick lift-off. Flying low over the jungle to pick up soldiers of the Mahar Battalion from their camp; they flew them back into the battle zone. Twenty fully armed soldiers on each sortie, with the Mi-8s setting up a virtual air bridge.

The last sorties brought in the tough men of the 9 Para Commandos.

Vavuniya was the HQ of the 4th Infantry Division. It had earned a reputation as 'Red Eagle' Div during World War II. Vavuniya also had the tactical HQ of 9 Para (SF).

Soon it got dark, but the sounds of fighting went on till late into the night.

* * *

Vinod, the Recruit
Vavuniya, August 1988

The humidity was suffocating. My face and neck flushed, I seemed to be swimming in my own sweat. The wet dungarees, holding a bucket of sweat, weighed me down. My rifle and pack straps had eaten into my skin. My raw shoulders stung away, prickled every time the salty sweat brushed against them.

Clamping my molars to steady the pounding in my temples, I had maintained a steady lead for most of the 40-kilometre endurance run. My nearest rival was a good 700 metres behind me. The rest of the Para probationers trailed much further down, struggling with heat cramps and dehydration.

Running on the tarmac of the Vavuniya airfield, with the finish line in sight, I collapsed.

After a while, I heard distant voices.

"Is he?"

"Check his pulse."

"He is alive, sir." That was the only sign of life.

"Okay great. He still has another test left."

* * *

Vinod

Unknown to Sudhir sir, a few months before he had reported to Sri Lanka, I had reported to 9 Para in Vavuniya as a young recruit. I had undergone basic recruit training at the Para centre in Agra and was in Sri Lanka for my extended probation.

I was a year older than Sudhir sir.

My friends told me I had the bright eyes of an optimist. I hated my thick eyebrows though. I was from a nondescript village near Naushera. Sudhir sir and I both came from humble backgrounds. We held that memory dear. We would never forget. We had that in common.

We would cross paths.

* * *

Vinod
Puthukkudiyiruppu (PKI)
28th October, 1988

The army has a knack of simplifying everything. So, the tongue twister, *Puthukkudiyiruppu*, was quietly nicknamed PKI. Situated on the north-eastern shore of the island, more than an hour's drive from Vavuniya, thick rain forests enclosed small lagoons, fringed by mangroves.

The lack of manpower in the hastily assembled IPKF (Indian Peace Keeping Force) was glaringly obvious. Volunteers for the 9 Para were far from enough. A progressive instructional process was not a luxury granted by the bloody jungle war. They had to employ every available man and baptise him through fire.

I cleared my probation and though a greenhorn, bounced into operations. This was my first encounter and it would remain imprinted in my memory like my first love – the girl from the village school.

An ad hoc team from 9 Para had set forth from our camp in PKI, under Maj. J.L. D'Cruz. We had planned to operate for 24 hours in the jungles – a typical search and destroy operation – and fall back to base.

The team ventured deep into the belly. Using *dahs*[24], we hacked our way through the humid, suffocating forests. After a day's march, with no break in the endless vegetation, we camped under the trees, conserving our sapping strength and depleting water.

* * *

By the morning of 29th October, our compass bearings went haywire. It was hard to tell due to the lack of landmarks, but we probably trudged in a forty-kilometre circle through the thick forests. Thirsty and famished, we camped for the second night, having finished our water and rations. The tall trees, dense vegetation and oppressive heat obstructed radio communications. Our desperate team leader radioed messages before the blinking battery died out.

On the third day, the team got lucky. Sig Int[25] at PKI received a single transmission racing over radio waves. Cracking and inaudible, the poor transmission was just enough to establish our approximate location. We had been lost for nearly two days.

* * *

"Hear that?" My ears on alert were straining to hear the sound again.

Chop, chop, chop, chop.

It was unmistakable. We heard it again. A smile broke out over my sweaty face. My buddy Joginder whooped with joy.

And then, like an angel in the sky, a heptr flew in over us. The machine with Indian army markings hovering over the treetops was a sight to behold. We hurrahed in joy and relief.

The heptr could not land because of the thick vegetation and a non-sanitised, hostile area. It, however, guided us towards the nearest track that would bring us home. After ascertaining that we had found the way,

---

[24] *Burmese word for long knife*

[25] *Signal Intelligence – A radio station monitoring radio signals*

it banked in salute and flew off.

The team was full of light-heartedness, our faces beaming with relief. Despite the long walk back, it was merely a few extra hours and a few more blisters. We would have to live with our painful parched throats a little longer.

Joginder and I led the way over the track as leading scouts. The track slithered like a giant python through the thicket. We walked through the first bend and into the second. Suddenly we both froze. Joginder's red-rimmed eyes opened wide; his hackles stood up.

Just twenty-five meters away, in the middle of the track, stood an LTTE cadre. He too had frozen on sighting us, two *patka*[26] clad paratroopers.

The experienced Joginder responded first. "*Bhenchod!*" I heard him swear. His rifle had jammed. I fired. The first burst kicked up dirt at the cadre's feet. Pointing my barrel up, I fired again, hitting him on the hip.

The cadre yelled, "*Ōu… Ōu, intiyanāyka!*"[27] He fired back, jumping into the forest. I distinctly heard footsteps and panicking voices further behind on the track.

"Oh god, there's a larger group." The thought raced through my head.

They, too, were not expecting the Indian Army. The LTTE group fired at us and ran into the forests. The team dashed in, tearing after the LTTE. Speculatively firing into the bushes, every few feet, alert for a response. We continued the drill for hours.

The jungles were too thick. We lost contact with the LTTE. Maj. D'Cruz reluctantly called off the chase. We had once again ventured in deep, straying off. Setting compass bearings, we wearily navigated our route back. Famished, thirsty and bone tired, we trudged through the humid jungles for hours. I had lost all sense of time.

* * *

---

[26] *Bandana*

[27] *"Run… Run, Indian dogs."*

The jungle was quiet except for our laboured breathing and the chirping of crickets. A wild trumpet startled the quietude.

The sound was menacingly close. Bracing against the unexpected call of a wild elephant, we tiptoed ahead. A second call made our hair stand up. It was louder and closer. We crept through the forest and emerged into a small clearing.

A herd of elephants, calves squealing in fright, were emerging from a green slimy puddle, surrounded by grey black slush. Two massive cows stood defending the herd, their ears flattened and tails held straight up.

We had apparently upset their afternoon siesta in the mud pool. Minutes passed. The trumpeting cows allowed the herd to melt into the forests. Shaking their massive heads as though warning us, they followed the herd.

A few moments passed. The air stood still. I eyed the green slime. So did a few other men. The same thought raced through every mind. Unmindful of the elephant dung, or the foul, pungent smell of the urine, we raced into the slush, and drank away.

It was only after we had quenched our thirst, did we hear the swearing and profanities being mouthed by Maj. D'curz. He was afraid we would all fall sick.

Much later, after his leave in India, he confided in us. He had heard someone crib in a bar, "Life is hard." It had tempted him to ask, "Compared to what?"

* * *

Raisina Hill, New Delhi
November 1986
(Six months before the accord)
The young waiter heard the voices behind the closed door.

G. Parthasarathy, the Prime Minister's Principal Adviser; Natwar Singh, Minister of State for External Affairs RAW[28] Chief Anand Varma;

---

[28] *RAW- Research and Analysis Wing, India's premier intelligence agency*

and J.N. Dixit, the Indian High Commissioner to Sri Lanka. They were all closeted in the room, with the young prime minster himself.

The concern was that the Chinese would show up if the Indians did not take a lead in ending the civil war in Sri Lanka. At its shortest point, the Palk Strait, which separated India and Sri Lanka, narrowed to a mere twelve miles.

"The only way to stop the Chinese is if they see us as equals," said a voice barely audible. "A regional power."

"That will help sweeten our oil deal with the Russians and… hopefully with the Iranians too."

"A regional power?" That voice probably belonged to Natwar Singh, an inner circle man. "That improves our equation with the US and…"

"Helps tackle the damn Pakis too."

"MGR's[29] been threatening. He feels we are betraying the cause," said the clipped voice.

The political alliance with AIADMK in Tamil Nadu was at stake.

"You can't be bowing to him."

"We no longer have that privilege," said the clipped voice. "The Congress needs him."

"Is that the urgency?" a voice whispered.

"Do I need to answer that?"

MGR pressurised New Delhi to support the Sri Lankan Tamils, despite its negative implications. He feared his political rivals[30]would accuse him of betraying Tamils. In a chess move of political brinkmanship, the Tamil Nadu assembly even announced aid to the LTTE at his behest.

"Rao…" the voice hesitated, "wants us to wait." The Minister of External Affairs, Narasimha Rao, not included in the meeting, thought differently.

[29] *MGR- MG Ramachandran. Founder of AIADMK (All India Anna Dravida Munnetra Kazhagam). He was a political heavyweight. His party was in alliance with Congress at the Centre.*

[30] *The DMK, Dravida Munnetra Kazhagam.*

"Ridiculous!" said the well-articulated voice, the tone distinctly underlined with anger. The waiter was certain it was the prime minister.

The tenor of the RAW chief 's voice was distinct. "We know these boys. They will listen to us."

The discussion became inaudible as garbled voices spoke in unison.

Suddenly someone said, "Madam had agreed." The reference was obviously to the previous prime minister, Indira Gandhi.

"Oh, really?"

"Well, training began in 1983 in Sarsawa." This was probably the RAW chief. "20,000 have trained so far."

"She sanctioned it?"

"Yes…yes, of course."

"And the instructors?"

"RAW agents, including some retired army officers and NCOs."

This was followed by some inaudible discussion.

An alarmed voice asked, "But armed intervention?"

"Just three or four days to wrap the island up…" The unmistakable voice of J.N. Dixit blurted out with misplaced confidence. "That's what we would take."

The talk veered on to an armed intervention in Sri Lanka with the Indian Army and LTTE fighting together against the Sri Lankan army.

"Will the accord not be binding?"

"That's for us to decide."

A murmured discussion followed. "But…but, the Indian Army? Are you sure?"

Afraid to hear more, the waiter leaned out, opening the window with an unsteady hand. What was being planned? The smell of fresh roses did nothing to quieten the ticking alarm inside.

The voices continued.

"What better way to secure the island than fight along with the LTTE?"

"Or with their support. After all, they are Tamils."

"Well, I am in charge now. But I agree with that."

They were planning to take over Sri Lanka, militarily.

Little did the coterie realise that their games would turn the LTTE into bitter enemies. The Indian forces would end up fighting the very people they had gone to protect and the mis-adventures would stretch to two years and seven months. India's losses in Sri Lanka between July 1987 and March 1990 would amount to 1,115 killed in action. In comparison, the 1971 war with Pakistan, which established an independent Bangladesh, cost 1,047 soldiers.

* * *

Just a stone's throw away, holed up in room 506 of Ashoka Hotel, Prabhakaran, the chief of the LTTE, paced the room. Clandestinely smuggled in, like always, this time New Delhi had brought him in with an ultimate purpose. He felt caged, unsure. The Indians had helped him so far, but he was uncertain how long it would last. He had played his cards well; he assured himself, ignoring his nagging fear.

* * *

"Okay, let's sign the accord and armtwist them to agree. Call for a cabinet meeting."

Everyone fell silent.

"And yes, get me the chief." He was referring to the Chief of the Army Staff, Gen. K. Sunderji.

The waiter tried to scuttle away, though not before an intelligence agent noticed him.

* * * *

Buddhist Sinhalese, the major ethnic group, dominated the government. The largest minority was the native-born Hindu Tamils in the northern and eastern provinces. Descendants of Indian plantation workers, the Indian Tamils lived mostly in the central province. Vavuniya, 140 kilometres from Jaffna, was further south. Sudhir was to cut his teeth in these tropical jungles with 4 Jat, an Infantry unit.

Commissioned from the Indian Military Academy on 11th June, 1988, Sudhir had travelled to Sri Lanka with his unit, as part of the IPKF.

* * * *

Entering the hut, the soldier glanced at Sudhir's back with respect. He placed the enamel mug in front of the mirror. The steaming tea frosted the image in the cracked mirror. Six months in the jungles had made Sudhir battle-hardened.

He had just returned from a mission with 47 InfBde, his uniform still covered in slush and sweat. The mission focused on ensnaring the LTTE in the humid jungles between Mullaitivu on the east coast and Vavuniya.

"Be careful, sir," cautioned the soldier, eyeing Sudhir's reflection. In the short time that Sudhir had spent in the unit, he had endeared himself to the soldiers. "We are already paying the price of a political game."

Sudhir raised an eyebrow.

"My retired cousin, an NCO, was their instructor, sir. He taught them about mines."

"We have a mission, Raghuveer. Let's not discuss what's beyond us."

"Even when they fight routinely from behind the cover of women and children?"

Sudhir nodded. "They aren't answerable. We are, to a nation."

Blowing steam from his cup, he continued to study his own reflection. "My only competition, Raghuveer," he said.

Sighing, the soldier shook his head. "You have enough courage, sir; you don't always have to endanger yourself to build a reputation."

Sudhir had by now become an indispensable part of 4 Jat – gaining intelligence, conducting raids and ensuring his men stayed alive. He was, however, yet unknown beyond 4 Jat.

* * *

Sri Lankan National Day
Vavuniya, 4th February, 1989

It was the Sri Lankan National Day and the Sri Lankan army had invited the Indian officers to the celebration. The function was bustling with Sri Lankan and Indian Army officers, filling the room with lively chatter. The crowd cheered when an officer from Sri Lanka sang an old Hindi song. The delight soon dissipated when the Sri Lankan challenged the Indian officers to sing a song in Sinhalese.

An awkward hush ensued. None of the Indian officers could speak Sinhalese, leave alone sing. The GOC 4th Inf Div turned in his chair, craning his neck, hunting for volunteers. No Indian officer would meet his eye.

A murmur broke out and yet no movement.

"I'll sing."

All eyes turned towards the young officer in the back rows. Capt. Yash Saxena from 9 Para Commando sitting a few rows away, recognised Sudhir from the NDA.

"... 72 Juliet," he whispered to his neighbour, referring to Sudhir's NDA squadron and course. "The boy has some balls, huh?" He was referring to Sudhir's NDA Squadron and Course.

Unknown to many, Sudhir had been learning Sinhalese on his own, carrying a book of translations picked up in Chennai during the unit's brief halt prior to induction into Sri Lanka.

The first lines of the song *'Sinhala avurudda ewilla'* had the Sri Lankan officers up on their feet, clapping. Composed by Rocksamy, a popular Sinhala composer, Sudhir had deliberately chosen the song for its popularity.

Everyone sighed with relief and cheered when Sudhir's raw Sinhalese song saved them from national humiliation. His attitude marked him as a perfect candidate for the 9 Para Commando Special Forces.

* * *

"You, Jackal! How did you do that?" asked Yash later, thumping him on the shoulder.

Sudhir's eyes twinkled. "Sir… I don't overthink."

"But you can't ignore people and what they think."

"The more I know people… the more I realise why Noah only let animals get on his Ark."

"That quote's not yours, Sudhir." Yash couldn't help laughing.

"Why reinvent the wheel, sir?" The twinkle in his eyes made him look like a mischievous schoolboy.

Meeting him when time permitted, Yash was soon guiding Sudhir, inspiring him to join the Special Forces. Sudhir, with the Ghatak platoon of 4 Jat, also trained with 9 Para (SF) for three months. Along with the special skills training, Sudhir also developed a deep fascination for the Ghost Battalion. He was yearning to be part of the acclaimed unit.

Unknown to Sudhir, Yash also spoke to his commanding officer, Col. H.D. Lidder about this young officer, who appeared to be a perfect fit for their set up – balanced, driven and focussed; and laced with a pinch of cockiness.

The shrill ring of the army telephone was jarring, but to the accustomed army ear drums, it was just a persistent white noise.

"Sir, call from CO, 9 Para," announced the operator.

"Yes, Hardy?" said Col Vijay, CO 4 Jat, "Are you coming over for a drink finally?" Friends from the NDA, they knew each other well.

"That will have to wait, buddy. We just got back from another gruelling operation in Vaani forest."

9 Para (SF) had conducted combing operations along with 4

Garhwal rifles in the Vaani forests, north east Of Vavuniya. Deep in the forest was the LTTE chief, Velupillai Prabhakaran's hideout.

"Yes I heard at the Bde HQ,[31]" said Col. Vijay, hesitating, a frown wrinkling his forehead. "He got away again?"

"Yes. They were bloody well-entrenched," said Col. Lidder.

"… and also out-gun us, Hardy."

"My Jat boys curse the 7.62 SLR[32]. It can't fire rapidly like their AK 47," cribbed Col. Vijay. "We need that for close combat."

"They are also getting—"

"Bolder?"

"Desperate," said Lidder. There was a moment's pause. "I need a favour."

"Shoot?"

"Ask Sudhir Walia to volunteer for 9 Para."

"He is one of my best cubs."

"Why do you think I asked?" chuckled Lidder. "He will do well with us."

Col. Vijay waited for a moment. "Hardy, I am short of officers."

"That's the story of the IPKF. Bad planning and too much… bloody hurry."

"Okay, let's at least finish this fucking jungle war first. And get back… alive!"

It was just a matter of time before Sudhir joined the 9 Para.

* * *

The Sri Lankan government had announced the general elections. The IPKF helped set up election booths and transport ballot boxes to ensure a fair and free election, despite LTTE threats. This would help diminish the LTTE's control.

The convoy of three vehicles followed a mud track, zigzagging

---

[31] *He was referring to 7 Brigade Headquarters.*

[32] *SLR- Self-loading Rifle. Replaced by the 5.56 INSAS Rif in Kargil*

between puddles. Lush paddy fields hugged the track on either side, as the lazy sun beamed back in happiness.

Sudhir sat in the first vehicle, a Jeep, eyes scanning the undergrowth. Four soldiers sitting behind were looking out, rifles cocked and ready to fire. Raghuveer, sitting behind Sudhir, touched him lightly on the shoulder, pointing with his chin. Sudhir followed his gaze. A lone man on a coconut tree was moving his arm, a fairly innocent gesture. Sixth sense nevertheless made Sudhir's scalp prickle. Something was amiss.

"Stop!" he screamed, simultaneously aligning his weapon, cocking it in reflex.

The Jeep jerked and slid sideways as the driver braked suddenly. His reflexes saved them from the landmine. Triggered remotely, it blew up in their faces. The pressure wave rippled their cheeks, numbing the ear drums painfully. The loud explosion threw up the mud-track, spraying the vehicle with mud and slush. The force flung the Jeep sideways as the rear vehicle skidded into the first, jolting them.

The men and Sudhir had already leaped out, firing.

"Shit, fucking shit!" cursed Sudhir, spitting out mud.

They had driven into an LTTE ambush. He noticed blood trickling from his colleague's ear drum, but there was no time to tend to that.

The rat-a-tat automatic fire of the machine gun thudded into the body of the vehicles, shattering the windshield. The fire was coming from dense undergrowth. Experts in mine warfare, the LTTE had been laying a network of ingenious mines, Improvised Explosive Devices (IEDs)and booby traps along the roads, mapping the countryside.

Unlike conventional metallic mines, these were heaps of explosives filled in plastic jerry cans. They used non-metallic objects such as coconut tree trunks to encase the explosives and connected them with wires. Some mines had up to 200 kilos of explosives, which is a kiloton explosive power. The Tigers kept a map of the mines and joined the wires whenever a suitable target passed by. The system had been in place to deal with the Sri Lankan army. It was now being used with devastating effect against the Indians, accounting for sixty percent of the casualties.

The LTTE machine gun fire had pinned down the men from the first vehicle. Sudhir scanned the jungle, his eyes glinting through his slush-splattered face. A machine gun mounted on the hood of the second vehicle fired back. A team from the second vehicle, not under direct fire, ran into the jungle to out-flank the ambushing party.

The LTTE machine gun shifted its fire and started raining fire at the second vehicle and the Indian Army machine gun.

No longer under direct fire, Sudhir quickly rolled over into the rice fields and crawled through the wet mud towards the LTTE position. Three men followed him. Crawling out from the edge of the field, the men crouched, taking up positions against the coconut trees on the fringe, reducing their silhouette. Covered in slush, their camouflage helped them merge into the foliage.

The second team had made good progress, closing in from a flank, but the LTTE were quicker.

Sensing enemy presence, firing quick bursts, they abandoned their position, swiftly withdrawing deeper into the jungle. The flanking team got bolder. Not drawing fire, they thought they had their adversary pinned. This is exactly what the LTTE wanted.

An excited young soldier, in hot pursuit, raced ahead. In a full run, his leg triggered the trip wire, cleverly laid by the LTTE, triggering a claymore mine tied to a tree.

"Down, trip wire!" he screamed in terror, forewarning his colleagues a moment before the mine exploded, spraying his body with pellets and shrapnel.

"Claymore, claymore!" yelled the man behind him, hugging the earth.

The young soldier screamed in pain, as parts of his rib cage and face blew away.

Gritting his teeth, Sudhir cautioned his team to be deliberate. *"Benchod, marna nahee, maarna hai!"* he yelled, cursing under his breath.

They trailed the LTTE men deeper into the forest. Leaves splattered with blood mapped the route for them. Clearly, the Indian army had drawn blood as well. Cautiously observing the dangling broken stem, he sniffed the sweet smell of a wild berry recently crushed. Sudhir inched forward with his team.

Suddenly, a shot whizzed past his ear, while another nicked a man on his leg. The fire was controlled and consistent.

"Pin him down!" yelled Sudhir.

The team fired back. Lobbying in a grenade, Sudhir and another soldier closed in on the LTTE cadre from a flank, firing controlled bursts. Outdone, the man fired his last burst. Firing from his hip, Sudhir and his colleague charged. A hail of bullets caught the cadre in the stomach and chest. It did not matter. The man was already dead. His frothing mouth revealing the cyanide capsule he had swallowed, instead of being caught alive, as was the LTTE code.

The fleeting fragrance of the wildflowers, mingled with the acrid smell of gunshot and fresh blood, hung heavy in the still humid air. The injured LTTE tiger had taken up a position, buying time for his colleagues to break contact.

The trail had gone cold.

Dusk was settling in. The team cautiously withdrew, carrying injured colleagues as they shuffled 35 kilometres back to the camp.

* * *

At its peak, the IPKF in Northern and Eastern Sri Lanka numbered nearly 100,000 men. It comprised four inf Divs—the 4th, 36th, 54th and the 57th—plus supporting arms and services, as well as paramilitary forces. 9 Para lost two JCOs[33] and eleven other ranks in Sri Lanka. It had

---

[33] *Junior Commissioned Officers*

many more injured.

The last fallout of the Sri Lankan adventure was the suicide bomber assassination of Rajiv Gandhi on 20th May 1991, fourteen months after the withdrawal of the IPKF.

The memorial at Colombo constructed by Sri Lanka in 2008, aptly cited the legacy of the IPKF. *'Valiant were their deeds, undying be their memories.'*

* * * *

Kashmir

1989

The year also marked a watershed in Kashmir. Rubaiya Sayeed – the third daughter of Mufti Sayeed, the Union Home Minister – was kidnapped about 500 metres from her home at Nowgam, by Yasin Malik led JKLF[34].The kidnapping blew the simmering discontent into a full-scale insurgency.

She was released a few days later in exchange for five militants held in Indian jails. This emboldened the perpetrators.

Kashmir would never be the same again.

* * * *

Chiseling the Diamond

"So we are off to Mhow for the young officer's course?" Yash smiled, eyes glinting.

"Yes, I have to bear with you now." Sudhir said, wrinkling his forehead. "The LTTE were at least lively."

Breaking out in a wide smile, Yash boxed him on the shoulder affectionately.

The Army HQ had detailed the two of them to attend the four months long Young Officers' course in Mhow at the Infantry School,

---

[34] *Jammu & Kashmir Liberation Front*

the first formal training after commissioning. Every infantry officer was required to attend, and expected to excel.

"And after Mhow?"

"We get buggered in the commando course, Sudhir." Yash winked. "Tally Ho to the Infantry School."

"I want to do well, sir. There must be a purpose to this."

"Why, Sudhir?"

"Because when you walk with purpose, you collide with your destiny!"

Amazed, Yash eyed his young friend with wonder. Nonchalantly, Sudhir just looked at the melancholy sun, dipping over the treetops of Vavuniya. His eyes mirrored the crimson colours of the burning sky, reflecting the resolve that burnt within.

* * *

The Infantry School, Mhow
January 1989

Jumping off the Malwa Express at Indore, Sudhir puffed his chest.

"This Malwa air smells good."

"Hmm," grunted Yash, biting into the famous Indore kachori, green chutney running down his chin. Ranjan was busy gorging on *mangodas*, a spicier variant of the pakoda, dipped in tamarind chutney.

They were off to Mhow, twenty-three kilometres away from Indore. It was home to the famed Infantry School, where the Young Officers course would be conducted.

"Mhow was the Military Headquarters of War?" asked Yash.

Sudhir tapped his book. "That's a backronym fuelled by student officers."

"Really?" said Ranjan.

"The Mhow cantonment was founded in 1818 through a treaty between the British and the Holkar…"

Yash looked up, enquiringly.

"... Maratha Maharajas of Indore, Yash," added Sudhir.

"Mhow finds mention in a letter from 1823 by a British lieutenant, Edward Squibb to his father in London," said Ranjan. "Rudyard Kipling wrote about Mhow in his books too."

"That's the professor speaking."

* * *

The course soon got the boys busy. Studying for the exams at night was laborious.

"So much science is not for me," Sudhir yawned, stretching his back.

"All this tech stuff about ammunition and weapons takes away the fun of shooting," remarked Yash philosophically.

"Thank god you did not study to be a gynaecologist," quipped Ranjan with a straight face.

Sudhir thumped the table. "Well said, professor, well said!"

Not yet giving up, a smiling Yash argued, "You never tire of certain things, professor. The gynaes have children too. That's proof that you don't get bored."

Ranjan arched his eyebrow. "There's a difference between duty and desire."

"Are you still afraid of heights?" asked Yash, his voice growing serious. "Does your duty force you to disregard your fear?"

"Fear will never be absent. It's always there. Courage is mastery over that fear," remarked Sudhir. "I learnt that in Sri Lanka."

"I have learnt to resist fear," said Ranjan," I know what a fucking devil it is."

"Your transformation is a pain-in-the-ass, professor. I am hit the hardest," joked Sudhir.

Ranjan had the best scores in the course by now. Sudhir was trailing behind and couldn't get past him.

Yash looked at the two. "Time does not change us; it just unfolds us."

"About time the professor stops unfolding now," smirked Sudhir.

Ranjan caught Sudhir's eye. "You are the one who requires unfolding, Sudhir. You are the one."

* * *

Popular for its traditional tailors and crocheted fabric, the narrow Mhow market streets were in sharp contrast to the drill-square whitewashed precision of the army cantonment next door. And while each lot depended on the other for its subsistence, the differing sensibilities occasionally triggered conflict between the Army men and the grounded townsfolk.

Most young Army officers were only temporary residents in Mhow, on a brief training assignment, while the townsfolk, in larger numbers, were sons of the soil, with properties, families and permanent interests but with lesser facilities and resources at hand. This only added fuel to the simmering divide.

It was Holi. Out shopping, a slur by a local goon turned self-styled social worker for a fellow officer's wife, infuriated a young officer. Not one to take the insolence lightly, the hot-blooded officer had an altercation with the goon. The heated exchange led to a tussle. In peak physical health, the recently trained commando not only overpowered the goon, but also his accomplices. A mob soon gathered, thrashed the officer, broke a rib, dislocating his shoulder. Refusing to take it lying down, the officer drove back to the cantonment and appraised his fellow student officers.

Faces smeared in Holi colours, two hundred enraged officers drove down to the market in search of the miscreants, vowing vengeance. The escalating scuffle turned into a street brawl.

No match for the commando-trained officers, the townsfolk suffered a rough deal. Vindicated by the trail of broken bones, noses and egos, the young officers finally withdrew from the scene silently, with operational efficiency.

The next day, the local papers screamed murder. The Infantry School launched a full-fledged investigation, a court of inquiry into the unsavoury incident. None of the young officers could be recognised. The well-planned strategy of Holi colours had helped. Individually summoned, each officer was asked to confess. None of the officers came forth.

"I will not lie, Yash," said Sudhir resolutely. "I cannot."

"But idiot, they will start a disciplinary action against you."

"I will argue. We went to defend our honour."

"What if they don't listen? Everyone has denied it."

"Truth is always the strongest argument."

"But there may be repercussions, Sudhir."

"Better to face it square." Shrugging his shoulders, he laughed. "I can't be shot for treason?"

* * *

Experience had wrinkled the senior officer's forehead, way ahead of his time.

The chief instructor glared at the young officer, the way a tiger watches a bunny. On the table was a written statement. Bunching his eyebrows, the chief instructor grunted, "Hmm... you are the only one who owned up."

Sudhir stared back without flinching a muscle.

"So you went there and beat these poor guys up?" The voice could cut glass.

"Yes sir, I did, but they deserved it."

"What the fuck?" He shot up from his chair. Words eluded him.

"I accept I did it... it's not about wrong or right."

Pointing a finger, the senior officer snarled, "You will do it again?"

"Yes, sir. Every time. I will defend the honour of the uniform," said Sudhir, hardening his jaw, defiantly.

The instructor's eyes carried a mixture of shock and barely contained anger. "I can have you sent back with a loss of seniority." The mouth turned up a fraction of an inch.

"That's your prerogative, sir. Mine is to stand by my comrade."

A wry smile touched his lips. "You are lucky. I have seen you in Sri Lanka."

Sudhir stared back without emotion.

"You are the idiot who sang that stupid song."

"Yes, sir."

The officer winked. "Did you make it up?"

Sudhir nodded, his eyes lighting up. " A little, sir."

The officer tore up the statement before him. " Fuck off."

Through the spotless window, he watched Sudhir's receding back. Catching his own reflection, he recalled. "I was once like him…"

He kept staring long after the sound of footsteps crunching the gravel had ended.

The babble of voices stopped as soon as they saw him emerge from the office.

"What makes him do this?" asked Ranjan, shaking his head.

"Strength and courage, professor."

"Fuck, that man seems untouchable."

* * *

New Delhi
December 1990

Sudhir and Yash had both got short leaves before the course. They planned to meet in Delhi and travel together by train to Belgaum for their training.

Organised and punctual, the greying gentlemen had arrived well before time. Standing on the platform of the New Delhi railway station, the professor observed the crowd. The train blew its last whistle. Yash, his future son-in-law was nowhere in sight.

"Where is he?" enquired his middle-aged colleague, a fellow academician. The professor snorted, shrugging his shoulders, wringing his fingers.

A loud commotion broke their quiet reverie. Two young men burst through the crowds, running at full clip towards the train, as it chugged away. Their baggage was presumably on the train, left with a few other officers who were also going to Belgaum. Yash had sneaked off to meet the professor's daughter, his girlfriend, while Sudhir was off wandering.

"Whoopee!" yelled Sudhir, more excited than distressed at the sight of the receding train.

Unaccustomed to abrupt developments and disorder, the two professors stared at each other, clucking their tongues. They had brought sweets for the journey. Eyeing the box, Sudhir smiled charmingly, "Sir, please give us the sweets and anything else you have brought along."

Tilting his head at the receding train, a speck by now Sudhir said, "Our money was on that train, too." Scratching his head, he continued, "We need to stay alive till Belgaum."

Yash shuffled, looking down, a warm flush on his neck, embarrassed to look at his future father-in-law.

"Are you sure?" Nudging the professor, the concerned friend whispered. "Your daughter… married to *him*?"

Sudhir strained his ears to catch the whisperings through the din of the station.

"They can't even catch a train… they have lost their luggage… money," whispered his friend, "and yet look at them…"

"Don't worry, sir, your daughter will be treated like a princess by my friend," said Sudhir, eyes dancing, a mischievous curl on his lips. "Won't you, Yash?"

The professor shuffled his feet and looked away, sighing.

"Sir, could you also lend us some money, please? Just enough to get us to Belgaum?" said Sudhir in his sweetest tone.

Yash wished the earth would swallow him.

* * *

The Commando School, Belgaum
December 1990

As they entered the gates of the Junior Leaders Wing, which housed the Commando School, Yash nudged Sudhir. They both chuckled as they read the sign overhead: *'Here we make men out of boys.'*

"Get ready for a thirty-five-day fuck, Sudhir."

Sudhir shrugged his shoulders. "Que sera, sera. Whatever will be, will be."

Regarded as one of the toughest courses in the world, it called for extreme physical and mental strength.

* * *

The next morning, the young, bleary-eyed officers attending the course stumbled in to muster.

"Commandos, wake up. It's a lovely early morning," barked the instructor at the squad.

"Early morning?" muttered an officer from behind. "Someone tell this chimpanzee it's 2 fucking a.m."

"A commando never sleeps. Now pick up your packs. Let's fill some healthy oxygen into your unhealthy lungs!" yelled the instructor.

The physical fitness session started at 2 a.m. with a pack weighing 5 kilos. The pack kept getting heavier as the course progressed. Most aspirants had the skin scraped off their backs, with painful ugly bruises because of the relentless pace of the course.

The squad ran past the signage.

"I don't want to be a fucking man, let me remain a boy," lamented

Ranjan, panting. A term senior than Sudhir, he hated physicals.

"You are wheezing like a bloody steam engine," said Sudhir, helping him. As they went around the loop for the fourth time on jelly legs.

"What do you fucking expect? A piano?"

"Well, at least a military trumpet," joked Sudhir, dragging him along.

"His rear sure sounds like one," quipped another officer, gasping behind. "He just farted like a bugle."

Everyone burst out laughing, forgetting their painful lungs.

The glaring instructor gave them three extra runs. "Let me see who laughs the loudest now," he added, smirking.

* * *

'When the going gets tough, the tough get going.' The second catchy slogan displayed prominently at many places would jeer them as they underwent the thirty-five days of endless gruel. Sudhir had aced the unarmed combat, day and night navigation, cliff climbing, weapons training and heliborne insertion into enemy territory. He had breezed past explosives handling, special operations and survival training, all part of the curriculum.

The squad was now undergoing the most daring part of the course. Called the Lido Jump, named after the hot and happening Lido beach in Venice, Italy, it was someone's dark humour at play. They said you could see bikini-clad women from up there. The Lido jump helped overcome vertigo and develop self-confidence.

Mind numb and feet wobbly, Ranjan slowly climbed the 55 feet tower over the huge square pool aptly named 'Lido Tank'.

"It holds the fears of a thousand souls," a young instructor had informed them. "You shed your fears here. It's a commando womb. You are reborn, better than at birth."

Palms sweaty, his throat felt painfully dry. Ranjan was afraid he would lose his grip and fall off the endless rails leading up the tower. Ranjan reached the top and dared not look down at the water. The wind whipped at his combat uniform. There was a hum in his ears. Closing his eyes, he muttered a prayer, feeling goose bumps on his arms and neck. "You can do this," he valiantly repeated, trying to bolster the sinking feeling.

Sudhir had warned him. "Just…don't look down."

Ranjan forced himself to look straight. Ahead was the 24-inches-wide plank on which he had to do a balanced walk. Big enough for his feet, but not an inch to spare. So fucking tiny and he had to walk on it. It stretched out like a bridge over nothingness. This was bloody crazy!

He thought he saw the plank sway. His chest heaving, he tried to control his jagged breathing. Arms outstretched, shuffling along the plank, he swayed precariously, cursing the day he joined the infantry. 'You are not fucking made for this!' a voice told him.

Halfway through the 40-foot long plank, Ranjan looked down fifty feet and lost his nerve. Looking down at the rippling water made you feel as if the plank was shaking and set off the vertigo. He still had to walk 20 feet and climb two flights of stairs, equally wide.

"C'mon, go on!" yelled Sudhir. "Don't bloody stop!"

Ranjan halted, and the squad held their breath. He sat down, clutching the plank; too scared to move.

An instructor yelled, "Get on, Commando Ranjan, or I am coming up!"

"Come up then, you bastard," muttered Ranjan, grinding his jaw. His eyes again strayed past the plank, 50-feet below.

The reflection from the water hurt his eyes. Nauseous and with his head spinning, he felt his bile rising. Distastefully sampling the leftover of the morning's breakfast, spasms forced the dribble out. The contents spattering into the waters below. His eyes widened, while his thighs trembled. White-knuckled, he held the plank till his palms soured.

Barely audible, his croaking voice filtered down. "I want to come down."

Unease hung in the air. The wind had stopped. Ranjan felt a warm wetness flow along his thigh. It wet the plank below and dribbled into the tank. He couldn't care less.

A chorus of voices arose.

"Get up, you'll break your family jewels!"

"You want to go through hell again?"

"Nooooo!" yelled Ranjan.

"Then don't give up. Think of your regiment!"

"Finish it and we'll never joke about your trumpet."

Everyone burst out laughing, including Ranjan 50 feet up. "You fucking bastards!" he yelled back. "I'll fall off, if you make me laugh anymore."

The bubble burst. Laughter had the desired effect and it triggered Ranjan to move ahead.

"Don't break your jewels. Think of your unborn descendants."

"Move on!" yelled Sudhir. "Don't fucking stop, Ranjan!"

"Fuck you!" yelled Ranjan, finally getting a grip of his fear. Sudhir smiled.

Ranjan, now monkey crawled along a 20 feet horizontal rope also hanging 55 feet above the water. Stabilising himself by locking his feet as two instructors tugged vigorously to dislodge him, he finally yelled his name and jumped down at the crack of a rifle shot.

* * *

Every weekend, as they went through the gruelling endurance marches, progressively moving from 10, 20, 30 and 40 kilometres, with personal weapons and loads of 17.5 kilos, Sudhir emerged strongest in the squad.

Awaiting their turns to fire their weapons at the range, the squad sat idle for the few moments of respite they had luckily got.

Sudhir lovingly wiped the bayonet from his weapon on his thigh. "I want that QFI[35]," he said, spitting out the straw he was chewing. Very

---

[35] *To be graded as 'QFI' (Qualified, fit to be an Instructor), a trainee had to clear all*

few trainees with the highest level of physical and mental ability had accomplished that.

Yash nodded. "You are already there. Just a little more effort."

Sudhir looked away. He knew where he lacked and it gnawed at him.

Ranjan looked at Sudhir. "It's a gamble… a chance."

Sudhir cleaned the glistening knife blade a little more and turned it around to look for dirt. "I hate to gamble, but if it's one thing I will bet on, it's myself." He held Ranjan's gaze as he spoke. Everyone was sure by now that Sudhir would get the QFI. He already was way ahead of the competition.

They just had one test left, the Battle Obstacle Course (BOC). The trainees would negotiate 22 obstacles in 18 minutes and 30 seconds, carrying their rifles and an additional Chota-Paploo of 3.5 kilos[36] in full combat dress.

"*Go!*" yelled the instructor, stopwatch in hand. Sudhir, ready like a coiled spring, jumped and took off. Nimble-footed, he negotiated the obstacles with ease.

Way ahead of the closing time, Sudhir reached a rope obstacle where he had to haul himself up and swing over. This was his weakness.

Failing in his first attempt, Sudhir attempted the obstacle thrice, losing precious time. He refused to give up and kept retrying. He finally crossed the obstacle, barely meeting the passing deadline of eighteen minutes and thirty seconds.

He had missed the qualifying mark for the QFI because of bad timing.

"Why didn't you just bypass it?" asked a surprised Col. V.K. Singh, a commando instructor. He would later rise to become the army chief. "You had enough points in hand. You could have skipped it."

"I could not just give up, sir. I had to overcome it."

"Even if it means losing out?"

---

parts with excellent timings.

[36] *A sand filled bag, nicknamed Chota-Paploo*

"This was only a grading, sir, but I have conquered…"

"Your weakness?"

"My vulnerability. My fear. My mind."

A smile broke out on Col. Singh's face. He tapped Sudhir on his chest, "Go on, commando."

"That boy has pep, sir," said another instructor who had overheard the conversation. "He'll do well."

"This confidence in your own ability is rare. A special courage. He is here to win."

＊＊＊＊

Recruits of Steel

Mahendra
Jhunjhunu
October 1990

He was Mahendra's hero.

Whenever his brother, a commando from 9 Para (SF), came home to their remote hamlet in the arid dust bowl of Jhunjhunu, Mahendra's dark solemn eyes would glint in reverence. He would often sneak away with his brother's maroon beret. Flaunting the beret perched at a jaunty tilt, he would swivel and salute, peering into the askew, half mirror.

He loved sitting under the stars, with the elders. Enveloped by the crackle of the warm fire from the hookah, he would listen to his brother's stories – his travels to Sri Lanka, his battles and the firefights in Vavuniya. He would listen to the anecdotes of 9 Para and the tales of brotherhood and comradeship.

It gave him goosebumps.

Even while feeding the camels or working in the small family field, his mind would wander, yearning to don the uniform and the maroon beret. Mahendra realised his dream when he qualified as a recruit and joined the para centre in Agra for his basic training. The second son from the same proud family had become a paratrooper.

Early in the same year, Kashmir had witnessed the exodus of the Kashmiri Pandit population. Following sectarian violence and ethnic cleansing, Jihad had killed Kashmiriyat, the centuries old communal harmony.

Kashmir was boiling.

* * *

Udhampur
November 1991

With enough motivation coursing in his veins to rouse his hamlet, he cleared the tough para probation in a breeze and joined 9 Para (SF) in Udhampur.

That year, Kashmir was burning. The government had announced the general elections for the 10th Lok Sabha in the country. The insurgency in Kashmir had reached a critical peak. Forced to declare a state of emergency, the Central government enforced the Armed Forces (J&K) Special Powers Act, enacted in July 1990, as the only means to douse the fire.

The general elections in Kashmir stood cancelled.

* * *

Something about Mahendra clicked in Sudhir. Not his strong heart, or his willingness to sacrifice. Mahendra's immense calm in tricky situations and his ability to think through danger made him a dependable buddy. The dependability evoked loyalty.

Mahendra became an inseparable shadow to Sudhir. He was not only Sudhir's buddy, but his radio operator as well. They often walked together as leading scouts, daring the unknown. Frequently compressed together, in the reactor of consistent near-death experiences, their minds created a partnership beyond natural horizons.

* * * *

Mukhtiar
Udhampur, May 1992

Raising an eyebrow, Sudhir peered at the squad lined up in front of him.

The faces reflected resolve, impatience, uncertainty. Fifty-three souls from across the Army stood before Sudhir in a motley bunch. They were volunteers for the para commandoes.

"Choose if you wish to live through hell or go back to your mothers," forewarned Sudhir, tipping off the weak-hearted. His eyes flickered past them.

Balking at his words, some men shifted their weight. Sweaty toes twitched undetected inside the boots. Their eyes caught the glint of the silver crest riding on Sudhir's maroon beret. With the wings, parachute and commando dagger, held in a scroll, the insignia of the parachute regiment challenged them to strive. Each man would undergo the mandatory probation of ninety days. Evidently, the worst nightmare imagined.

The Parachute Regiment were the elite volunteer force of the Indian Army. Because of their pivotal role, the regiment demanded the greatest level of efficiency and physical fitness. This made recruitment as a para commando difficult and rewarding.

They would test each man beyond the limits of endurance, challenged psychologically and intellectually. Their spirits would succumb to the lowest point. Their will would be broken. And then, nudged a little further.

The aim was to break their boundaries and recalibrate their minds. Hereafter, nothing would limit them. Not even their minds.

"You will be called upon to accomplish missions that ordinary men will find impossible. Your start line is where they end. They will never pat you for your triumphs. You will never find glory. Largely, the world will never know about your exploits."

Experienced, he recognised only the toughest would survive. Only the finest were to be cherry-picked. The special forces were an exceptional force and it became Sudhir's responsibility as the probation officer to keep it that way. Every man had to earn the right to wear the maroon beret.

"You need the resilience of a dog, the ferocity of a tiger, the speed of a cheetah, the swiftness of a gazelle, the guile of a jackal, the eye of a hawk and the survivability of a cockroach. You will scavenge like a hyena and fight like a lion!"

The words arrested every man. On cue, a flap of black wings squawked angrily. Eyes scarcely darting, Sudhir bared his teeth.

"No omens, no gods can help you. Only your own grit, your weapon and your buddy. Hungry, exhausted and tired beyond death, we will still expect you to rise and beat the enemy."

Gritting, he hissed, "Not everyone has it."

"Go back! Grow old, retire and earn your pensions."

Smarting under Sudhir's stare, the crowd shifted uneasily. As reality sunk in, so did their enthusiasm.

Sudhir's eye caught a young Sikh soldier standing casually in the rear row. Hardly a man, his scraggy beard and slight frame made him look far too young. The thin upturned moustaches never-the-less gave away his intentions.

"Where are you from?"

"Jogger, Sir," said the young soldier, holding Sudhir's gaze steady. "Tehsil Pathankot, District Gurdaspur."

"Jogger? Never heard of it," quipped Sudhir, a curl touching his lips.

"You will now, sir," said the soldier under his breath.

"Your name, young man?"

Gaze unmoving from Sudhir's Balidan badge, the soldier retorted, "I am Sepoy Mukhtiar Singh from 17 Punjab."

The Special Forces had a distinct insignia called Balidan. A commando dagger pointed downwards, with upward-extending wings extending from the blade. A scroll superimposed on the blade with 'Balidan' inscribed in Devanagari; set in silver metal on an upright red plastic rectangle. Only the para commandos could wear the badge. Balidan, or sacrifice, determined the ultimate cost of the inexpensive insignia.

"And you think you can wear this badge?" challenged Sudhir, touching the badge on his chest with reverence, as he followed Mukhtiar's eyes.

"I am here. I will earn it," declared the young man resolutely, a quiver defining his voice.

Though straight-faced, Sudhir's heart skipped a beat. The boy had nerve. "Okay then, let's meet at 3 a.m. tomorrow, Mukhtiar Singh. Rest. This is the only rest you will get for the next 90 days."

Freezing in the chilly mountain air, their feet crunched the frosty grass the next morning, while the world still slumbered in its warm bed. 20 kilometres of race, carrying 30 kilos on their bloody backs. Deprived of sleep, minds numb with exhaustion, their muscles screamed from the endless speed runs in full battle loads.

The last phase of the arduous probation crept up. A few had given up, unable to bear the extremity of the physical demands. Others had broken down, unable to handle the psychological pressure.

Having cleared his physicals with a hundred percent result and his written exams with equal elan, young Mukhtiar once again stood before Sudhir.

Wincing, Sudhir noticed the tender pink skin peeping through a broken nail as Mukhtiar saluted. The slim frame had turned rugged, the body gaunt. Peeling lips and the weather-beaten face, however, could not dampen the fierce pride that shone through the eyes.

"You have done well in your 30- and 40-kilometre speed marches. Your skills at communication, navigation, map reading, first aid and medicals are clear," said Sudhir, glancing at the score sheet with interest. "Your firing is exceptional. You almost got caught in the escape and evasion exercise, though."

Mukhtiar's boyish face broke into a smile as he remembered the night.

Left deep in the jungles, post a simulated 72-hour combat exercise, they were now expected to survive another 96 hours, without food, living off the jungle. They were prisoners of war, escaping from an enemy prison. If caught, it would be the end of the probation.

Mukhtiar had battled four soldiers who had crept up on him as sleep caught up. He had finally jumped into a gorge dense with undergrowth to evade the trackers as he made off.

Sudhir studied the high mutual assessment scores, frowning, eyebrows knitted. "Either you are a terrific team player or a sly fox. Who are you?"

A pan-faced Mukhtiar tilted his head, gesturing towards the team with his chin, "Trusting them was my decision. Proving me right was their choice."

Despite just three and a half years' service, Mukhtiar had also aced the 12 IQ tests and was running first in the group. He now had only one test more to prove. The psychological test.

Sudhir knew he had found a winner.

"As a soldier, you hardly earn a few thousand rupees in salary. What if you are called to desert and join the Khalistanis? You will earn millions. Why wouldn't you go?"

Mukhtiar bit his lip. "Sir, the uniform gives me *izzat*. If I die, I will go home draped in a tri-color. I can never earn that elsewhere, despite my millions." Mukhtiar's eyes blazed with passion.

"You need to kill and not die for your country, Mukhtiar," roared Sudhir, his fist banging the table. The blaze in his eyes equalled Mukhtiar's. Straightening his spine, Mukhtiar took in a deep breath.

Acknowledging the lesson of life. One of many he would learn from this remarkable young officer.

Eyes softening, Sudhir removed the badge and slid it across the rough table. "Jogger, your village will be proud of you…" he drawled, pursuing his lips.

A shaking *kada* was the only emotion that escaped, as the steel hand proudly clutched the reward in a vice grip.

Sudhir handpicked Mukhtiar. He became not only part of his B team, but part of the inner circle, the Fifth troop. They would now be inseparable, parting only when death did them apart.

* * * *

An instructor read out the names. Only seventeen soldiers had cleared the probation. Amongst them were two officers, Capt. Negi, a medical officer, and Capt. Arun Jasrotia.

Arun and Sudhir would forge a friendship for life.

Commissioned in 8 Bihar in 1989, Arun Jasrotia had earned a Sena Medal before he joined 9 Para. The only son of Lt. Colonel Prabhat Singh Jasrotia, his grandfather had also served in the Army as a Lt. Colonel with the 2nd Dogra Regiment.

Those selected would now go through another gruelling training of nine months. 50 jumps from 33,000 feet at the Air Force Training School in Agra and skilled to fight in the water, they would qualify in the Naval Diving Training School, Kochi. They could not only fire, but also strip every weapon, blindfolded. Not only survive, but they were also now trained to hit back with a violence that few could fathom.

* * *

Vinod

I heard the shocking news in the unit. Along with two of my colleagues, we rushed down to the military hospital at Pathankot.

Just that morning, Sudhir sir had sat on the scooter, revving it up.

"I'll be back soon, Vinod." He smiled with a twinkle in his eye.

"Go, enjoy your Diwali, sir." His energy was indefatigable, infectious. "You need the break."

Off on a quick leave, Sudhir sir had borrowed a scooter to travel down to Palampur. He waved in response to my salute and set off from Udhampur on the jaunty ride. Near Hira Nagar, short of Pathankot, he collided with a buffalo. In the freak accident, the scooter caught fire. Sudhir sir got severe burns on his thighs and back. He remained scarred for life with those wounds.

Covered by a raised sheet because of the burns, we found him peppy and grinning in the officers' ward of the military hospital.

"Painful?" I asked him, concerned.

He shook his head, smiling. "I feel like an overdone steak."

Eyes crinkling with mischief, he turned his head towards us.

"The nurses here are beautiful," he whispered. "You should get admitted too."

We discussed operations and intelligence inputs as he directed us to follow leads. Despite being burned and in considerable pain and discomfort, his fertile mind was never at rest. We spoke for hours. The nurse on duty had to push us out after the visiting hours were long over.

Not wanting to alarm his parents, especially his mother, he did not inform them but continued to wrestle with the painful burns by himself. We admired his grit. And his indomitable spirit. His mother found out later and hurried down to see him by herself. He had inherited her strength and her resolve.

"You didn't inform me?" Her eyes flashed fire, as she barged in.

Sudhir sir smiled tenderly. "Ma … I'm ok."

"Is this how … ?" She squared her jaw, overcome with anger.

"Yes, that's how I honour your love and values, Ma."

He had inherited both, her strength and her determination. She had ingrained that in him. "Uphold the honour of a mother's milk," she had often inspired him. And he did just that.

The doctors thought it would be a considerable while before he could get on his feet. But who could hold down Sudhir sir? He couldn't wear trousers because the wounds hadn't healed. Even that did not stop him. He was on his feet, strutting around, much to the astonishment of the doctors, with a wrap around his waist.

KASHMIR

Jihad-e-Kashmir

The crisp clean mountain air carried the smells of the night drizzle, mogra and blooming roses. Pakistan's independence day was always a sensitive one in the valley.

An early riser, he sipped his morning tea. He looked at the picture of P.V. Narasimha Rao on the cover of the 31st July 1993 issue of *India Today*, sitting on the elaborate veranda overlooking the manicured lawns of the Raj Bhavan in Srinagar.

Characterised as indecisive and a bumbling ditherer, the prime minister, after completing two years in office, was now stained with the added ignominy of being labelled a bribe-taker. In the dock for the biggest scam in the Indian stock markets, Harshad Mehta had accused the Prime Minister of India of taking a bribe.

Shaking his head, he read the bold headline, 'Can He Recover?'

Raising an eyebrow at the incessant ring, Gen. K.V. Krishna Rao put away the magazine. He noticed the old gardener from the edge of his vision, snipping away the tulip bulbs with precision. He was preparing for the coming year.

"Yes," he said gruffly. The secretary hesitated, sensing the general's irritation.

The ruling Congress government in Delhi reappointed the former Chief of Army Staff, Governor of Jammu and Kashmir in March. He shared a close rapport with P.V. Narasimha Rao.

Intelligence had forewarned Gen. Rao of trouble. Inputs suggested miscreants would unfurl and hoist the Pakistani national flag. They had expected some trouble, but nothing so appalling.

In New Delhi, Shankarrao Bhavrao Chavan, the Home Minister was just about waking up from sleep. Spilling the glass of fresh milk from his favourite cow, the phone call from his secretary banished his sleep completely.

* * *

Kishtwar
14th August, 1993

The stench in the *dhok* with its mud rammed walls and animal dung plaster was offensive. The stench of animal and human faeces in the foul air was aggravated by the pungent unwashed body, saturated with dried sweat, high on substance.

Barely thirteen, she was skinny. Her penetrating green-blue eyes and sharp nose affirmed her Gujjar-Bakharwal lineage.

Naturally auburn, her hair was matted red. The crimson mark on the rough wooden door testimony to her heroic struggle. Her skin prickled as she sensed his gaze scorch her bare back. Her muffled sobs were more from shame, than from the sheer pain between her legs. Violating her adolescent malnourished body, he had mounted her all night. His teeth marked painful welts on her growing breasts, stomach and thighs where he had bitten, like a beast.

Drawing up his grey salwar, Langrial kicked her naked butt, leaving a red welt on her white skin. "Get out!" he barked roughly. "Go back!" She scampered out with her clutch of torn rags, spasming through her convulsing breath.

Brushing his greasy shoulder length hair away from his forehead, he wrapped his black turban roughly over a cap and let the extra tail fall on his shoulder. Picking up his AK-47, standing vigil at an arm's length, he sneered, recollecting her cries of pain.

They had forcibly taken food from the pitiable hutments just a kilometre away. Looking at the girl as she brought in the milk, he had clutched her shivering wrist and dragged her out. A gun pointed at the father's head halted the wailing mother midway.

Puzzled, Abdul Bari, the young engineering student from Taif in Saudi Arabia, looked askance. Noticing the frown lines on Bari's youthful face, Langrial raised two fingers. "It serves two purposes," he derided, ever ready with advice.

"Her family will not utter a word to the Indian dogs till she comes back," spat out Habibullah. "She will keep us safe."

From Wakan in Afghanistan, Habibullah rarely spoke. He had been with Langrial through the fighting and the guerrilla wars. Habibullah was like a coiled spring. He only exploded with violence when needed.

"And our bodies can have some rest, as we serve Allah's will," smacked Abdul Hameed the Turk, lecherously.

"Inshallah," responded Nasrullah Manzoor Langrial, pulling on his beard. The boys were learning.

ISI wanted to send the message that Kashmir had now become the focus of an international jihad. The presence of the foreign recruits served the game plan.

Kishtwar, barely seven kilometres away, had 41% Hindu population. The dhok overlooked the Kishtwar-Sarthal Road.

24 kilometres away, Sarthal was a picturesque meadow, very popular as a tourist spot. The Sarthal road intersection was a perfect site for their plan.

At 0615 hrs, the lookout gave a signal as the rickety passenger bus came into view. Bound for Jammu, the bus screeched to a halt as a masked man stepped out in front, holding an AK-47.

Two more masked militants got in, as the bus stopped.

"All kafirs get out," barked the militant, standing next to the driver. He pointed his weapon at the nearest man, poking him in the ribs. A cackle of scared voices shrieked in unison.

The second militant had walked down the aisle, pointing his gun, identifying victims.

Her father just had time to enough to keep his palm on her head. Her scalp ached every time she thought of it. Etched for life, a young, bewildered Madhu would never forget her father Keshav Nath being kicked out. Her mother whimpered silently, nails digging into her sweaty palms.

Bound for Jammu for cancer treatment, Raghbir's wife seized his wrinkled hand, trying to hold on to the fifty years they had spent together. Her feeble efforts were wasted.

A resisting Girdhar Lal, accompanying his pregnant daughter, was hit with a rod. As the daughter tried to protect her father, she was kicked in the stomach. The jarring pain embedded in her soul. Pupils dilated, Manoj watched the terrorist step on to his second year Physics book. Perspiring despite the early morning, he tried to control his trembling fingers. Wobbling on jelly legs, his childhood friend and roommate, Abhaya, let out a small cry, oblivious to the darkening patch in his pants. His mother's love, enclosed in the small tiffin, sat sadly on the seat, abandoned.

Teeth chattering, the two poor labourers fell in the mud, begging. Mud caked their faces, stained with tears and spit.

Three bangles broke, as she clung to her husband. Her red dupatta tore, dragged by his thick kada, when he stood up in a huff. They followed him as he stiffly walked down the aisle. That would be the only memory of her brief marriage.

Satisfied that they were no more Hindu men inside, the terrorist stepped aside and signalled the driver to drive off. The sixteen passengers who had been taken off the bus were told to line up along the road.

The four masked men switched their weapons to automatic.

From the Harkat-ul-Mujahideen, Arif Hussain looked up at the dark figure obscured by the pine tree. The man nodded, not wanting to reveal himself yet. Arif walked up, looked into Manoj's terrified eyes, a smile touched his mouth as he pulled the trigger. On cue, the other four terrorists mercilessly gunned down the hapless passengers. They made sure they fired a second time over, spraying the bodies with more automatic fire.

Deed done, they silently climbed up the slope and melted into the deep forests that hugged the road.

* * * *

The governor called for an emergency meeting. Rao noticed the glum expressions of the Director Gen. of Police, B.S.Bedi, a 1961 IPS batch officer. Next to him sat the Chief Secretary, Sheikh Ghulam Rasool, a Kashmiri. P.C. Dogra, Additional Director-Gen. of the BSF and Gen. Mohd. Ahmed Zaki, the Security Advisor to the Governor.

"Members of one community…" said Rao, voice low and gravely. "Killed in cold blood?"

BJP and some parties had organised bandhs. Five districts were under curfew.

Commanding the valley based 15 Corps, Gen Sundararajan Padmanabhan leaned forward. "The Kishtwar killings have added two new perilous dimensions," he warned. "First is the communal tinge given by the Harkat-ul-Mujahideen."

"But, Paddy, this isn't new." Stroking his nose, Rao shook his head. "The Kashmiri Pandits and their exodus two years back? That was communal too."

"But this is different, sir," said Gen. Padmanabhan, tapping the table with his finger. He looked around, noticing little support.

"Second, the fire's spread to the Jammu region."

Rao looked at him wryly. "It happened on our watch. We have blood on our hands."

Curiously, the police chief was born at Daska in Sialkot, present-day Pakistan, home of one of the perpetrators of the massacre. "Possibly your old neighbourhood," winked Paddy, as they broke up.

While Governor K.V. Krishna Rao was all for holding elections later that year, Minister of State for Internal Security, Rajesh Pilot, felt normalcy needed to precede democracy. As the government dithered, terrorism widened its reach and escalated its violence. The state slipped further into the abyss.

* * * * *

New Delhi
16th August, 1993

A heated debate ensued in Parliament. BJP stalwart Madan Lal Khurana, MP, questioned the government. Sadiq Ahmad, part of a sleeper cell of Jaish-e-Mohammed in Delhi, had ordered his favourite biriyani. The stale smell of rolled beedi clung in the small unkempt room.

He watched the recorded tape of the debate, smuggled out through his contact in Doordarshan, India's public service broadcaster. The cold Pepsi left a puddle on the newspaper where the incident had found a small mention. Sadly, Harshad Mehta's exploits made better headlines.

Eyes wide, Sadiq watched as L.K. Advani, another stalwart MP, stood up. He spat in disgust as he saw Advani. "Mother fucker!" he abused.

"We will get you too, you dog," he swore under his breath. Advani had been under threat for his pro-Hindutva views.

"Mr. Deputy Speaker, we demand answers. The house needs to be appraised of the facts."

There was a disturbance as the Congress MPs shouted Advani down. Sadiq looked on.

Rajesh Pilot stood up to make the statement on behalf of the government. Sadiq smacked his lips and smiled. This was good. He took a sip from the Pepsi bottle, eyes still riveted to the scene in front, scratching his beard.

The house sat aghast, listening to the account of the carnage. The cameras captured the statement without missing a blink. The house knew the passengers had been all Hindus.

Rajesh Pilot spoke, his tone stiff. "They killed 14 people. Two injured. One died in hospital." He looked up as the house sat in stunned silence.

"The security forces have been told to ensure such incidents do not occur again."

Clapping his hands, Sadiq shrieked in childish glee. The macabre chuckle resonated off the bare walls. The biryani forgotten, he rushed down to the nearest PCO to make a phone call. He dialled 01342, the STD code. Bijnor flashed on the display, a town in Uttar Pradesh, near Moradabad.

Time for congratulations. Nasrullah Mansoor Langrial had made his mark.

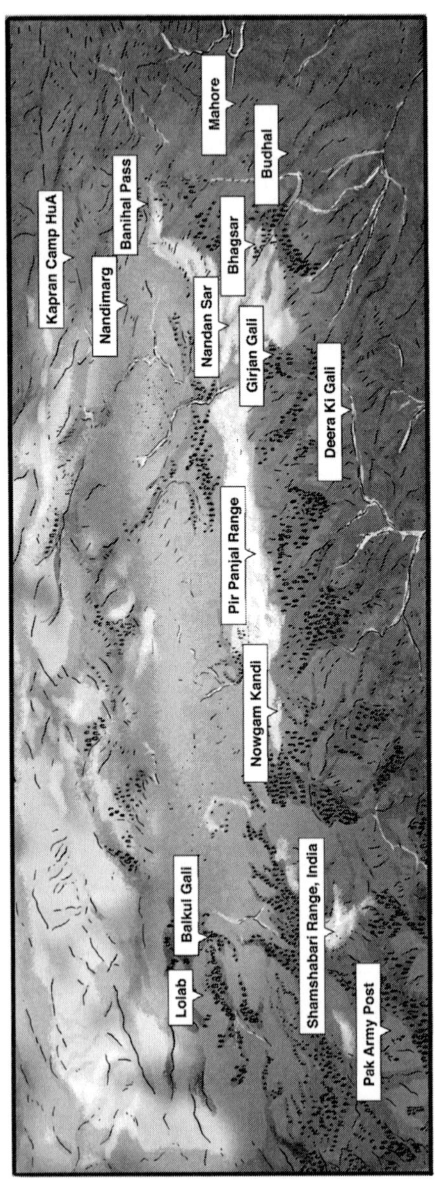

Shamshabari, Kapran, Pirpanjal, Banihal

Muridke, Pakistan

December 1990 (Two years before the bus strike)

"The jihad needs to endure," appealed Merajuddin alias Col. Assad. Apparently of Kashmiri origin, he oversaw the political cell of the ISI. "The flames need to spread further across the valley."

Col. Assad, along with three ISI brigadiers, played a major role in Kashmir.

He was speaking at the Markaz's[37] *Alsanawiu*, the annual meeting in Muridke. It had money pouring in from its global benefactors.

Lowering his voice, Mustafa alias Brig. Tariq hissed to the man next to him.

"Experienced men," he said. "And … they need to heed orders."

"Basically, morons who will act," replied Brig. Salim Khan under his breath, placing his palms on the table. "Exactly on our orders."

Peering at the gathering, he pointed with his chin. Mustafa followed his gaze.

Jalaluddin Haqqani, the infamous Afghan mujahideen, sat in the first row. Next to him, the HuJI[38] leader, Maulana Arsalan Khan Rehmani[39]. On his left sat Nisar Ahmed Bhatt. He would play a critical role in the Mumbai blasts.

The Saudi delegates sat to the right. The rich Arabs only paid the sponsors. Personally, they were disinclined to fight the jihad.

"Kashmir needs to boil. Our timetable unfolds early next year," proclaimed Numanaka Brig. Farooq Ahmad, the third brigadier.

A murmur broke out through the crowd. The brigadiers looked at each other.

Treading carefully, Brig. Salim waited for the perfect moment. "The mujahedeen…." he paused and looked around hesitantly. "Need to

---

[37] *Propelled by the ISI, the Markaz-dawa-ul-Irshad (Centre for the Propagation of the Right Teachings) became one of the most vibrant pan Islamic organisations*

[38] *Harkat-ul-Jehad-e-Islami*

[39] *Future Afghan deputy prime minister*

embrace Kashmir." He raised his voice above the din.

The gruff voice was arresting. "And the jihad in Afghanistan?"

Brig. Salim looked at the tall figure with his shawl and a black turban. Gulbuddin Hekmatyar[40] of Hizb-e-Islami, an Afghani terror outfit, looked formidable.

"Our support to jihad there will continue, but Kashmir needs to be stoked." Mustafa held Hekmatyar's gaze.

Abdul Rehman from Bahrain stood up. "India is the centre of *kufr*… infidelity." He looked at the crowd as a buzz broke out. "It requires cleansing. Jihad."

"I will go into this land of kafirs." All eyes turned towards Gulbuddin Hekmatyar, his imposing frame towered over the gathering. He raised his thick fist in the air. "I will cleanse Kashmir," he growled.

"I will be the *the* volunteer." The shawl slipped from his broad shoulders, revealing his gun belt and weapon. He was never without it.

"My mujahedeen will protect Islam," Maulana Arsalan Khan Rehmani raised his voice.

The echo of gunfire reverberated in tune with the announcement, accompanied with a cry of, 'Allah-hu-Akbar.'

The brigadiers finally smiled.

Rubbing his hands gleefully, Tariq murmured to Assad. "These guys are ideal. They are primed."

Hiding a sly smile, Assad whispered. "Ideologically committed and militarily seasoned, what more do we need?"

"More fighters. The fire must spread with speed," spat Brig. Salim, overhearing the muffled conversation. As a fallout of the meeting, several foreign mujahedeen were funneled into Kashmir by the ISI, as its trump card.

---

[40] *Hekmatyar oversaw four training camps: Khost, Cheherabagh, Tremangal and Jalalabad. The best-known camp, the Illaqa-e-Gair (forbidden area), was part of an army cantonment, on the road between Islamabad and Attock.*

* * *

The ISI soon got more fodder. They got plain lucky.

Brig. Tariq looked at his boss, Lt. Gen.Asad Ahmed Durrani, the ISI chief, "We have over 20,000 hanging around."

The premature shutdown of the Afghan war had rendered these jihadis jobless.

Brig Farooq Ahmad said, "There are two kinds, sir."

The ISI Chief nodded, asking him to go on.

"The poor illiterate who require the money," glancing over his glasses, he continued, "even as they further Allah's will."

"And the educated ones who need to be convinced that Islam is in danger." The ISI chief looked at a smiling Brig. Tariq as he spoke.

"Use them well," winked the general, beaming broadly. "Allah has been merciful."

Rushing back to his office, he was keener to read the letter from his son studying in Harvard.

The ISI used the Jamaat to convince the *Ulama*[41].

"Faith knows no boundaries. Any true believer should come to the aid of the religion anywhere in the world." The word of the Ulama was final.

Earlier, the inspiration for jihad was against the Soviets in Afghanistan. It was now against India. Most required little convincing. The ready availability of women and a debauched life was bait enough for these hardened men.

* * *

Mountains of Kunduz, Northern Afghanistan

The pungent smell of hashish hung in the air. Back in his camp, after the Muridke meeting, he had gathered his henchmen. Reciting the

---

[41] *The ulama are the guardians, transmitters, and interpreters of religious knowledge in Islam, including Islamic doctrine and law.*

Kalima, he settled on the carpet. Prayer bead in hand, Maulana Arsalan Khan Rehmani looked at the faces of his commanders as they sat in his mountain hideout.

As the supreme commander of HuJI, it was his responsibility to convince them.

"Only our relevance to ISI will guarantee our survival," said Rehmani.

Dropping a pellet of hashish into the glowing embers, he sucked up the vapours through a straw. Letting out a small puff, he grumbled, "But it is not our fight brother?"

Rehmani glared at his younger brother, Abu.

"We need the money." The opium trade had helped them survive and profit. The trade with the Baloch tribes along the Iran border could only continue if the ISI turned a blind eye. "Our supplies of opium need to continue."

"… the Uzbeks?" Abu suggested. "They will buy from us? They are closer, just across the Amu Darya.[42]"

Abu looked at his brother.

"I have spoken to them."

Spitting, Langrial took off his shawl, keeping his weapon aside.

"Undependable mother fuckers," he sputtered out.

Tapping his chillum on a rock, he let the burnt residual fall out. Removing a cloth pouch from deep inside, he refilled the chillum with great care. "And they fleece us."

Abu studied Langrial with swelling unease.

"We will even lose the *usher* if we continue like this," spat out Langrial, grinding his teeth. He was referring to the 10% they collected from each farmer growing opium.

He glanced at Abu, drawing back his lips in a snarl, challenging him. Stiffening his shoulders, Abu felt his ears burn. How dare Langrial speak

---

[42] *The Amu Darya running towards the Northwest was also famous for the Friendship Bridge over which the Soviets had finally withdrawn.*

to him with such insolence? He was the supreme commander's younger brother. Langrial had to go.

Snapping his mouth shut, he glanced at his brother, beseeching help.

Rehmani studied Langrial. 'If only my brother was more like him.' The thought compelled him to linger on Nasrullah Mansoor Langrial. One of his best commanders, Langrial had fought in the Afghan jihad through most of the 1980s.

Langrial spoke through the smoke cloud. "Jihad in Kashmir will give us power."

Rehmani nodded.

"It will ensure our survival in the *majlis* of Kabul too. "He was keeping a tab on his political ambitions.

Cupping his hands, Langrial drew deeply on the chillum. Rehmani watched his prodigy's bobbing Adam's apple. "Kashmir is our nijaat, our salvation."

Rehmani stole a glance at his younger brother. Blood was thicker than water. He had to make space for his brother to take over the HuJI after he moved to Kabul.

Langrial noticed Rehmani share an eye-lock with Abu. He saw Rehmani abruptly stand up and walk towards him. Puzzled, he squinted up to see the hard expression on Rehmani's face.

He stood up. Rehmani held him by the shoulders. "Lead the jihad."

A surprised Langrial peered into Rehmani's dark eyes. A muscle in his jaw twitched as understanding dawned on him.

His mouth set in a hard line. "*Kha... tashakor kha.*"[43]

He faked a smile. It did not touch his seething eyes.

"And … when will you leave?" Rehmani forced a smile. "Visit Jalalpur before you go into Kashmir."

Langrial closed his eyes, trying to recollect his village Jalalpur in Tehsil Jattan in the Gujarat district of Pakistan's Punjab. He couldn't

---

[43] *Okay. Thank you very much indeed.*

recall anything.

He just ground his jaw.

Langrial kissed Rehmani on the cheek as they parted. He knew what it meant. Politics and family loyalty had denied him a future in Afghanistan. He had to seek his destiny in Kashmir.

****

Leepa Valley, Pakistan
November 1992

"We will go through there." Langrial pointed his finger towards Chanian. The 10 men looked towards the Line of Control. Beyond rose the formidable Shamshabari ridge on which was deployed the Indian Army.

Well-positioned machine guns covered gaps in nallahs. The criss-crossing fire would cut them like ribbons. Barbed wire obstacles, mines, traps threatened to maim them if they came out alive. Snipers could pick them off with night vision.

They had risked it so far. The sinking feeling was infectious.

Sipping salted tea, they relished the hospitality of the Pakistani army. The last act of hospitality of the Pakistani army would be to fire on the Indian positions, giving them space to make a free run.

Sitting at the Pakistani post of Kaiyan in the Leepa valley, the eight Kashmiri and two Pakistani militants had an early dinner. They had a long night ahead.

Thankfully, it would be moonless, with a cloud cover obscuring their movements. Some 83 kilometres from Muzaffarabad, they had taken the famous 72 U-turns to reach the village.

Hopefully, they would get the 72 Hoors[44] in Jannat if they did not survive.

***

Asked to focus on Southern Kashmir, he based himself in Kapran. Here

---

[44] *A beautiful fair-skinned woman in heaven*

he gathered up his *lashkar*[45] and led it in operations across the Pir Panjal in the Doda district.

His close friend, the one-eyed Ilyas Kashmiri, an Ex SSG[46] commando, was already active in Kashmir since 1991[47]. Kashmiri was, however, still relatively unknown to the outside world.

Apparently, the Harkat-ul-Mujahideen, an offshoot of the HuJI, used some of its trainees to set up local cells in Doda and Udhampur districts.

* * *

Dal Lake, Srinagar
1990

Nudging him with her elbow, she chuckled, "You are such a scoundrel, Sudhir," recalling their first meeting.

Keeping aside the book, he snickered, "How dare you, Taslim?" A voracious reader, Sudhir never travelled without a book.

"You read my mind. It wasn't a coincidence?"

He grinned, shrugging his shoulders. "Well, I am trained to foresee. And react. Just used that to my benefit." He went back to his reading.

Blowing over the steaming noon chai, she recalled, the memory still fresh.

It was just four months ago. Negotiating the Delhi morning rush, he had barely made it to the airport. Anxious, with his haversack and two heavy bags slung over his shoulders, he looked unwieldy.

She, nevertheless, recalled his neat appearance and clean-shaven look.

---

[45] *Army*

[46] *The Special Service Group or SSG is a special forces unit of the Pakistan army*

[47] *Named as the most dangerous man on earth by CNN, Kashmiri rose as a possible successor to Osama bin Laden. He was David Headley's handler and was associated with the 2008 Mumbai attacks, the 2010 Pune bombings and assignation of Benazir Bhutto. He founded the 313 Brigade under the HuJI.*

It made him stand apart. She smirked watching him grapple with his falling bags. Fumbling, he watched her gracefully sashay past him.

An alluring perfume lingered faintly behind her. A peeved Sudhir felt his neck prickle. Squaring his back, he lumbered away, trying to assuage his belittled, testosterone-fuelled masculinity.

He smelt her before he noticed her, up ahead in line. Jumping the queue, he elbowed past a group of squabbling women and stood right behind her. Ignoring his presence, she walked to the nearest counter, feeling his gaze scrutinising her. Check-in done, she stared back at him, her forehead wrinkled in distaste and walked away quickly, clutching her bag tightly.

Her boarding pass stared him in the face, forgotten on the countertop. He read the name. A wizard at seizing fleeting opportunities, he accosted her at the security check. "Clumsy Taslim!" He fanned his face with her boarding pass, a grin touching the corners of his mouth.

Her lovely almond eyes blazed in indignation.

"Don't be cheeky," she said, snatching the pass and stomping off. Unbalanced by her stance, she tottered on her heels, grimacing, knowing Sudhir was watching her and smiling.

A motorboat with security personnel cut through the waters of the Dal Lake, causing ripples in the placid waters, rocking the houseboat gently.

The rocking brought her back to reality. The weekend was over, and she would go back to her campus, the University of Kashmir, close by, where she was pursuing her MA in Economics. He would go back to his unit.

"I am adopted," she said suddenly, watching the receding motorboat. The almond eyes clouded with tears. "They killed my parents."

Reaching out, Sudhir touched her shoulder, tenderly, unsure of what to do.

"It's been a bloody struggle ever since." She bit her lip, still gazing out. She laughed.

"Nothing's been easy." Sudhir gulped his tea, not wanting her to notice his own discomfort. Her words had touched a nerve.

"The need to prove yourself every day. At everything. When the others have it so easy." She scowled, tightening her jaw. "I was just 12." As if that explained everything

Jerking back from his touch, "You struggle too, Sudhir." Her eyes sought Sudhir's. "You just hide it."

"No," he lied. "I don't know. Maybe." Again, too rapidly. The casual half shrug a piece of armour.

Delving into topics she cared about, but didn't want to comment on, she stared at him, unblinking. Uncomfortable under her unrelenting gaze, he nodded, reluctantly. "Okay…yes." A rare moment of truth.

His voice hardened as he spoke.

"Walking to school in a government school uniform and sandals…" His voice trailed off, leaving her to make conclusions.

His fixed expression looked at a place somewhere over her shoulder. "The other kids…" He paused, tightening his jaw. "Went in private uniforms." He had the resigned stare of people who weren't getting far enough fast enough, she figured.

"Is that why you are constantly proving yourself?"

"I was born common. I don't want to die common. Untitled. Unheard."

"Well, it gives you the edge, Sudhir." She touched his nape, ruffling his hair.

"And also the ghosts that I fight every day," he said, emptying the tepid tea in the lake waters, his mouth curling.

* * *

Taslim introduced Sudhir to her batchmate and friend Aslam Beg. Interested in conservation and heritage, Aslam was involved in setting up INTACH's[48] J&K chapter.

"We have no disaster management here," he rued. "Should a flood or earthquake happen, everything will be a ruin."

Stuck by his boundless naiveté, Sudhir winced, shaking his head.

"When a state is grappling with its existence, who cares about heritage or conservation, Aslam. There are more pressing matters."

"But someone's got to look out for centuries of heritage."

"I agree." Sudhir nodded indulgently.

"Now there's a movement afoot to destroy the Buddhist statues in Bamiyan in Afghanistan." Aslam threw his hands in the air."Assholes … 1500 years of heritage being pulverized!"

Sudhir sighed. Quoting Oscar Wilde, he said, "Youth is wasted on the young."

Not taking anything lying down, Taslim retorted, "With age comes wisdom, but sometimes age comes alone."

Catching Sudhir's puzzled frown, Taslim said, "Oscar Wilde again."

Putting out her tongue, Taslim concealed a smile, "You aren't the only one well-read here, Sudhir Walia."

They burst out laughing, following it up with another round of *kulladh*[49] tea.

Aslam would meet Sudhir whenever he passed through Srinagar. The friendship gave Sudhir rare insights into the torn fabric of Kashmiriyat, and glimpses into the reddened waters of the Chenab.

Taslim and Sudhir found little time together. However, even these moments of togetherness were often eclipsed by the shadow of the conflict that loomed over Kashmir.

* * *

---

[48] *Indian National Trust for Art & Cultural Heritage*
[49] *Earthen cup*

Kupwara
May 1993

Something about the ringing sounded ominous.

"Sudhir, Professor…" said Yash speaking in a voice Sudhir couldn't decipher.

It blew Sudhir's sleep away.

"How badly injured?" Sudhir's voice was low, tone uncertain. He waited. A long silence at the other end screamed back into his ears.

He tensed, massaging the back of his neck.

"Rajnan fought till the end…" The words clawed their way out of Yash's throat. Sudhir could hear pain in his voice, and anger.

Sudhir struck the unyielding wall with his fist, his body convulsing in pain.

Outnumbered and outgunned, Professor with a small team had walked into a large group of militants in Wariban forests. They were operating incognito, impersonating as militants. With reserve troops unable to reach them in time, the party expended their ammunition. The militants finally captured them alive.

"The bastards tortured…" hissed Yash, swallowing a string of profanities.

Shocked, Sudhir didn't realise he was holding his breath. "They found the bodies mutilated." He heard Yash's voice from a distance. "With signs of torture."

Sudhir's head was reeling. He drew in a long breath, gripping the handset till his knuckles hurt. "I'll visit his parents," whispered Sudhir in a tone flat and steady, but taut as a guitar string. "We owe him that."

* * *

"You are fr…ree to choose…" said the whisky-soaked voice, "but you're not free from the consequences of your choice." The words slurred and lisped.

Bathed in moonlight, the rooftop was perfect for a night drink. The sweet-smelling jasmine clinging to a wall, adding to the charm.

Taking a sip, Sudhir looked over at his childhood friend. He seemed about to speak, but the thread eluded him. Sudhir looked at the twinkling lights of Palampur instead. "Do they always dance?...these lights?"

The friend shook his head, but it took him a moment to find his voice. "And this constant risk? Is this your…" His voice trailed off.

Sudhir thought of Professor. His hair bristled. He took another long swig from his glass.

"I get my high when I'm in the moment," said Sudhir in a calm, unhurried voice. The tone said order could prevail over chaos.

His mother had been unwell. Asha, his sister, had been constantly pestering him to come home. He had combined the leave with a visit to Professor's home.

Back in Srinagar after the visit home, he was itching to rejoin his unit. "Withdrawal symptoms," his friend had said sourly, the playfulness falling away like a discarded cloak.

* * *

On the way to his unit, Sudhir took a detour to meet Taslim and Aslam.

Taslim was fiercely progressive, driven by a desire to see positive change in Kashmir, a place plagued by years of conflict. Sudhir, on the other hand, was committed to his role in the Valley. This often placed him at odds with those who questioned the Army's presence in Kashmir.

Their disagreements grew more frequent and impassioned. She believed that the Army's presence was a hindrance to the peace she yearned for. He saw it as a necessary force to combat militants and maintain order.

The harsh realities of their respective worlds kept pulling them apart.

Caught In the Crossfire

Zainakote, Kupwara.
July 1993

Responsible for operations in Kupwara district, the Kilo Force was at Divisional Headquarters. It operated under the XV Corps at Srinagar.

9 Para was located within shouting distance of the Kilo Force Headquarters.

The Bravo team had formed a far-reaching intelligence network. Interestingly, rumours spiralled about a rift between the Al-Badr and Hizbul Mujahideen. Apparently, it seemed to be a turf war.

"We can take advantage of this," suggested Sudhir to his CO during his intelligence debrief.

"Wait and see," advised his second in command, Lt. Col. Mohan, experience on his side. "Don't jump to conclusions too soon."

Far from taking advantage, Sudhir had no clue he was about to become embroiled in a feud between the two gangs, being shot at from both sides. A hilarious hell-raiser, life was stranger than fiction.

*** * ***

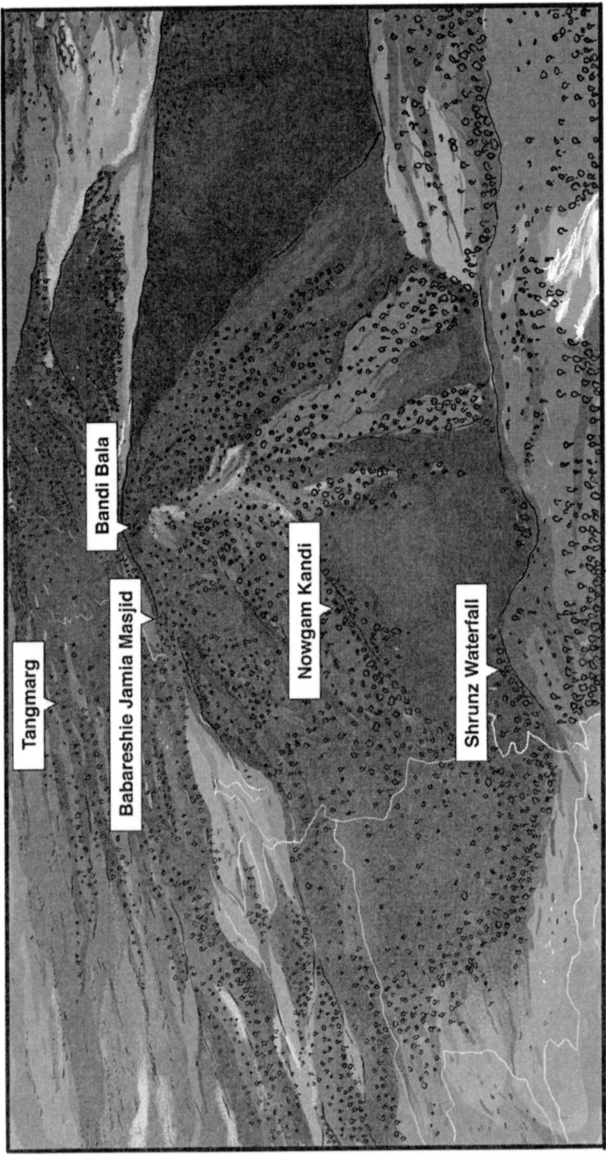

Nowgam Kandi, Baramulla

Enchanted by the majestic deodars, he had allowed his mind to drift, recalling the letter from Delhi. Remembering the tiny silver nose stud as she wrinkled her nose, made him all fuzzy.

A sudden bump broke his reverie and the clattering vehicle dragged him back to the intelligence input. The team had scrambled after they received the intelligence tip. There was some meeting being planned. They expected militants in a group. Their tanzeem, however, was unknown.

They were driving along the Zianakote-Gulmarg road, headed to Nowgam Kandi, a remote village surrounded by deodar and pine forests. Located eleven kilometres north-east of Gulmarg, it was close to the famous Shrunz waterfall. The slopes of the forested spur-lines rose to a flat top that towered over the valley below.

This was a groove near Nalasar, a small hamlet in the valley. A boulder-ridden stream separated the forest beyond. Greeted by the gurgling sounds of the fast-flowing stream, the team hopped off in muffled silence to the smell of the pines. A quick last check, cocking their weapons, they walked over the pine-needle-strewn forest floor.

The stream drowned their splashing as they navigated the chilly waters and entered the forests. They walked for the next three hours in silence, avoiding goat trails and tracks, making their way to the pre-selected ambush site.

Sudhir had organised the team into two squads. One squad had been arranged near an undulation in the terrain, close enough to hear the nearby waterfall. Pushing into the undergrowth, they had camouflaged themselves.

On the opposite side of the undulation, the second squad covered the reverse slope. Mukhtiar, with a radio set on his back, was in the second squad, led by Hav. Balwinder Singh.

Sudhir was positioned with the first squad.

Taking turns, three men slept, their breath visible in the chilly night air as the other three stayed alert. The night grew long and quiet. Disturbed by the intrusion, the crickets, which had abruptly stopped chirping, resumed their singsong once again. Seasoned hunters, the squad lay in quiet wait for the kill. With an uncanny knack for camouflage, the squad had melted into the foliage with such subtlety that it rivalled a leopard's.

Unsure if it was the chill or his buddy's hand, Sudhir felt his skin prickle. Abruptly snapping his eyes open, his gaze followed the track as his buddy pointed. Instinctively, he reached for his weapon, finding comfort as his fingers touched the cold steel. Wide-eyed, the squad rolled into firing positions, observing the spectacle before them.

"*Bhala Sipahiya Dogriya*[50]," Sudhir heard the singing before the man came into view. Merrily singing a popular Punjabi melody, a militant trudged up. Two other militants trailed him closely, their features concealed underneath balaclavas. Intrigued, the team sat holding their breath, as two more shapes gradually materialised out of the darkness.

The team peered through the bushes. A singing militant coming up close was an amusing sight. Something they had never encountered.

The oblivious singer stepped closer to the bushes, feeling the rough bark of the tree as he leaned his weapon against it. They could now smell his rancid body odour. Lowering his salwar, he peed in the bushes, the yellow trickle slowly meandering its way towards them.

The other four militants stood in a huddle a short distance away, their conversation a quiet buzz.

Sudhir licked his lips, an amused twinkle in his eye. Kneeling squarely, he readied his weapon and let out a whistle.

They could see the whites of his eyes, as the closest militant swirled, face contorted in terror.

Waiting for a moment for the militant to grab his weapon, Sudhir pulled the trigger, shooting the man through his head.

A flutter of angry wings churned the air as the random scatter of

---

[50] *A popular Dogri folk song*

fire from the militant's weapon thudded into the undergrowth. A tiny feather drifted slowly down, its descent full of indignation.

The other militants spun around, their eyes wide with surprise, fumbling to point their weapons. On cue, the squad unleashed a heavy volley of fire, giving the militants no escape.

Caught in the perfectly laid ambush, they killed three of the militants instantly. With one swift jump, the farthest militant disappeared into a gully, the dense undergrowth muffling his movements.

"Stop!" yelled Sudhir, ordering the squad to cease firing.

Treading cautiously, the squad emerged, scanning through the undergrowth tinged with the harsh smell of gunpowder.

* * *

On the other side, alerted by the firing, Balwinder and the squad were ready. "Check the area," Sudhir instructed Balwinder on the radio. "He's probably run towards you." Sudhir organised his squad to take up a dominating position while Balwinder's squad searched.

Balwinder ordered his squad into an extended line and went in for a deep search to flush out the militant. Combing the forest, step by step they crept ahead. Soon they were directly under the top, which loomed above them.

Suddenly, Balwinder felt the sharp sting of a whizzing shot as it ricocheted off the binoculars around his neck. He heard a thud as it buried hitting a tree.

Yelling, "Fire!Fire!" he dived for cover.

Shaken but lucky to be alive, he sought protection, as did the rest of the team. Sounds of automatic firing echoed as death rained down, pinning them. Unable to lift their heads, the team desperately tried to ascertain the direction of the fire.

They realised the fire was coming from the flat ridge top. A PIKA gun was firing down accurately. They had unknowingly walked into a violent ambush. Regaining control, the squad started striking back. Aiming at the intermittent flashes, they had to fire up-slope in low light, towards the sound. It was challenging.

Sudhir's squad was still in position, unsure.

A movement caught Mukhtiar's eye. "Balwinder!" he yelled, pointing. Right under their noses, close to the village, a group of twenty militants were scurrying away, some curiously firing back towards the top.

The machine gun on the ridge top suddenly shifted its aim and fired back at the escaping militants.

The entire scene was a wild melee of chaos. Sounds of gunfire reverberated everywhere. Ubiquitous, trigger-happy militants seemed assembled for a jamboree.

The volley of automatic fire and the reverberating noise of the barrage finally died down after about forty minutes. Ensuring that it was safe to venture out, the Balwinder's squad stepped out warily.

They had barely gone a few steps through the foliage when out stumbled the escaped militant like a scared rabbit. Caught in the crossfire, he was injured. His leg was bleeding.

"Janab, don't kill me," he pleaded, throwing away his weapon, raising his hands. "This is my village."

Hand-bound, Balwinder dragged the militant to Sudhir as the two squads joined up.

"What the fuck was that?" asked a bewildered Sudhir, tilting his head.

Nostrils flaring, the militant clenched his jaw and spat out, "Madarchod[51] Hizbul Mujahideen, janab."

"And you are?"

"Al-Badr," he said dryly.

"What the fuck?" Furrowing his eyebrows sceptically, the story did not convince Sudhir. "Why was Al-Badr here in your village?"

---

[51] *Mother fuckers*

"To avenge my brother," blurted the militant, his eyes vacant.

Stupefied, Sudhir asked, "Hizbul?"

The militant nodded, wiping his nose, "They killed him… Haramuk[52]." His voice wavered.

"And those fuckers running away?" asked Balwinder, jerking his head towards the village.

"They came to help my… my tanzeem," said the militant, swallowing hard.

Under further questioning, the militant revealed the entire story. He had gathered his cronies from Al-Badr to avenge the killing of his only brother. Al-Badr, itching for a fight, wanted to settle old scores with Hizbul Mujahideen.

Forewarned of Al-Badr's plans through a Hizbul Mujahideen. sympathiser in the village, Hizbul Mujahideen had taken up a dominating position on top of the ridge, to ambush Al-Badr.

"Why did your friends enter the village?" asked Balwinder, scowling.

"They wanted to kill the Hizbul sympathiser."

"So why didn't they fight the Hizbul Mujahideen?" asked Sudhir, eyes boring into the militant.

"You came in between…," said the militant shakily, but the corners of his mouth twitched.

Dumbstruck, Sudhir gaped at the militant. Balwinder's gaze met Sudhir's for a moment. No words passed; their eyes said it all.

"Bloody hell!" said Sudhir, slapping his thigh. A grin replaced his frown. "The Hizbul mistook us for Al-Badr." The woods resounded with his distinctive laugh.

"And we saved Al-Badr from getting fucked in the ass, sir," guffawed Balwinder, doubling over.

"And almost got fucked ourselves," butted in Mukhtiar, rolling his eyes, joining in.

---

[52] *Bastards*

"Don't laugh so hard, Balwinder, you'll pee yourself," warned Sudhir, laughing so hard his shoulders shook.

The militant's face was a mixture of curiosity as an uncertain smile flashed and disappeared on his face.

Sudhir said, "Hey, give the guy some water!"

Disbelief limped across the militant's face, startled by the abrupt change in fortune.

Mukhtiar's stony gaze fixed on the militant as he gulped the water. "There's a thin line between luck and fuck," warned Mukhtiar, winking at the militant. "Two sides of the same coin. Depends how it will land."

The militant tossed his greasy hair and scraped dried blood from his neck. "You will learn," whispered Mukhtiar, taking his flask back.

* * *

The team got ready for the long walk to the pickup point. Though exhausted, the team took turns in carrying the dead weight down the slopes. The militant shuffled between them; head bowed. He had been tethered to a soldier to prevent him from running away.

To stay safe, they had to be unflaggingly vigilant for any sign of an ambush. The leading scouts alert, weapons ready for action, led the way. The team followed with their eyes peeled. A two-hour walk brought them to a flat clearing bounded by a deep gorge.

The militant made a fatal mistake. He mistook the temporary friendliness for casualness. Wanting to escape, he jumped down into a gorge, dragging the soldier along. Two perfect headshots had him somersaulting down in a heap.

"Now we have to carry this bastard too," grumbled Balwinder, eyeing the dead body.

"Just a flip between luck and fuck," said Mukhtiar philosophically, tugging the body, trailing the tangy metallic smell of fresh blood.

Sudhir felt the sun on his back as he walked down the goat track and surveyed the lush and serene valley below. A thought crossed his mind, It's all about finding calm in the chaos. "Yep," he said to himself, "It's all about finding the calm."

The operation finally gave Sudhir much-deserved recognition. They awarded him a Sena Medal for gallantry which he received in January 1994.

* * *

Srinagar, Sher-e-Kashmir University.
October 1993

The winds were just right and the air was scented with falling leaves, earthy pumpkins and squash.

Autumn had turned the massive chinar trees on the university campus into a spectacular painting. Resplendent in hues of gold, orange and red, set against the magnificence of the distant mountains, they made you pensive. Nature's hush against human yearning.

Looking up from the journal, Aslam Beg nudged Taslim, gesturing with his pen. From her perch on the veranda, observing Sudhir make his way through the deep red carpet, she sat up straight.

That day, talking of Kashmir and its people, Sudhir and Taslim had yet another argument.

Despite their affection, the weight of their backgrounds, beliefs and the ongoing conflict proved insurmountable.

Their feelings were a poignant reminder of the complexities of love in a region marked by turmoil, where the pursuit of peace sometimes comes at the cost of personal sacrifice and heartbreak.

Very soon, realisation struck that their profound feelings could not bridge the gap between their worlds.

"We give it some time?" she finally asked. It was heart-wrenching, but they understood that pursuing their individual paths was the only way to honour their commitments and salvage their friendship.

Summitting the Brammah

Vinod
Base Camp, Brammah-II
23rd August, 1993

I silently thanked Sudhir sir for bringing me along. I was super excited about the expedition.

Leaving the vehicles behind, we walked up from Suid Village with mules loaded with our supplies. We crossed a precariously hanging wooden bridge over the Nath river, the only access to the redolent Dachhan valley. Enveloped by coniferous trees, a heady scent wafted through the valley.

We passed through ancient villages, the wooden architecture as intriguing as the ancient secrets they held. Even though we had seen it all before, the sights, sounds and smells of the Dachhan mountains still enthralled us. It was a different world.

Now and then, lovely clearings popped out of the forests. At other times, sunlight streamed in through the trees in wonderful layers. The constant burbling of the Nath river accompanied us through the first two days of the trek.

By the third day, as we climbed higher through the lush greenery, the river sounds became a distant hum. It was now accompanied by an enthralling melody. Pairs of shy, bright yellow-breasted golden orioles sang in perfect harmony.

I watched Nk Jagmel walk strong and fluid. Never breaking a sweat, his steady gait revealed his steel nerves and iron resolve.

Nk Jagmel had lost a leg in the in the killing fields of Vavuniya. Refusing a cushy job, he had volunteered to remain with 9 Para, pushing his artificial limb beyond the limits of its mechanical endurance. Walking alongside his able-bodied colleagues, Jagmel inspired belief and diehard pride.

Tapping Jagmel on his shoulder, I saw Sudhir sir look into those eyes with respect. A respect that is born in men who serve. Jagmel saheb's deep eyes radiated a fierce, uncompromising attitude. And yet he carried the scars of the war deep inside. He would never be the same.

I, too, was not the same. I, too, often relived Sri Lanka. War does that to you.

Though not qualified in mountain warfare, I had pestered Sudhir sir to take me along. He had finally given in.

"Only because of your resolve."

Saluting him crisply, I had smiled broadly.

"And you can stop following me around now, you idiot."

Unknown to me, Sudhir sir was not detailed for this expedition. He too had persisted. Initially detailed to lead, Lt. S.S. Dahiya had stepped back, allowing Sudhir sir to take over as the expedition leader. In fact, the Lieutenant had spoken to the CO and convinced him to allow Sudhir sir to lead.

* * *

"There is the Hudh Mata temple," said Munir, the Muslim porter, gesturing with his head, looking at the ridge line. Sudhir sir looked at him, bewildered. "Mata Parvati," he continued, his voice low and serious. "I used to come as a child with my father."

Sudhir sir looked at me. He knew. "You want to go and pray?"

My eyes lit up, I nodded excitedly.

"Mission… first, Vinod."

Seeing my crestfallen face, he kept a hand on my shoulder.

"Religion is secondary. The mission is our salvation."

My face flushed. I nodded, embarrassed by my naive stupidity.

* * *

"This was the land of Shiva," said the porter spreading his hands wide.

An amused Sudhir sir smiled.

"They ruined everything. Centuries of Kashmiriyat."

"I am not sure about the Shiva part," whispered Sudhir sir to Lt. Dahiya. "But I know Shaivism flourished in Kashmir."

"How long back, sir?" asked Dahiya.

"From the last centuries of the first millennium AD, through the early centuries of the second."

The mule shifted as Dahiya heaved a sack off its back. "I didn't know that, sir," he said breathless, face reddening with the effort.

On the fourth day, the clear waters of the Brammah Sarovar shimmered with the last rays of the late afternoon sun. "It will cleanse your sins," said Munir, jerking his head towards the water, his eyes glowing with reverence.

"Want to try?" chuckled Sudhir sir.

"Fucking hell," yelped the young officer, dipping his hand in the freezing waters.

"Will come back in a few years," he groaned, warming his frozen fingers.

"Perhaps you should," Dahiya snickered saucily.

Sudhir sir glared at him in mock anger before they burst out laughing.

* * *

In between the thick maples, walking through the birch trees, we burst on to an extensive grassland, Kidhaar maidan. A whispering breeze carried the smell of the silent river as the grasslands embraced us.

A local herdsman and his two young sons, sprawled out on the soft, cushioned plateau, surveyed us with curiosity.

Toothy grins and shy smiles accompanied Sudhir's attempt at conversing. The family, generous despite their meagre resources, offered us warm cups of a peculiar-tasting tea.

The herder showed us the best route to an impressive, lush grassland.

The locals called it Sattar-Chin. "You can pitch your tents here," he said. It was perfect – an idyllic altitude meadow with freshwater springs. The carpeted grass was soft like a cushioned mattress.

The locals used Sattar-Chin as a summer pasture.

"You know why the locals stopped coming?" boasted Munir. His eyes searched our faces for an answer.

We shook our heads.

"The mujahid used to play cricket here."

Dahiya gave him a look of disbelief.

"They would come down from those mountains," said Munir, pointing. "When they got bored."

"Even they love cricket?" My eyes widened in disbelief.

"At the basic level, everyone is human, but it's our job to single out the less human."Sudhir sir's voice was thick with conviction. "And send them back to God to straighten out the flaws."

Nk. Puran Mal Gunjal bared his teeth in a wide grin. A tough highlander from Uttarakhand, he was accustomed to the terrain.

"Well, we will also have our base camp here." Sudhir sir announced smugly, pushing his trekking pole into the soft grass." And play cricket, too."

* * *

We carried out acclimatisation for a full twelve days at Sattar-Chin, walking up to the base of the terminal moraine every day.

"This is the debris left by the moving glacier." Sudhir sir explained, showing the rocks and soil. "Like the river silt."

The moraine stretched all the way up, between the two peaks of Brammah-I and II.

"Push yourselves," exhorted our instructor, Hav. Vinod Sharma. He was a qualified instructor and mountaineer, certified from the High-Altitude Warfare School (HAWS). "Your lungs need to breathe normally in the rarefied atmosphere and low oxygen levels up there."

Sharma instructed the men on ice craft. He made us memorise the rock pitons, ice pitons and ropes. We had to deal with Belay devices, slings, knots and harness. It was tough.

"This climbing rope is made of polyester," he instructed, kneeling, holding the rope. "It elongates under loads—"

"But, why not the normal rope?"I interrupted, eager to learn, hovering over his shoulder.

"Static…static rope." Sudhir sir corrected me. "Static rope does not stretch."

The instructor continued, his tone grave. "The greater stretch allows a dynamic rope to absorb the energy of a sudden…."

"Fall?" I blurted out enthusiastically.

"Yes," said the instructor, with a weary resignation. "This reduces the peak force on the body."

"And therefore, the chance of catastrophic failure," added Sudhir sir, peering into the audience.

"Oh…like a broken spine." I remarked, squeezing in the last word.

The instructor eyed me from under his brows. I wondered why he was peering at me. Did I put him off? I guess I had. Acutely aware, I inched back slowly, trying to make a run.

Sudhir sir watched us, his eyes twinkling.

"Come," he said, drawing the instructor away before he censured me with a punishment. "I need to discuss something."

The instructor walked away with a grimace of a man reminded of his age, like when he couldn't understand the noise they called music.

I scampered like a rabbit, lucky to have escaped the baying hound.

Brammah I and II loomed large, casting a shadow over the valley. Sudhir sir on impulse looked up at the massive peaks. They seemed to cut attitudes and egos to size.

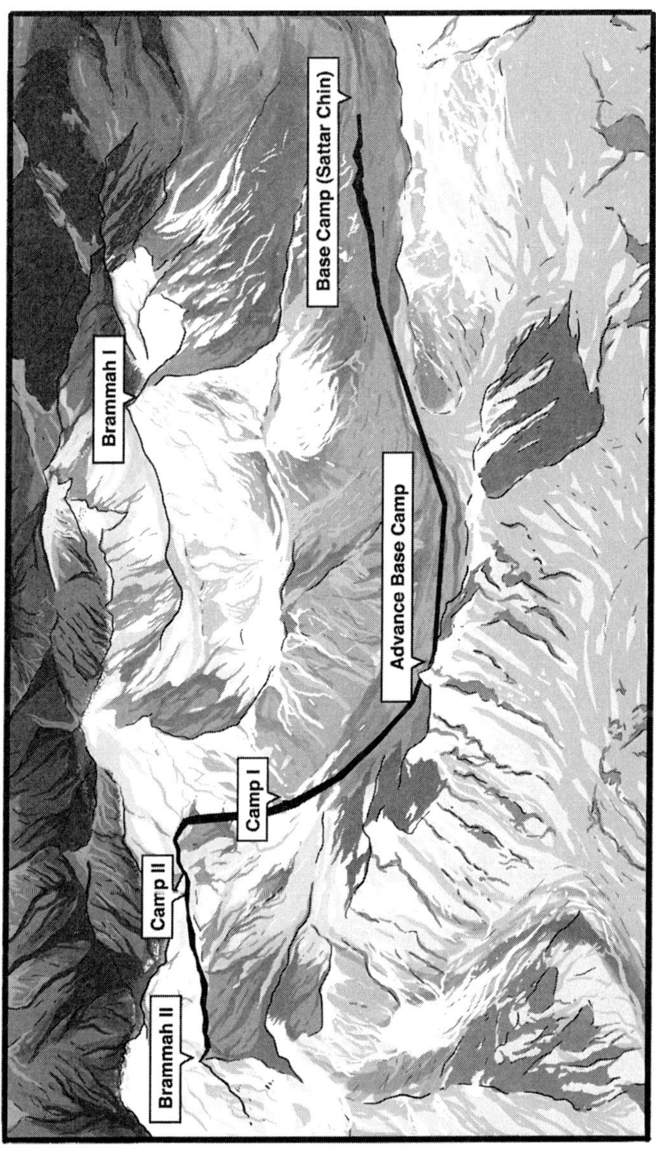

The Brammah Expedition

Advance Base Camp
8th September, 1993

Standing under the northeast face of Brammah-II, Sudhir sir craned his neck up at the massive peak. His eyes travelled up the spires of naked rock thrusting into the sky so high that one would believe they had pierced the very heavens. His breath spun white, then evaporated in the chill. At 13,000 feet, the air was frosty.

Because of the tortured, rock-strewn surface, we had found the last piece of level ground only at the head of the glacier. It nestled in a steep, confined valley.

"This is where we start our climb," he said, pointing his ice-pick towards the saddle between Brammah-I and II. "Let's open the route."

The problem was the icefall.

"We'll have to fix the ropes, sir," said Sub. Laksh, "At least ten to eleven." He too was an instructor from HAWS.

Sudhir sir nodded. I glanced at the sheer slope. The ropes would have to sustain the logistics of the climbing team and also evacuation in an emergency.

Sub. Laksh and a team of paratroopers worked hard, their hands slipping as they pushed the rock pitons into the slim crevices, despite the wet and windy weather. Over the course of three days, they toiled away to fix the eleven ropes.

Eager to get going, Sudhir sir had ordered an early start. We were ready before the night had even evaporated. Standing below the icefall, the men looked up as the cloud mist lifted, showing them a slice of the sky.

We gained the South Col[53], traversing a series of ice gullies and loose rock ridges on the left side of the icefall. Roped at the waist, we scaled step by step as much as our lungs would enable us, gasping and exhaling white puffs.

---

[53] *The lowest point of a ridge connecting two peaks.*

Heads bowed against the gusting wind, we trudged through deeper snow as we climbed further along the sheer ridge. Up ahead, the ridge steepened like a knife's edge.

Surrounded by only rock and snow, we established a camp just 500 metres short of the steep incline of the saddle.

Zipped up in his sleeping bag, Sudhir took in a few moments of solitude. Her face came into view. He thought of Palampur and his mother. He looked up at the thin oscillating fabric of the bivouac sheltering him from the enraged winds outside.

A smile settled across his face as he snuggled back into the sleeping bag.

*** * ***

Camp I
13th September,1993

"We don't have any food left, sir." Puran Gunjal cupped hands to his mouth, trying to keep them warm. We needed to survive for another four days. The situation was critical.

The weather had turned foul. An avalanche warning prevented any movement from the advance camp.

"Well, we just wait. The link patrol will come up tomorrow," said Sudhir sir.

Carrying just our personal loads and two days' rations, we had climbed up the treacherous ridge on the ropes to reach Camp I.

We had already spent two days at Camp I. Acclimatising, we were getting ready for Camp II and the final push up the summit.

"They are hungry, sir," said Sub. Laksh, his voice laced with concern, watching us pitch the small tents. At 17,000 feet, in glaciated terrain, the absence of fuel for the body could be lethal.

"Okay gather them … after they finish," said Sudhir sir with a twinkle in his eye.

After we had settled, Sudhir sir spoke, summarising the situation. We exchanged sullen glances with each other in the silence. My stomach was already growling.

"This fight with hunger calls for mental toughness," said Sudhir sir, motivating the men. They had to quell the hunger pangs.

"Okay let's sing," he said. Taking the lead, he belted out some popular tunes. We started clapping, joining in the chorus. We soon competed against each other, singing out our hearts. The riotous cacophony continued for hours.

Puran requested Sudhir sir, "Sir, your favourite song…please." Some of us had already heard it in a regimental get-together, the Bara Khana[54]. We clapped and laughed.

Sudhir sir cleared his throat, and like a seasoned opera soloist, sang the humorous articulated lyrics. He started off in Tamil, then switched to Malayalam, then Kannada, then Tulu.

I watched Puran listening in rapt attention, a wide grin covered his face. I tilted my head, eyebrows furrowed, "Can you…?"

Puran shook his head, laughing. "Fuck no, I only know Pahadi and Dogri."

"You think he is fucking with us?" I whispered, smirking. "Not one idiot knows all these languages."

Puran nodded, grinning. "He can even fuck with the devil and get away with it."

Sudhir sir continued his singing. By now shifting to Bengali, Marathi, Gujrati, Konkani, Bhojpuri, Rajasthani, Punjabi and all the way up to Kashmiri and Tibetan.

We guffawed and hooted. It quietened our growling stomachs. Exhausted, we retired to our tents.

---

[54] *Dinner with troops, on special occasions, where officers and their men share a special meal informally.*

By morning, a wedge of sunlight burst past the mist clinging to the cliffs. "They are here!" shouted a young soldier on duty. The mist parted to reveal the link patrol with Lt. Dahiya in the lead, walking up along the knife edge ridgeline. Excitement aroused the camp. Prodded by their appetites, men tumbled out of their sleeping bags. Never was a team welcomed with such enthusiasm.

"No way!" Sudhir sir exclaimed, his laughter ringing out as he watched the display of emotions, "Hungry is a feeling!"

* * *

Sudhir walked over to Jagmel, crouched over a kerosene stove.

"You can't climb any further, Jagmel," said Sudhir, holding his shoulder. Sudhir tried to break the news as gently as possible. The call was tough.

Jagmel had expected this. A muscle in his right cheek flexed. He shifted his weight, letting the order sink in. He couldn't risk the lives of his colleagues.

A long silence followed. Sudhir could smell his frustration, like booze on breath. The smell of frustration accumulated over the years. He had been a full-bodied man once. Jagmel nodded. He cocked his head. A bitter expression and a curious smile played out. He saluted stiffly, then walked away with laboured dignity.

The team soon got busy preparing to set up Camp II.

* * *

Camp II, 18,700 feet
15th September,1993

Circumventing the massive rock, we had walked up ahead to reconnoitre the route to Camp II. Sudhir sir surveyed the ridgeline, his face hardened in concentration. We had studied the maps, flown over the area and read reports. But nothing had prepared us for this.

Ahead lay five hundred feet of hard snow. The silence screamed at us.

Stamping my crampon feet, I leaned on the ice pick, shifting my weight. My toes felt stiff. The wind icy and withering, sneaked in through our layers of clothing, attacking seams and zipper tracks and spots of thin insulation.

Staring into the distance, Sudhir sir blinked as his eyes adjusted. Beyond the snow, he could see the sharp rock edge extending for over a thousand feet. Thin white puffs of fresh snow hovered over the knife's edge. Picked up by whistling winds, the fine flakes hung in magical streams before plunging over the suicidal slopes into a never-ending fall.

The glamourous, National Geographic moment could turn into tragedy in a minuscule moment of sloppiness.

I felt a chill run through me. I stared at Sudhir sir, clamping my teeth. He just glowered ahead, breathing thoughtfully.

Four gendarmes[55] blocked the thin rock edge at intervals. We could make out three. Mist partially obscured the fourth.

"There is no option. We have to get past those," said Sudhir sir without looking at me, his tone flat.

I shuddered, feeling goosebumps on my neck and arms. I was certain it wasn't the chill that made me quiver.

"But there isn't enough..." I stared wide eyed, at the vertical rock pinnacles blocking our narrow path. "... for even a foot."

Sudhir sir shrugged his shoulders. "We must risk it, Vinod. We just have to..."

I peered sightlessly at the vicious vertical monoliths, standing fiercely at guard, daring anyone to cross their path.

"So we select only the sure-footed?" Sub. Laksh said softly, hardly daring to breathe.

"Find me men not intimidated by that mountain," said Sudhir sir,

---

[55] *A Gendarme is a pinnacle of rock on a mountain ridge. The name originates from the French Alps, where they were seen as resembling the French Gendarme police.*

pointing with his ice pick, "but inspired by it."

The wind picked up and the swirling snows allowed us a quick peek at the last gendarme.

Eyes locked on like magnets, four pairs of eyes blinked in unison, mouths gaping open. We studied the vertical rock with unwavering attention. It revealed itself shyly. Lives depended on the decision.

"My god," muttered Sub. Laksh under his breath. Colour drained off his face. The gendarme rose five hundred feet in the sky; the sight terrifying enough to strike a bolt through any heart. The mists enveloped it again like a shroud.

Icicles had crystallised on his nostrils and eyebrows, but Sudhir sir brushed them away, waiting for his breath to stabilise. "Get me ordinary men who hunger for the extraordinary."

I noticed Sudhir sir's clenched jaw, his breath streaming in the air. Infused with his silent authority, any doubts that we harboured melted away like snow in a fire.

Ready the next morning, the handpicked men stood in line, even before the fused warm light of dawn crept down from the summit. We passed the ropes in silence, each lost in thought. Either we would all come back or…

Snow pelted our faces. I saw Sudhir sir pull up his zipper to shield himself from the bitter cold. Looking back through my foggy goggles, I saw mists bellow over the slopes, hanging low, masking the camp in a ghostly grey. And the ghostly figures of our men, much closer, closing in like zombies.

We made steady progress. Walking on the knife edge was tough, but tackling the vertical rocks was defying death. Like trapeze artists, backs pressed into the rock, we inched our way, one at a time, daring the white hellish vortex of nothingness. The surface was loose. Dislodged rocks kicked off by our feet, spun off into the twirling depths, bringing in the surreal reality of the risk.

Puran, his face shiny with sweat, slipped on a loose rock. He flayed his arms madly to gain balance, precariously bent forward. He hung there frozen, weighing between life and death for what seemed a lifetime. A fresh drop of sweat teared up on his brow and made a slow, wet path down the plane of his cheek. Rolling down his chin, it fell into the white void.

It was all in slow motion. Anchored at the waist at either end, the rope team held on, wheezing, putting their muscles to test. Puran's rucksack rode up and slipped off his shoulders. Tumbling, it fell with a dizzying speed, carrying precious rock pitons and hammer. A strong tug on the safety rope finally helped him shift his weight back. Regaining balance, he hauled himself back over the precipice, crossing back from death to life.

Steadying his heaving chest, he made it to the other end. Gratefully, he grabbed my flask. Gulping down a swig to ease his parched throat, he sank down to quieten his frayed nerves and wobbling knees.

Shoulders touching, I just sat there next to him, quietly.

He swiped his mouth after another swig, squeezed my shoulder and smiled. I smiled back, patting his arm. We really didn't have to use any words.

A snowfield stretched beyond the fourth vertical rock all the way to the summit. The team made it to the bottom of the snowfield and bivouacked by afternoon. Darkness quickly settled round us. Thick clouds masked out the moon, enveloping the white field in a bluish haze. We had turned in early after a frugal dinner.

* * *

Laying inside his bivouac, Sudhir swallowed down a soupy broth, with a strong whiff of kerosene lacing the bowl. Nauseous, he brought up the contents.

What could go wrong? And the consequences? Thoughts rushed

through his mind in a hallucinogenic kaleidoscopic, cramming his brain. He felt lightheaded and his vision swam. He broke out in a sweat.

The light-headedness was because of low air pressure at 18,000 feet and the insufficient tissue-level oxygen supply. The low air pressure prevented oxygen from permeating into the blood.

Sub. Laksh brought him an oxygen cylinder. Grabbing the cylinder, Sudhir pressed the mouthpiece to his mouth and nose. Pressing the push button, he inhaled, feeling the oxygen rush to his head. The oxygen helped him ward off the early signs of hypoxia.

An instinctive process forced him to shut down his wild thinking, let his mind go blank and deliberate on the ascent.

* * *

The Summit; 21,050 feet
17th September, 1993

We had all got used to living with a dull headache that occurs at extreme altitudes. The night before the summit was unending. A stimulating brew of ecstasy, awe and the unknown surged through each man. Tossing and turning, we awaited dawn, like our hair was on fire.

The narrow ledge allowed little privacy. It only provided nature's business to be conducted naturally, with a simplicity that was absent of any fuss or puritan values. Survival was the prime focus here. The rest was trivial.

The 3 a.m. sky was clear, allowing a few stars to peek out. Packing up our frugal lives, we abandoned the rucksacks at the camp as we needed to travel light. Equipped only with ropes and climbing gear weighing us down. A silver-white moon still hung in the sky as we began the deliberate walk, crunching across the 1,500 feet snow-slope.

Obscured by a velvety darkness, the summit was only a shadowy silhouette, almost entirely lost to view. The initial shallow snow gave way to deeper drifts, making the ascent laborious. The gentle climb soon became torturous.

Muscles aware of each foot traversed in lateral distance and lungs in each inch climbed vertically, we drew on our last ounces of willpower and grit, having exhausted our cache of physical energy long back.

We reached the final vertigo-inducing ice wall. Sub. Laksh and Sudhir sir stepped forward and stuck their ice picks in. Hauling themselves up, they braced their bodies from falling debris, pushing against the bluish white ice wall. Retrieving pitons hanging from a carabiner at their waist, they searched for crevices, clubbing them in with a rubber handle hammer.

The spindled climbing ropes ran through the pitons, fighting gravity, holding the lives of trusting men in their 10 mm fibres. As compared to smelling roses in the park, well, it could be risky. But for men tempered by danger, thriving on peril, inhaling risk like oxygen, it seemed routine. Death was always a nuisance, looming a breath away.

We fixed three ropes with help from Rajinder Singh, Dharma Lingam and Sub. Laksh Singh. Their rasping breath and heaving chests foretelling the story of their effort. The climb demanded complete concentration. Belayed by safety ropes, we made the ultimate ascent, using our pick axes and crampons. Our hot, vaporised breath froze faster than it was exhaled. The only sound was a soft clink when metal clashed on rock and the heavy breathing of men intent on victory.

The sun was climbing out of the deep well of snow, but still felt brutally cold.

I remember when I rested, I was lifeless. Except that my throat burnt when I drew breath. I could scarcely go on. No despair, no fear, no anxiety.

I had not lost my feelings, there were actually no feelings. I consisted only of my will. After a few metres, this too fizzled out in unending tiredness. Then I thought of nothing. For an indefinite time, I remained completely immobile. Then, I would take a step again, driven only by the motivation of not letting down my colleagues.

We made it to the top after seven hours of exhausting climbing. Puran fell to his knees in the snow, overwhelmed. Heroics apart, his heart burst with pride.

The clouds cleared for a few moments. A golden shadow, not three inches from Sudhir sir's leg, spread out, revealing the brilliant peak. The magical moment infused us with joy and exhilaration. We smiled, thumping each other, hugging in a tight embrace. We all smelt tangy. But it did not matter, we all had the same strong odour.

Sudhir experienced déjà vu, as often happens when you experience an intense moment. He felt a sudden calm. Closing his eyes, he breathed in the wholeness of the nirvanic experience.

We planted an Army flag, fluttering in the misty winds. Powerful gusts swirled the snow, masking out the light in a grey haze.

"Let's get—" ordered Sudhir sir. His words drowned by the winds. He signalled with his hand. With a final salute to Brammah-II, we turned around.

Down to life and further adventures.

We had conquered more than just a peak. This was a triumph of the human spirit. We felt like kings.

* * *

Walking through a snowstorm, we reached Camp I by nightfall. It felt like home. We had been walking for almost seventeen hours. Exhaustion coursed through our bones. Our feet felt dead, our minds felt numb. If ever there was a point beyond tiredness, we had reached it. Reaching the camp, we tried to sleep. Surprisingly, it eluded us. The pain in our bones and the excitement of our achievement ensured that.

An eager Capt. Negi, the doctor, greeted us at the advanced camp the next day, with a royal meal of Maggi noodles and chicken broth. We gulped down everything with a hunger that was ravenous. We could have easily passed off as survivors from a concentration camp, with sunken cheeks, shaggy beards and eyes rimmed red.

What we needed was a deep slumber. And a bath.

We smelt like we hadn't washed in a month. Sweat, anxiety and fatigue set off an odour that required deep cleaning. Negi sir wondered if he smelt like us.

We had set a record of sorts. All thirty-three members of the expedition had ultimately scaled the peak. A riotous campfire, complete with dancing and singing and much ribbing marked the last night. A matter still weighed on Sudhir sir's mind. He walked over to Lt. Dahiya and poured a drink into his glass.

"Thank you, mate."

Shrugging his shoulders, Dahiya smiled, "Not needed, sir."

"You gave up on a chance to lead … that was selfless."

"You making it sound big, sir." Dahiya gulped the drink, "I didn't think much of it."

Reluctantly, Sudhir had to admit that the younger officer had given him a valuable insight into leadership. Sometimes leadership was about giving the best man a shot, even if it meant stepping out of the limelight.

Sudhir sir kept a hand on Dahiya's shoulder. "It's not always about winning." He affirmed softly, more to himself.

The expedition could not have been completed without the unwavering support of the logistics team. Sudhir sir acknowledged that.

The Times of India and other dailies carried our worthy exploits soon after. The team finally reached Srinagar on the 1st of October.

For having led the challenging Brammah expedition and conquering the indomitable peak, the Indian Army again awarded Sudhir sir with a Sena Medal, non gallantry. His second.

* * *

At NDA as a cadet *(second from right),* Dinner night, Term VI.

Commissioning at IMA, being piped by his parents.

Then Capt *(later Col)* Rajesh Tyagi *(right)* with then Lt *(later Maj)* Sudhir *(second from left),* relaxing after an operation in Sri Lanka as a part of 4 Jat *(picture courtesy: Col Rajesh Tyagi).*

From left: Col R.S. Gill, Col Britto, Maj Walia and Col K. Bhushan, 9 Para (SF).

With the then Chief of Army Staff,
Gen V.P. Malik, as his ADC.

Receiving his second Sena Medal.

Speaking at the Pentagon, USA, after being adjudged the Best Student.

With an instructor of the US Military Intelligence Corps.

With international student Officers, USA.

Maj Sudhir Walia *(top centre)* at Zulu Top
(Vinod with climbing rope, second from right).

Maj Sudhir Walia *(rear centre)* with his team,
the morning after the capture of Zulu Top.

At Mhow, during the Junior
Command Course.

At Dehradun, as an
Instructor at IMA.

After operations in
Pir Panjal.

Capt Arun Jasrotia,
before joining
9 Para (SF).

The coveted
Balidaan Badge.

Then Nk *(now Hony Capt)*
Mahendra Singh,
KC in Kashmir.

Then Nk
(now Maj) Vinod.

Then Nk *(now Hony Capt)*
Mukhtiar Singh, SC.
Ski training in Manali with
Capt Sudhir Walia,
December 1994.

Nk Kheem Singh,
(Posthumous) SM.

Mortal remains being escorted by colleagues
to his home in Palampur.

Sub Maj Rulia Ram
(*father of Maj Sudhir Walia*)
receiving the Ashok Chakra
from the then President,
Sh K.R. Narayanan.

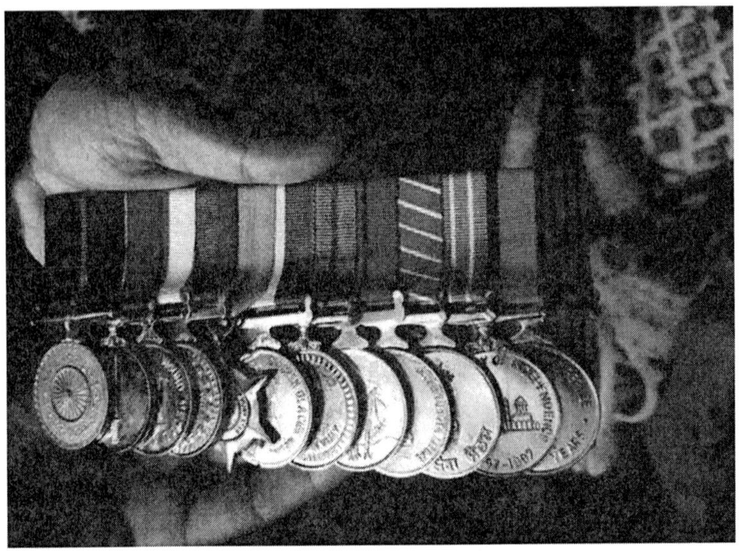

Maj Walia's medals of honour *(picture courtesy: Vikas Manhas)*.

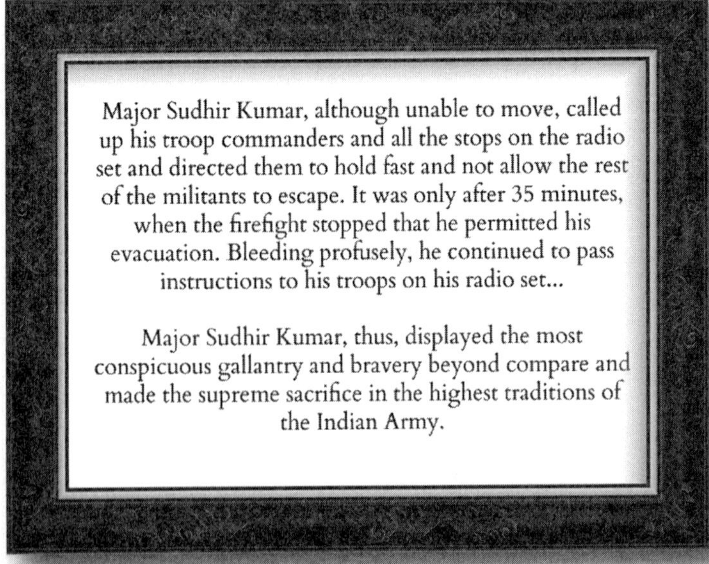

Major Sudhir Kumar, although unable to move, called up his troop commanders and all the stops on the radio set and directed them to hold fast and not allow the rest of the militants to escape. It was only after 35 minutes, when the firefight stopped that he permitted his evacuation. Bleeding profusely, he continued to pass instructions to his troops on his radio set...

Major Sudhir Kumar, thus, displayed the most conspicuous gallantry and bravery beyond compare and made the supreme sacrifice in the highest traditions of the Indian Army.

Excerpts from the citation when awarded the Ashok Chakra.

She gave him a once over. A conscious Sudhir rubbed his nose.

"Your skin matches the colours of the chinar." A sly smile lurked on her lips. "And your nose, the bark."

Aslam picked up a chinar leaf. "And this is a symbol of Kashmir."

"Tan... the climb," said Sudhir, touching his cheeks. His nose had turned grey black from acute sunburn.

"You're getting so red," said Taslim giggling away.

"I'm not blushing!"

"Yes, you are." She glanced at him, her eyes teasing.

Sudhir stared at her. His expression dulled. He had figured it would never work between them. Their realities were too different.

Fiddling with her earring, she stared at him. Their eyes locked in a moment of understanding.

Losing colour, she took in a long breath and lowered her head, hiding her eyes.

The two months of absence had finally afflicted their resolve to continue. They both had time to introspect.

The silence was so icy it could have frozen the Dal Lake.

"So, you especially went climbing?" Aslam's hesitant voice struggled to break the stillness. "Why always push yourself?"

"I wasn't just born to pay bills and die," Sudhir snapped, bunching his brows. It was clearly one of those weaponised sentences that gets flung out to hurt, to end whatever existed. It wasn't directed at Aslam.

He was angry because whatever little existed with Taslim was ending. Angry because he had no control over the forces that had killed it. At himself. At her. For them. The struggle just spilled out in misplaced emotions.

He realised that his mission and her vision were the same. And they cared for each other. Yet, it just wasn't enough.

Taslim stiffened.

Gripping the armrest, Sudhir eventually regained his composure and attempted to make conversation. "Only two ascents have been made on Brammah-I. In 1973 and 1979." He fidgeted with his collar. "Two British climbers died in the 1979 attempt."

He crossed his legs, then uncrossed them. "And we were the first Indians on Brammah II."

He seemed about to speak more, but the thread eluded him. He was still struggling.

Aslam noticed Sudhir's discomfort.

"So what did you conquer, Sudhir?"

"It's not the mountains we conquer… but ourselves," Sudhir spoke quietly, almost to himself. His voice trailed off; the conclusion was inescapable.

The honking of the jeep brought him back.

"See you guys. I've got to get back."

A misty-eyed Taslim stared at Sudhir, the corners of her lips twitched. Their eyes met, but Sudhir broke away. He lifted his shoulder in a half shrug and with a dismissive wave of his hand, reeled and walked away.

Aslam watched his receding back. She sensed he was struggling too. She hoped he would look back. He did not.

"Did something happen?" Aslam turned to Taslim. He looked past her brave smile, at her wounded eyes.

"Nah." She hadn't realised she was holding her breath.

She wrapped her hands around herself, rocking back and forth.

"We weren't meant to be together. It's better this way, just as friends."

Though no longer a reality, the fleeting love story was a testament to the sacrifices made in the name of principles and duty and the hope that one day, the conflict in Kashmir might yield to a more prosperous and peaceful future.

* * *

Azadi at any Cost

Joint Intelligence North, ISI, Islamabad
December 1992

The JIN (Joint Intelligence North) handled Jammu and Kashmir operations. Infiltration, exfiltration, propaganda and other clandestine operations. It was part of the ISI.

The ISI Colonel put his palm on the map, "This is where we need to focus, now. Incite them."

"Your fat palm has covered the entire district, Assad." Brig. Tariq smiled as Assad removed his palm. He stared at the map. Shaking his head, he pursed his lips, "Doda is difficult to cover." Tariq's code name was Mustafa.

"Didn't we try this in '65 too? Operation Gibraltar?" asked Brig. Mohd Salim Khan. "We had sent in fighters through the Pir Panjal."

He looked at them over his glasses.

"Yes, to incite rebellion. Operate around Ramban and Banihal. Cut off their fucking National Highway... the 1A."

Mustafa looked at Assad. "It failed and led to..."

"War?" said Assad, pre-empting him.

"A debacle, Colonel," said Mustafa. "The uprising never took off. The Indians got wind of it and the war started." He spat out in disgust, curling his lips. "My father..."

"Oh, I am sorry, sir... I didn't know he died in the '65 operations."

"He was a major in the Northern Light Infantry."

"Doda can tie down the Indians disproportionately... almost indefinitely." All eyes turned to Numan. "That leaves the valley to us. That helps." Numan was the code name of the third Brigadier.

"Exactly my point, sir," said Assad, a half-smile sneaking out hesitatingly.

"We should bleed them on the NH1, too. It's easier." Mustafa looked at Numan. He studied the map, chewing his lip. "We should have control over the Pir Panjal. That's crucial for us."

Assad nodded. He knew what Mustafa meant. Encircling the valley, the Pir Panjal facilitated unfretted access.

"What's the update on HuM?"

"Langrial is setting up the training camp at Kapran," said Assad, pointing to a location west of the National Highway. "Here, close to Banihal."

Langrial had built barracks and a parade ground. It was a well organised training camp for recruits.

Lighting a Camel Lights, Numan blew away the smoke. "We need more brotherhood among our fighters." Following Brig. Salim's gaze, Numan slid the pack towards him, smirking. "My son's on vacation from Yale."

"The camp will train Al-Jehad, Hizbul Mujahideen and of course the HuM." Mustafa informed the other two brigadiers. "That's how we will get our synergy."

Nodding his head, Numan said, "Give him all the resources." He crushed the cigarette. "This is important."

Clearing his throat, Brig. Salim had the last word. "Right, let him focus on South Kashmir."

* * *

The Pir Panjal is a sub-range that stretches from Murree in Pakistan to the Rohtang Pass in Himachal Pradesh. The seamless connectivity makes it ideal for infiltration in Kashmir. The gigantic range separates Poonch from the Kashmir valley, receiving more snow than any other range in the Himalayas. Its spires are the first white walls encountered when venturing into the vastness of the northern mountains.

An 84 kilometre road runs through the Pir Panjal, connecting Poonch to Srinagar. Emperor Akbar stretched the road to Lahore as an imperial route. The historic Mughal route has several passes, the highest being Peer ki Gully. Gujjars and Bakharwals have used the route for their seasonal migration.

The Pir Panjal was a safe haven for militants because of its savage ranges.

* * *

HQ XVI Corps,
Nagrota, North of Jammu
October 1993

The 16 Corps had a pivotal role in safeguarding the sensitive and strategic LoC from Akhnoor in Jammu district to Poonch and the areas south of the Pir Panjal range.

The meeting had a large gathering. Winters were setting in. The lifeline to the valley, NH1A had to be kept operational under all circumstances. The General Officer Commanding, Delta force, responsible for Doda, gave his brief. The Jamaat had stepped up its activities and were recruiting in Doda.

The nodal group in Doda, however, was the Al Jehad.

"And their leader?" asked GOC Romeo Force. He handled Rajouri and Poonch.

"A local."

"Harkat-ul-Mujahideen has set up cells in my areas," said GOC Uniform Force. He handled Udhampur and Banihal.

The Army had noticed an alarming new trend. The new militants were no longer rookies. Someone was training them better. Emboldened by better training, the militants had fired at the BSF post at Ramsoo in Ramban, with precision and planning.

"And Dessa…" said GOC Delta Force bitterly, "Operation Huntdown."

False info misled a BSF column into an ambush in Dessa, near Doda.

The militants had held one constable captive.

The BSF Commander looked on either side before speaking. "We lost 20 boys… that bloody day."

Silence followed. All eyes in the room turned towards him. He took a deep breath, trying to steady himself before continuing, "It wasn't our fault entirely. If only we had more experience and better training."

The gathering knew what he meant. Constant deployment and relocation had affected training and an unclear chain of command. Often deprived of Army privileges and resources, it led to disastrous operations. And yet, the BSF always bore the blunt for lacking professionalism.

They had paraded him in chains in front of local journalists.

"And exhibited him like a bloody trophy." His face was a mask of anger and rage, his jaw set in a hard line. Pushed to his emotional limit, the BSF commander was simmering to take action.

The GOC 16 Corps winced. His shoulders stiffened at the thought of Head Constable Bikash Nazary, captured by the Harkat. They had gouged out his eyes and pulled out his skin, before beheading him.

The room fell silent.

"We must each bear the cross," the GOC's words hung in the air, "Of our decisions."

After an agonising silence, the GOC 16 Corps placed his palms on the table.

"I have called you all precisely for this reason. We need to hunt down that animal and find this camp."

A unspoken singular thought raced through every mind. The GOC 16 Corps echoed it out loud. "Hunt down Mansoor Langrial!"

* * *

In early November, the Signal Intelligence unit intercepted messages between the clandestine stations operating in the Pir Panjal and one just across the LoC in Kotli. Kotli, part of the Mirpur Division of PoK, was only 41 kilometres from Rajouri.

Clandestine station 1:*Janab, Indian dogs have launched massive sweep operations… both sides of Banihal and the Jawahar Tunnel."*

Controlling station, Kotli: *Troops?*

Clandestine station 1:*We escaped… Gurkhas… janab.*

The messages were frantic…

Clandestine station 2:*Three of our mujahideen got martyred… yes, we will avenge them.*

… and desperate.

Clandestine station 1:*Control one, Allah-u-Akbar, control one. We had a firefight in the Mahu Mangat area, west of the highway.*

Controlling station, Kotli: *Where… near Banihal?*

Clandestine station 1:*Yes, yes, on the southern side of the tunnel.*

Controlling station, Kotli: *Injuries?*

Clandestine station 1:*Two mujahideen brothers injured… one missing… other ate cyanide to avoid capture.*

Controlling station, Kotli:*Who?*

Clandestine station 1: *Abu Afghani*

Unknown to them, the Army was interrogating the missing militant. The militants were feeling the heat… but Langrial was still elusive.

* * *

Finally, 16 Corps launched the third phase of operations. The GOC planned to push in a team of 9 Para Commandoes.

Positioning techniques that triangulated radio signals and narrowed down the approximate locations were applied. Militant's intel added another layer to the confirmation.

"They are somewhere here, sir," said the signals officer, circling his marker along the rugged mountain ridge with sharp slopes. It was a long shot.

Pinching his lips, GOC 16 Corps removed his glasses. "That little circle you drew covers two valleys and a major ridge line."

"Besides a two-day walk from the road in the toughest terrain…" said the Colonel, CO 9 Para (SF) curling his lips.

The CO looked at the General. "We don't mind the walk, sir… it's the loss of surprise. That's concerning."

"I'm concerned too Colonel, but what's the option?" The corps commander glanced at the map.

The flat expression of the intelligence officer was not heartening. "We corroborated the intelligence with a Gujjar whose wife they had picked up, sir."

"How authentic is this Gujjar?"

Deliberating, the intelligence officer shrugged his shoulders, "We just have to take that risk, sir."

Adjusting his maroon beret, the Colonel's scowling eyes bore into the intelligence officer. He knew what it meant. His boys would have to risk their lives on yet another convoluted intelligence input.

* * *

Kapran, Ramban
November 1993

The vehicles dropped off the 9 Para team on NH 1A, close to Ramban. The sun had already set and the sky was darkening.

"So everyone clear?" asked Maj. Anil Nair. "Any doubts?" Sudhir shook his head, as did the other two officers, Capt. K. Bhushan and Nirmal Dhaliwal.

Appearing more like savages with their faces smudged under camouflage paint, they quietly slithered away to their smaller groups for a last check.

The infantry units had moved in and laid a cordon west of the national highway. They spread the nine hundred troops in small teams to prevent the militants from running through.

Left at the mercy of the elements, the biting icy winds and the freezing frost would test them. Without rest for the next four days, only consuming the provisions each man had packed. They had just their breath to prevent their trigger fingers from freezing.

Waiting until it was perfectly dark, dark shadows crossed the Chenab over a river bridge that swung dizzyingly over the frothy water. The moonless night had been specially selected for the sanctuary it offered, the cloud cover a perfect foil for the operational surprise.

Unmindful of their heaving lungs or sore hamstrings, the men kept up a relentless pace. They could endure strain. Sweat soaked despite the sub-zero temperatures, they carried their battle loads with life's essentials – ammunition, first aid, radio set batteries and finally, survival rations, in that order. Ankles hard wrapped in thick bandages called 'putty' prevented painful twists and ligament tears.

Reassuringly caressing their weapons, cocked for immediate use, each man had his instincts primed. Ears prickled for the slightest sound, noses twitching for unnatural smells, their eyes scanned every innocent bush and rock, their feet lithe but sure.

They continued their ascent, making steady progress.

* * *

Just before first light, the leading scouts Anchal and Bijli spotted a dhok. Obscured in the false dawn, its silhouette jutted out beyond a massive rock.

On a silent signal, the squad melted. Using the frozen rocks and scrub, they fused into the landscape, blending in like chameleons. The dense pine and deodar treeline on the lower slopes had given way to a more open vegetation, scraggy shrubs and larger rock-faces. The sting from the cold was sharper. An occasional angry screech from a night bird or a flap of wings disturbed by the intrusion rented the air.

Nothing else moved. If it did, it would be hostile.

Mukhtiar crawled ahead and approached Anchal. He sniffed the air. His nostrils only detected the smell of fresh pine. No smell of smoke. He turned to go back and froze, sharply drawing in his breath.

"Bhenchod," he muttered softly. Arrested by a sight, he craned his neck. A cigarette stub, carelessly thrown.

'It's fresh.' The thought raced through his mind, ringing alarm bells. Innocent elsewhere, its foreign presence in this remote desolation was a screaming warning.

He looked further and detected signs of human manure. Hackles raised, Mukhtiar signalled the team to fan out. As per practised drill, kneeling down, the scouts, Anchal and Bijli, covered the front door with their weapons to prevent an escape. There was still no sign of life in it.

Sudhir padded ahead and tapped Mukhtiar on the shoulder.

Communicating briefly, Mukhtiar exchanged information, half in sign language, the rest through telepathy. Sudhir knew exactly what he meant. Like between a whale and her cub, or between identical twins. Trapped in the extreme pressures of endless near-death-situations, you forged a kinship. It enabled psychic communication, beyond verbal conversation.

Sudhir and Mukhtiar guessed the hut was a lookout post, probably with no more than two people inside. Sudhir soaked in the unfolding situation. Eyes locked in silence; they studied each other. A series of thoughts crossed back and forth. Sudhir thrived on uncertainty while Mukhtiar bemoaned his youthful zeal.

A protective Mukhtiar did not want Sudhir to defy luck again. But the job had to be done. Someone had to risk it and Sudhir knew what it would take. Nodding at Mukhtiar, without waiting for an answer, Sudhir slithered ahead. With grudging admiration, a silently protesting Mukhtiar followed. He wouldn't dare leave the young officer's side.

Using the undulating bumps and scrubs, they closed in on the hut. Anchal shifted his position to adjust his weapon, cracking a dry stick below his knee. In a quick retort, the crackle of the AK-47 fire thudded into the bark above his head, fanning his forehead. He fired back in reflex action, as did his buddy Bijli next to him.

Cursing at the loss of surprise, Sudhir inched towards the door, hugging the wall of the hut. Fierce fire from the scouts kept engaging the door and a windowless open cavity now. On reaching the corner, Sudhir lifted his hand in a signal. The scouts held their fire. Sudhir kicked the door, Mukhtiar threw in two grenades in quick succession. They waited for the thump of the grenades and barged in swiftly, weapons blazing.

Over in a quick blur, the action was swift and surgical. A makeshift straw bed and stale smell of food carried the account of the revelry; the smell of hashish, the indulgence to debauchery. Of the two bullet-ridden bodies, one apparently was an Afghani. His girth, clothes, footwear and hands clearly established his rank. He was not an inconsequential expendable terrorist.

A hysterical Gujjar woman ran into the soldiers in the outer ring. Left to herself, she had forced her way out through the rear window of the dhok when the firing started.

Digging her toes in, mumbling inconsolably, she had refused to go near the hut. They still needed her for identification. Glancing around, not focusing on anything, her grey eyes widened in alarm as they forced her inside.

She had shut her eyes, when forced to identify the dead body. Her broken lips trembled. "Farooq... Farooq Teli," she blurted out hesitatingly. She belonged to a nearby village. The Afghani militant had raped her.

Farooq Teli aka Mohammed Suleiman was an Afghani training instructor, helping Langrial. Employed to train the endless supply of recruits, he was an important asset. The confirmation came as a relief. They were close.

Stiffening her back, when questioned about the location of the camp, she shook her head in denial. She was terrified. A bloodied eye, however, darted towards the ridgeline across. It was a further day's climb.

Seeing her pitiable state, Sudhir shook his head. "Let her go." Kheem Singh released her. Curling his upper lip, Sudhir spat out, "Fucking animals!"

* * *

The sound of distant gunfire alerted the sentry, sitting guard in his makeshift dhok. The news travelled like a jungle fire across the camp.

Langrial's gaze followed Habibullah's calloused fingernail, as it pointed towards the thickly wooded ridge line.

"That's where Farooq Teli went, yesterday," Habibullah spat in disgust. "With Suleiman and Wasim."

Suleiman was Habibullah's younger brother, who had recently joined them as a young recruit along with Wasim.

"Farooq Teli's balls are always swollen," hissed Habibullah in Pashto. "He can fuck with his own grandmother.

Habibullah's voice was low, but the menace in it was unmistakable.

Aware that his Lieutenant was growing ambitious, Langrial had to find a way to cut him down. He could not allow Habibullah to challenge his authority.

Langrial glanced at the mark on Habibullah's forehead.

A five-time *Namazi*, Habibullah bore the *zebiba*, a dark callous mark on his forehead below his Hazara styled turban. His reward for decades of at least thirty-four *sajdas*[56] each time he prayed. In the past few months, his beard had grown long, his cheeks had sunk in and his eyes glinted with fanatical fervour.

"Is our location compromised?" Filling his chillum with tobacco, Langrial glanced up at Habibullah.

Langrial wanted to pin the blame on Habibullah. Habibullah,

---

[56] *Prayerful prostrations*

however, smoothly sidestepped.

"I will kill Wasim myself if he has compromised us." Habibullah held Langrial's gaze. "Even Suleiman, my brother... if required."

The static tension between them was electrifying. The unspoken more powerful than the stated.

News travelled up. The lower slopes had security forces swarming in large numbers. The camp's location had still not been found by the Army.

"Tell the scouts to signal the moment they move upwards. Be ready to abandon the camp," Langrial ordered.

"We fight, Commander. We will not run from these dogs."

Langrial gazed at Habibullah. Convincing and controlling him was becoming increasingly difficult. "Our recruits are raw. This appears to be a large force."

"Allah is with us. This is our Jihad."

"But we need to live for that... not die."

"*La ilaha illallah.*[57] I have already declared my *Shahada*[58] Commander. I am ready to face death."

"Habibullah, do as I say." The icy tone was unmistakable. Langrial removed the black Glock 26 Gen4 9 mm Luger from his waistband and laid it out on the rock before him.

Eyeing the Glock, Habibullah's eyes strayed back to Langrial.

He lingered on for an uneasy second, weighing the options. Stroking his beard thoughtfully, a sneer finally slithered out. The gaze, however, was cold as steel. "Okay Commander., whatever you want."

As Habibullah sauntered away, Langrial's gaze scorched into his back.

*** * * ***

---

[57] *There is no God but Allah*
[58] *Declaration of faith in one God (Allah) and His messenger.*

Warming themselves against the inclement weather in the dhok, the commandoes rested, recouping their strength. They waited for nightfall to start the hunt for their quarry. A half-crested moon moved between the trees, casting long shadows. Except for the sound of crickets, they could hear little.

Bijli and Anchal had taken up their positions as leading scouts. Using a combination of map reading techniques, training, instinct and geography, the squad moved with caution.

The challenge was to shun established trails. They had to maintain tactical domination by moving along the crestline to avert being fired upon, and yet, maintain surprise while moving with speed.

Bijli moved a step behind Anchal. Enveloped in the eerie hazy glow, he watched Anchal's surefooted shadow jump nimbly between rocks like a silent cat. A warrior from Arunachal, Anchal was a hunter, used to stalking prey since childhood. Anchal's deadpan face broke into a toothy grin as he heard Bijli slip on an algae covered rock, scraping his shin painfully.

The smile, however, masked the deep respect he felt for Bijli. From Rajasthan, Bijli carried his nickname with ease. Noted for his lightning movement and quick reactions, Bijli could shoot blindfolded. Anchal could bet his life on him.

"Stop grinning, you ape!" whispered Bijli, elbowing him. Eyes narrowing into slits, Anchal grinned more. Anchal's smile broke the tension, easing the moment.

Unknown to them, a third terrorist named Wasim had also escaped along with the Gujjar woman. Hiding in the undergrowth, he had managed to escape the soldiers placed around the dhok.

Keeping up an unflagging pace, the squad made swift progress, reaching a mountain stream by first light. Daybreak was still a few minutes away. Anchal saw something move while he walked across the bridge of logs and boulders.

A Gujjar cowherd was observing them. Signalling Bijli, Anchal broke into a run.

On seeing the soldiers, the Gujjar started gesticulating loudly. He slapped a herd of cattle and pack horses, goading them to run downslope. He followed the melee as it ran down. They overpowered the man quickly.

Bound and quizzed, he eventually admitted to being a look-out for the camp. The cattle running down the slope was a signal, forewarning the camp that the Indian soldiers were closing in.

Another set of camp look-outs sitting across the ridge could clearly observe the cattle in sudden flight. They would relay the warning of impending danger. Surprise was clearly lost. Pressed for time, the squad now raced towards the camp with greater urgency.

* * *

Struggling up the precipitous slopes, Wasim made a run for the camp. The pain from his broken knee was jarring. He had bitten his tongue when he had fallen down a rock. Painfully stuck in the rock crevice, he had lost his shoe when he pulled out his leg. His squashed toes peeped out through the torn socks.

Terrified, cold and exhausted, he cursed his luck. Mind numbed with fear, barely nineteen, he had no stomach for this Jihad.

They had paid his family a measly sum for his involvement. Smiling through his gold-capped teeth, the tanzeem agent, a present-day slave trader, had winked, "It's your *meher*, for marrying Jihad." It was a cruel joke. They paid *meher* to the bride during the marriage.

Overpowered by the lookouts, they led him to Habibullah, bound in ropes.

"You vermin! Did you lead the dogs here?" Habibullah kicked him in the stomach. Wasim sprawled on the ground, doubling in pain.

"No… no, please … don't!" whimpered Wasim clutching his stomach.

Holding him by the hair, Habibullah yanked his head up, slapping him hard, kicking him in the groin.

Wasim gulped, wheezing. Habibullah kicked him again, this time harder.

"Suleiman? Farooq Teli?"

Habibullah continued kicking, only stopping to get his breath back. A red patch spread in Wasim's salwar.

Exploding in pain, Wasim hugged the ground, sobbing. Spittle dribbled on the frozen earth, caking his face with mud.

"Both dead… killed!" he screamed out.

Jerking Wasim's head upright, Habibullah forced a finger into his mouth. Crooking his finger, he tugged at Wasim's cheek, tearing the tissue. Wasim screamed.

"Who killed Suleiman?" The voice was icy. This time Habibullah kicked him in the face, breaking his front teeth.

"A captain. I am not sure." Blood dribbled down his chin.

"*La ilaha illallah!*"

Eyes narrowed to slits, face pulled in a snarl, Habibullah hissed. "You too should die, you bloody dog!"

Continuing to hold Wasim by his hair, Habibullah pulled out a glistening knife and deliberately slid it across Wasim's jugular. He watched as the warm blood ran down and Wasim struggled in his death throes.

"I will kill that Indian dog!" he swore. "I will avenge my brother."

Letting go of the quivering body, he wiped his bloody fingers on Wasim's shirt.

A man ran up. "Cattle… cattle… the signal!"

"What? Did you see the herd run down?"

"Yes… yes!"

Slinging his rifle, Habibullah ran to Langrial.

"*Prekhudal… prekhudal!*"[59] he shouted. "The infidels are coming!"

---

[59] Abandon

* * *

A deserted camp site greeted Sudhir and his team. Encircling it from another flank, Maj. Nair and Capt. Bhushan approached the camp with caution.

After the build-up of the past few days, this was quite a dampener. Noticing Sudhir's stooping shoulders, a wistful smile spread across Maj. Nair's face. "But such is the game of the hunter and the prey, young man."

He thumped a crestfallen Sudhir on his back. "But look at what we found."

The camp had army-style squad posts for carrying out weapon trainings. A small firing range for conducting live firing practices. Ropes strung across trees and logs for an obstacle course, for physical training. A small ground for drill stood in the centre.

There was literature on Jihad and Islamic indoctrination, pamphlets on weapons and making of explosive devices. There were quarters to house recruits and cook houses and inside were radio set batteries, ammunition, medicines and first aid boxes. They left bags of rations behind along with photographs of families and some hearts etched in wood.

This was the biggest camp discovered, the huge haul a dividend for the efforts.

Langrial had escaped. Once again.

* * *

A fortnight later, Arun Jasrotia barged into Sudhir's room.

The corners of his eyes crinkled. "Did you hear?"

Sudhir glanced up from his book. His forehead puckered. "What, Happy?

"Langrial and Ilyas Kashmiri bumped into a roadblock."

"Dead?"

"Arrested by the Gurkhas."

"So unbecoming? After all the drama. They didn't fight? Both are Afghan Mujahid."

"Not even a shot fired." The corner of his mouth quirked up. "Someone's loss is someone's gain."

"What are you hinting at, Happy? That I fucked up? And they got the catch?"

Arun shrugged. He gave Sudhir his lop-sided grin.

Screwing up his face, Sudhir threw the book at him. "Get out!"

Arun caught the book neatly and walked out grinning, ear to ear.

Mansoor Langrial's arrest and detention triggered a chain of events that shook India.

* * *

Arun and Sudhir were having breakfast. Arun stirred powdered milk into the dark liquid until it turned the colour of caramel. Sudhir wrinkled his nose, watching Arun sip the concoction. Clearly, they did not share the same view on healthy eating. Arun gave him a toothy smile.

A commando brought them the Corps Sit Rep.[60] Sudhir's eyes grew dark, as he read the report. He gritted his teeth, "Shit."

Sajjad Afghani, an area commander of Harkat-ul-Ansar had executed a Maj. Bhupinder Singh.

Arun glanced at the report.

"Isn't he the same bastard who attacked Elahi Bagh Camp on 16th January?"

"Yes, Langrial's old crony. He's gone rabid and needs to be shot." Sudhir swore under his breath.

"Did he have a demand?"

"Langrial's release."

---

[60] 15 Corps Situation Report which had a summary of operations and intelligence of the area. It was circulated to units.

"So he executed Maj. Bhupinder when the Army refused to negotiate?"

Sudhir nodded. He pushed the plate away, having lost his appetite.

* * *

January 1994

Sajjad Afghani's actions were creating concern back in Pakistan. Harkat had planned to lie low to seek entrenchment in South Kashmir, but Afghani refused to toe the line.

ISI dispatched a maulvi to India to discipline Afghani. He was also tasked to merge the HuJI, HuM and HuA into one group. The overweight, bearded maulvi, along with Sajjad Afghani, unfortunately ran into a BSF patrol in Anantnag when his car broke down. He was Maulana Masood Azhar, notorious as the limp maulvi.

ISI audaciously attempted Masood Azhar's release several times; from capturing British citizens in Kashmir to American backpackers from Paharganj in New Delhi. Al Faran, a front organisation for HuA seized six western tourists in Pahalgam, on orders from ISI, but in vain.

The final and most dramatic attempt was ultimately successful – the Kandahar hijack in 1999. India released Masood Azhar and two others, both Harkat members, in an exchange for the hostages. Masood Azhar became the most wanted man in India. He who swore to break India up.

Curiously, the hijackers didn't demand the release of Langrial, whose arrest had triggered the entire chain of events. India repatriated Langrial in 2011 after he spent 18 years in jail. Sajjad Afghani was killed during an unsuccessful jailbreak attempt from the top security Kot Bhalwal Jail in 1999. He lies buried in a Jammu graveyard.

* * *

ICE AND FIRE

Srinagar
March 1994

Towering above them was the historic Hariparbat fort. A honey-sweet fragrance hung in the air.

Sudhir inhaled deeply. "Jasmine? Lily?"

"Almond blossoms," said Aslam, "*Soonth* is here."

Sudhir looked at him. "Spring," Aslam explained, "Soonth was once celebrated in Kashmir."

They walked through the historical Badamwari Garden, built in the centre of Srinagar by Jehangir, the Mughal emperor.

"Ammi would get a *samovar* (metal urn with an arched neck) with namkeen tea." His eyes softened as he watched the flowers. "And we would sing the *wanwun*."

"A Kashmiri lullably," he added.

"We should also visit the Tulip gardens," said Sudhir, cleaning his green Ray Bans.

"Why?" The tone was weary but cheerful. Overhearing the conversation, a hunched old man, Abdul Samad, a friendly shikara owner, butted in.

"There's only cold beauty there…no soul."

They were the only people in the deserted garden. "New Delhi and the Wahabi Islamic thought killed Kashmiri identity."

Sudhir realised the Kashmiri culture, the world Abdul had known, had vanished – the political class, the rule of law, the Hindu inhabitants, alcohol and cinema. The cricket matches, picnics by moonlight in the saffron fields, schools, universities and an independent press were things of the past.

"Everything's dead," Abdul spat out, his hands shaking in a palsy of rage.

"See," he indicated, spreading his arms "The Tulips are here, but no tourists."

The empty line of bobbing shikaras in the Dal Lake and the skinny riding ponies munching on lost dreams, a sad metaphor for the drowned hopes of an entire Kashmiri generation.

"Our reality has reduced," said Abdul, his vision narrowed to a pinprick. His voice was soft and measured, like someone trying to overcome a stutter. "It's no longer defined by our gardens, agriculture, music, or our handicrafts, or cuisine."

He screwed his eyes shut.

"It's just defined by two bodies that confront each other…without a mediator."

Opening his eyes, his gaze pierced Sudhir. "The mosque and the army camp."

He scowled like a man who had bitten into a rotten apple.

* * *

Lolab

April 1994

The heptr landed. And Sudhir grinned mischievously.

"Will you fit?"

Mahendra's gravelly voice let out a rough laugh. They dashed in and settled down.

Squeezed between Mahendra and the heptr frame, Sudhir shot a glance at Mahendra. His close-cropped head nearly touched the roof. Sudhir could feel the bristling muscles, as their shoulders touched. The massive barrel chest took up most of the space.

"I am glad you are with us."

"And we are proud that you lead us, sir." The rare acknowledgement thrilled Sudhir.

Despite being a man of few words, Mahendra was larger than life and dwarfed most men.

* * *

Sudhir's eyes flickered on 'D… Dagger,' scribbled behind the helmet. The pilot was Sudhir's course mate from Delta squadron, NDA. He smiled. The 'Deadly' had peeled off.

When you looked down from the helicopter, the mountains enveloping the Lolab valley looked like a curved sickle.

"Looks like a snarling lionhead." Speaking into the microphone, Sudhir pointed down.

The pilot craned his neck, casting a sceptical eye through the visor. "That's very extreme, Sudhir," he said amused, "The forests are innocent."

He banked the helicopter like a swooping eagle, giving them another view of the wooded mountains.

"Hungry to devour anything that walks through its open fangs," added Sudhir above the whirr of the rotors.

Sitting next to him, Mahendra nodded, completely agreeing.

Mahendra peered over the treetops, making a note of the ridge lines, as the light utility helicopter, Cheetah, flew over. The Mujahid infesting the forests were far from friendly.

"It's like gladiator games," Sudhir said, smirking wickedly. The tone oscillated between sarcasm and humour. "We are the gladiators. We need to kill them before they kill us."

"And the ringside audience?" asked the pilot, humouring along.

"The people glued to TVs watching prime-time news," said Sudhir, bleakness darkening his eyes, the playfulness falling away like a discarded jacket.

* * *

Manganwadi Top Encounter
April 1994

They walked from Mohalla Shalpora along the ridgeline, straight up towards the Manganwadi top.

Spring was everywhere – from the smell in the trees to the gurgling springs and the sprouting soft ferns. And the smell of wildflowers.

"This is Soonth," Sudhir smirked, showing off to Mahendra, leading him through the lush greenery. Mahendra barely noticed the landscape. His deep-set eyes were focused on what lurked behind the trees. Mahendra's powerful aura ensconced Sudhir in a blanket of safety. The strong square jaw line enhanced his ruggedness. The boxer's nose dared anyone cross him. The AK-47 looked puny in his large hands. Each time Sudhir witnessed Mahendra in action, a profound respect almost bordering on reverence welled up within Sudhir.

Sudhir and Mahendra, as expected, showed the way as leading scouts. The moon sliver dipped behind the ridge lines by the time they reached the bald patch on top of Manganwadi. It left a faint afterglow.

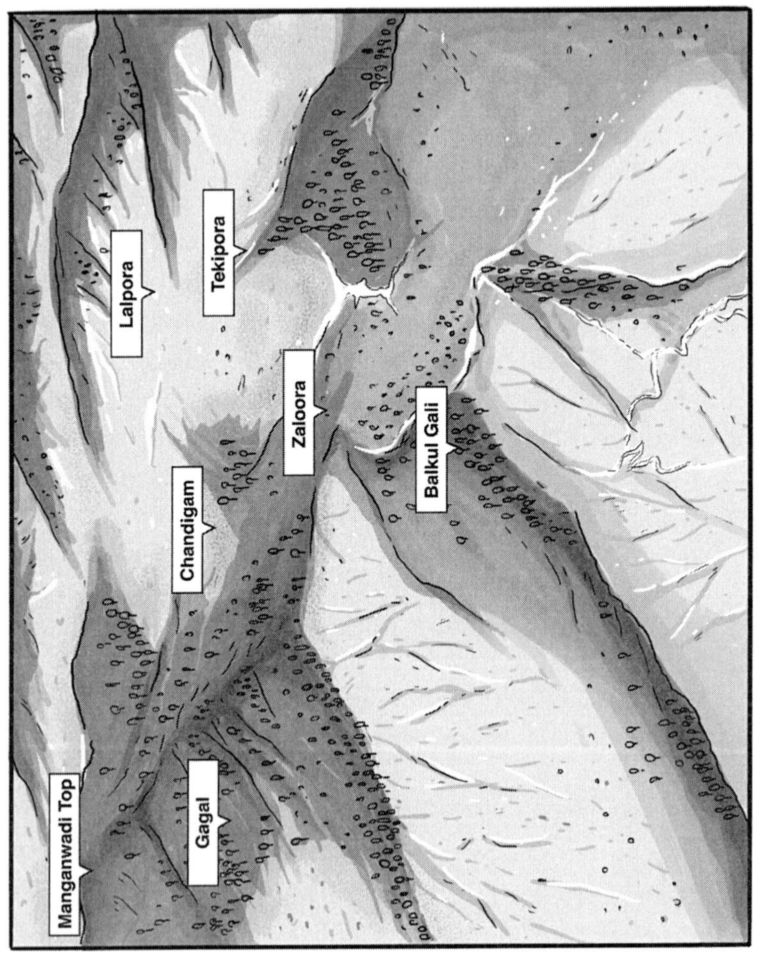

Manganwadi Top, Chandigam Balkul Gully, Lolab Valley

Mahendra could see the dim silhouette of the two dhok huts against the night sky. They could smell cow dung. Following their practised drill, the team crept ahead and listened. Complete silence. They waited. Nothing.

The team finally searched the huts. They were empty.

The mountain top was cold. They had walked for nine hours so the team wanted to rest in the warm dhoks.

"No," objected Sudhir, setting his jaw firm. "We will go into the trees. They cannot surprise us there."

Moving back into the treeline, they moved below the crest, away from the skyline. Sudhir ordered a break. They deployed lookouts, shed their loads and rested.

Turning over against his pack, Sudhir dozed off, snatching a quick wink. It always did him good. He could even sleep standing up. He had learned that in the NDA as a cadet.

A thin whistle warned the team. An alarm. The sentry had spotted hostile movement. Before the team could stir, Sudhir was already up and running. He checked his magazine, shifted the safety catch to automatic and aligned his weapon, all in one movement, as he flew past.

Spurred into action, Mahendra raced behind Sudhir.

Perched on a tree, pointing his weapon, the sentry indicated the direction. Sudhir dashed swiftly. Jumping over boulders, he vaulted over a broken tree.

A few steps behind him, Mahendra saw Sudhir race through the undergrowth without breaking stride.

In a flash, before Mahendra could react, he saw Sudhir hoist up his AK-47 and let off two quick bursts. Sudhir followed it up with another long, staccato bursts of automatic fire. Feeling the thorns prick at his skin, Mahendra too broke through the bush. Sudhir was studying the bushes ahead with a predator's unwavering attention, holding his weapon ready for rapid fire.

Across a small rivulet, one terrorist lay dead face down, a little further Mahendra could observe a sneaker clad foot sticking out. Two dead.

From the edge of his vision, Mahendra saw a lifeless bloody arm clutching a weapon. That was three dead. Moving ahead, Mahendra and

Sudhir carried out speculative fire. By the time the team caught up, they had already scoured and cleared the immediate area of danger.

"Don't you know fear?" Mahendra finally muttered, unable to contain himself.

Sudhir jerked his head towards the bodies. "These bastards come with a voucher…to get killed."

Mahendra stared wide eyed. He opened his mouth to speak. Words eluded him. He clamped up.

Sudhir half shrugged, "What's there to be afraid of?" He gave a dismissive wave of his hand.

Operation over, Mahendra pieced the action together.

Sudhir had sensed the militants, even before he saw them. Like a magnet drawn, he had charged ahead. He spotted the five terrorists walking, their faces covered in shadows. His speed, and audacious move helped him shoot down three terrorists. Two had jumped down into the bushes, making it impossible to track them.

They had walked down from the direction of the dhoks. Sudhir's astute knowledge of militant temperament had saved the team from being surprised.

Sitting round the campfire during dinner, the conversation turned towards Sudhir. "He's like a bloodhound," remarked Mahendra.

"Exactly," chimed his colleague. "He could smell out the militants today."

"Every time…" Mahendra corrected, his tone reflecting admiration and a hint of disbelief. Sudhir's uncanny ability to detect danger and hunt out militants was acquiring the status a campfire legend.

* * *

Snow and Survival

Operation Meghdoot
The Ice Wall
July 1994

He struck his toe into the ice wall, embedding the protruding steel teeth of the crampon bound under his snow-boots. The crunch in the ice barely audible, he reached up and heaved the ice pick above his head. It held. Bringing up his right leg, he repeated the action with his other foot.

The echoed clinking of the ice pitons and carabiners hanging on his waist marked the steady progress of his laborious climb. Using a combination of two ice picks, he climbed the sheer eighty-degree ice wall slowly.

Depleted oxygen at 19000 feet made breathing difficult, sapping his energy. Halfway up the ice wall, he rested for a minuscule second, closing his eyes from the stinging wind. Denying him the solace, guilt barbed his mind awake, dislodging the snowflakes settled on his closed eyelids. Fatigued from the exertion, Sudhir laboured on despite his heaving chest and aching muscles. Time was crucial. Lives depended on it.

Peering through the blizzard, he sensed Hav. Sonam ascending about ten feet above tirelessly. A Ladakhi, his lungs and muscles were genetically modified by his birth and further strengthened when he joined the Ladakh Scouts.

As leads, Sudhir and Sonam were fixing the ropes on this uncharted route. The team waited below , impatient to start the climb.

* * *

Sitting in the adjutant's office, drumming his fingers on the table, Sudhir fixed his gaze on the board, reading the names of previous adjutants, waiting for the major to read his application.

Scowling, the major held up the paper and looked up at Sudhir. "The

Old Man may not like it." He was referring to his commanding officer.

"I want to test myself, sir," said Sudhir, returning the application. "I can explain…"

He was soon ushered into the CO's presence.

The hard-nosed colonel examined Sudhir without twitching a muscle. In pin-drop silence. Sudhir stared back; gaze unwavering.

"Why?" The voice was far from friendly.

Gulping, Sudhir focussed on the Balidan Badge, averting the CO's eyes.

"They need volunteers, sir."

Dropping his half glasses lower, the Colonel peered over them. "Really?"

"I need a break, sir. And this would do me good."

"Now that's an honest thought," said the Colonel straight faced. "But a break in Siachen?"

Sudhir nodded. His eyes crinkled, displaying just a hint of excitement.

"You've served there before?" More an affirmation than a question.

"Just a few weeks, sir. That too… as a replacement."

"By the way, you did well on the course."

"Thank you, sir. Siachen will help me hone my skills."

As the best student, Sudhir had topped the tough mountain warfare course conducted by HAWS in Gulmarg. He was also detailed for the advanced course.

The fuss was over an application volunteering for a stint in the Siachen Glacier.

* * *

76 kilometres long, the Siachen Glacier was strategic to India. Indian troops under Operation Meghdoot pre-empted Pakistan's Operation Ababeel by just one day to occupy most of the dominating heights on

the Saltoro Ridge to the west of Siachen Glacier.

This was in 1984. Since then, troops positioned here played Russian roulette with death every day, fighting a trigger-happy enemy who was itching to ingress on Indian territory and confronting the weather, which snuffed out life in an eye-blink.

Even Warshi, the last Ladakhi village, was a good 10 kilometres downstream from the base camp. No life was expected to exist beyond.

But at the glacier, the men of the Army, drawn from every Indian state, had pledged to defend the honour of a nation, defying logic and the circumstances of their genes.

* * *

Though confounded by his strange request, Sudhir's zest finally edged out the Colonel's reluctance. The eyes crinkled, warming up.

"Must you always be proving something, son?" The whispered words probed Sudhir's heart.

"I didn't come this far, only to come this far, sir."

Keeping his glasses aside, the Colonel stared at Sudhir in silence. Nodding, he finally picked up his pen.

"Ok, fuck off!" he said, dismissing Sudhir with a nod.

"Thank you, sir." Sudhir beamed, saluting crisply.

"… And good luck, boy." The steady stare held a hundred thoughts as the door closed behind Sudhir.

On the way out, Sudhir beamed at the Major. "I promise to get you some pure *shilajeet*."

The mountains around the Siachen were famous for the prized shilajeet, the potent aphrodisiac mentioned in Ayurveda.

"You'll need it yourself to thaw your audacious balls from the sub-zero temp, Sudhir," scoffed the Major.

* * *

Siachen Glacier

It had been three months.Devoid of vegetation, just barren rubble and rock, the lunar landscape was stark white.It was so bloody cold that skin would peel off if a soldier accidentally touched his steel barrel with bare fingers.

Every man who served here would go back, altered physiologically and psychologically, most temporarily, some permanently. The price of defending a nation.

Unable to sleep, Sudhir stepped out of his cramped fibre glass hut. The snowstorm had eased up. Though still dark, stars peeped out shyly, seduced by the soft glow of a reluctant moon. And the overwhelming silence. Almost a perfect night, the absence of crickets chirping and sweet smells made the scene more eerie than pretty.

Walking towards the rear, Sudhir unzipped his feathered down trousers to pee. "Shit," he exclaimed, feeling goose bumps on his genitals from the icy sting. Chuckling, he remembered the last conversation with his adjutant. No longer surprised to see the frozen yellow puddle at his feet, he knew even shit froze faster than it was excreted. Not only were you expected to live here, but fight too.

And in his case lead too. There was no room for weakness.

Back inside his small hut, he zipped the sleeping bag up to his nose. Used to the nauseous smell now, he barely registered the odour of kerosene as it dripped, drop by drop into the crude army issue heat stove called Bukhari. The smell of kerosene was everywhere, pervasive. The clothes had it. The water. The food. You could even taste it in your bile when it came up.

Settling down, he slowly drifted into sleep, thinking about the air hostess he had met in Delhi.

A shrill noise ruined his dream.

"Avalanche. Avalanche!" The radio set suddenly crackled, "Eastings 354…"

An avalanche had swept an infantry patrol. And they expected him to rescue them, if possible, alive.

He sighed. "Braves never rest," he reminded himself.

* * * *

Barking orders, strapping on the crampons, adjusting the snow goggles over his forehead, Sudhir slipped the avalanche beacon around his neck. It tracked signals from similar beacons buried in the snow.

In the light of a kerosene-lit lantern, he examined the map, marking out a route. They would have to take the ice wall to save time. It was a risk, but then everything was risky here. Risk was routine.

Miraculously, two survivors had radioed the details back to base. Muttering a small prayer, he hoped they would be alive. He had met the young officer just a few days back. Barely out of the academy, this was his first posting. He had trained some of those men. Teaching them mountain craft, Sudhir was teaching them to fight on the world's highest battlefield.

The rescue party was ready. Ropes, safety gear, harnesses, first aid kits, oxygen cylinders, radios, immobilisers, alpine stretchers, weapons and ammo. Everything strapped on.

Sepoy Shiv Pandey, a devout Hindu from Mathura, touched the small pebble. He carried the talisman in his pocket. Plucked out from the mazaar of a peer baba in Kashmir, he sought divine assurance through a different link. Religion was never an issue in the Army. When one was confronted by death, beliefs were trivial, survival was primal.

Their all-white attire was a camouflage against the snow. There was still the enemy to deal with.

* * * *

He was almost near the top. Two more swings and he would be up. Sonam was already up, waiting. Arching his back, he swung the ice pick above him. The ice cracked, fracturing vertically. Without checking, swivelling with his right arm, Sudhir dangled his body weight on the pick. It was a perilous mistake.

He heard a sound, like Velcro and then the ice block smashed into his face and shoulder. Tipped backwards by the force, he wobbled like a pendulum, pivoting on his wrist.

The ice pick slipped out of his free hand, falling down into the white abyss below. Red saliva dribbled from his mouth, marking his boots and trousers. His bloody tongue touched a loose tooth. Dizziness hit him as swirling, blurry images flashed before him. He tried to regain control.

The blackout was sudden. He fell free, barely conscious.

The sudden jerk snapped him back to consciousness. The belay rope, anchored to the pitons, taut with his body weight, burnt into his waist. Luckily for him, the ice pitons that he had hammered in while ascending had held on to the crevices, adamantly.

"Sir... sir..."

Deliberately hauling himself up, he heard Sonam calling out to him. Sonam threw down another rope, which had been secured. Half climbing, half being dragged up, Sudhir made it to the top with sheer grit.

Sonam finally yanked him up unceremoniously. They both fell in a heap, gasping for breath.

"You picked a funny time to do rope yoga, sir," ribbed Sonam.

"I wanted a lateral view," grimaced Sudhir still gasping.

"Yes, perhaps it helped you view yourself in ways you never imagined."

Still wincing in pain, Sudhir grinned, "Stop. Please stop!"

The rest of the team climbed up soon enough.

* * *

Five men anchored in each rope team, they set pace for the avalanche site, keeping eight metres between each man. It prevented falling down in a crevasse. Keeping a sharp lookout for avalanches and crevices, the team made steady progress.

The men watched snowflakes drop off into the bottomless abyss of the crevasse they were bridging. Combating vertigo induced by the sheer drop, they shuffled over the steel ladder thrown across the wide gully.

"C'mon. Stop strolling in the park," coaxed Sudhir, egging them on.

The two hours' trek through waist-deep snow would normally have taken twenty minutes of brisk walking in the plains.

A snow boot protruding through the snow and sadly mauled backpack was the first sign of the calamity.

The two survivors had dug out one colleague. Those closest were best suited for the quickest rescue, ensuring survival. Huddled in a bunch, their hysterical eyes and voiceless mutterings on seeing the rescue team were unsettling. A young soldier was hyperventilating.

"My god, trauma…" whispered Sonam under his breath. Sudhir nodded, surveying the moonlight snows for tell-tale signs of life.

Signalling with his hands, Sudhir gave a series of orders.

Hypothermia was setting in on the survivors. Their bodies were losing heat faster than it could produce, plummeting their body temperatures. Finding the remaining victims was important; sustaining those alive was imperative.

Dragging them into a makeshift bivouac, the rescue team administrated essential fluids.

"Where was the last sighting?" asked Sudhir gruffly. The last sighting before being buried helped narrow down the search location. The information was crucial.

Vacant eyes stared back at Sudhir.

Grinding his teeth, Sudhir again asked, "Where was the last sighting?" Bringing his face close enough to feel the man's breath, he shook the soldier by the shoulders roughly. Impassively, the man lifted a finger and pointed.

"Show us. C'mon, get up!" Sudhir pushed his knee into the soldier's back. Regaining his composure, the man nodded and walked out of the bivouac to join the rescue team.

Sudhir spread the rescue team in probable locations. Hoping for success, they pushed in the thin avalanche probes. They prayed it would hit something solid.

Sudhir tried his transmitter. No beep. Eyes dark, Sonam too shook his head. Never was time so cruel. Each ticking second nailed into their hearts painfully.

"I found something!" The sudden eager cry galvanised them.

Using snow shovels, the team dug in frenzy. Regardless of fatigue, muscle cramps, blisters and a clawing dread. The corner of the jacket showed up. "He's here!" a wistful cry went out. Fiercely digging they found a glove. Then goggles and an ice pick. Glazed eyes and a mouth full of ice surfaced out gradually. The soul had abandoned the still warm body just minutes before. The demanding glacier had claimed yet another sacrifice as restitution for violating its sacred sanctity.

Suddenly a beeping sound drew their attention. The transmitter around Sonam's neck jumped alive. His gaze sought Sudhir's in affirmation. Nodding, Sudhir felt his neck prickle with goosebumps. He licked his lips nervously. Like a baby's first cry, the 'bip bip' sound sent a thrill down the spines of the battle-hardened men. They attacked the snow with new-found fury.

In a cavity next to his dead colleague, they found the exhausted victim alive, gasping. His frozen buddy had shielded him in death. An oxygen pocket had kept him alive. Examining him for injury, they realised he had a broken neck. A broken neck was a small price for life, reflected Sudhir, as a medic rushed in with an oxygen mask and a cervical immobiliser.

* * *

"Help… Help!" A bleak cry resonated from an overhang.

Scarcely inches from the edge, Sudhir and Sonam found the victim painfully wedged between two rocks. The rock had prevented him from going over.

A broken rib cage and a dislocated shoulder had the man writhing in pain. Coughing blood, droplets had turned the snow red.

Organising themselves with trained readiness, they set to work. The sharp pain of the needle administered by unaccustomed hands was insignificant compared to the pain from his breathing.

They fitted a brace around his chest. The brace constricted his chest. It made breathing difficult, but prevented jagged ribs from puncturing his lungs by sudden movement. Placing a lookout for avalanches, Sudhir ordered Sonam to anchor himself and get the man roped up.

Now came the challenging part. They tied another rope to the chest brace. Bracing themselves, digging in their feet, Sudhir and his buddy, using their body weight, pulled on the rope like in a tug of war. They had to maintain balance, ensuring their own safety. Even a near miss would be a certain fall to death.

Inch by painful inch, the weight moved. Struggling, with their breaths jagged, they tried again. And finally he was free.

Fatigued by their efforts, both took a breather. Sudhir closed his eyes for a second. Suddenly roused by the distinct sound of clinking, blinking his eyes open, he yelled out alarmed, "No... No! Stop... Stop!"

Lucky to be unbound from the rock, and to unfetter his restricted breathing, the just-freed man had unhooked his uncomfortable chest brace. He let go of the rope. Trying to stand up, he tottered and slipped.

Horrified, they watched him slowly glide downwards, skidding over off the edge. There he hung like a rag doll, oscillating. Still tied to Sonam with the safety rope.

On cue, in a moment of perfection, the mountains rumbled.

"Avalanche... Avalanche!" screamed the lookout. Blood drained from Sudhir's face as he saw a white cloud hurling down towards Sonam.

It was the toughest order and perhaps the bitterest. "Cut the bloody rope Sonam, cut the rope!" yelled Sudhir. Sonam was still tugging at the rope, trying to pull the man up.

"Bhenchod, cut the fucking rope," Sudhir screamed again. A reluctant Sonam looked at Sudhir for a final confirmation. Sudhir yelled, gesturing frantically. And Sonam cut the rope just moments before the cloud hit him.

Clenching his teeth, Sudhir clasped a fistful of snow, seeing the cloud devour Sonam. He waited for it to pass. He could only wait.

Miracles happen. It affirms our belief in the inexplicable. This was a day of providence. The avalanche was not big. Split by a huge rock, the fury of the avalanche passed by Sonam. He emerged like a white ghost with his toothy smile. The cut ropes had tangled in yet another rock, easing the man on a smaller ledge. He was alive and smiling when they found him. He had cheated death twice that day.

"Let's get back," said Sudhir, blinking as the first rays hit his eyes.

Back in his fibre glass hut, Sudhir studied himself in the small mirror. "I am the storm," he breathed, "I am the storm. And I am not done yet."

* * *

Blood in the Gully

It was just a week ago. A rare, serene evening.

Catching a lull in the storm, Sudhir and Arun had sat down for a drink. The erratic electricity had appeared and disappeared characteristically. The generator in perfect sync had packed up.

Life simplified by circumstances, the two friends sat in the soft glow of the trusted wick-kerosene lamp, ignoring the shadows on the walls that tried to eavesdrop on the conversation.

Munching roasted ground nuts sprinkled with chopped onions and green chillies, they talked quietly and drank the dependable Old Monk rum.

As the night deepened Sudhir gazed into the flickering flame of the kerosene lamp, his mind drifting. He had always found solace in the simplicity of his upbringing rooted in a small town.

Usually reticent, Arun read his thought.

"You know what your strength is?"

Sudhir took a sip and shook his head. He smiled disarmingly.

"That you embrace your background."

"And what is my weakness, Happy?

Arun munched on some nuts, weighing his words. "That you are in a constant battle with the world. Even with yourself."

Taken aback by Arun's directness, Sudhir looked into Arun's eyes. "What do you mean?" He said gruffly.

"It's your Achilles heel."

Sudhir paused for a moment, contemplating Arun's words. He sighed. His carefully hidden vulnerability exposed, for once.

"It's not that simple Happy. The world I know has its own demands. Sometimes I have no choice." He took a deliberate sip. "You didn't have to claw your way out. I had to."Arun popped in another nut. "But I too..."

Sudhir cut him off. "Live up to a family tradition? That's different."

The contrast between the simplicity of life in that moment and the complexities they discussed was intriguing.

"One thing we certainly agree on," said Arun, smiling.

Sudhir raised his glass. "Cheers to that." They didn't have to spell it out.

Few people realised that beneath his affable disposition, poise and old-world charm, Arun possessed an unfaltering zeal.

A soldier stepped in, saluting them. A source had come to meet Arun.

Arun excused himself and walked out. Sudhir could hear some inaudible conversation.

Arun returned, took a deliberate swig and settled down. Sudhir waited impatiently, bouncing his knee.

"I have credible Int."

Sudhir sat up excited. His eyes sparkled. "Go on."

"20 fuckers."

"20 fucking motherfuckers?" Sudhir's voice was barely a whisper, eyes ablaze.

Arun nodded, "And where exactly, Happy?"

"Balkul Gully, Lolab." The quiver in Arun's voice made Sudhir's nape prickle.

* * *

Analysing the intelligence, they thought it best to act. While taking a hot water bath, Sudhir tried to punch holes in the plan. He found none.

"Okay Happy, we'll go," said Sudhir, frowning. "But you owe me a drink if we get nothing."

Arun chuckled. "By that reasoning, you'll owe me a liquor store."

Maj K Bhusan had been made in charge.

All three officers got their men ready. They had a troop each to lead. As they prepared for their mission, Sudhir couldn't help but smile. "Alright Happy, let's come back with more than just stories."

Arun smiled. "And I promise you a drink you won't forget."

* * *

Balkul Gully, Lolab
15th September, 1995

They travelled in vehicles to the de-bussing point. Chandigam, named after the Goddess Chandi, was 20 kilometres east of Kupwara, deep inside the Lolab valley, there was a BSF post close by. They left the vehicles at the BSF outpost.

The mosque in the centre of the village thrived as people went about their business. A man pounded corn. The sound of the mallet striking the grain accompanied the sharp sound of an axe cutting wood and the laboured heave of the man wielding it. The noise of shrieking children mingled with the *azaan* from the minaret. A donkey brayed.

A little further up, they crossed a small temple which stood deserted. Bushes and brambles grew against the door, with green slime on the walls.

Stepping up closer, Mahendra noticed a small earthen lamp abandoned in an alcove. Clearly, it had been months since it had been lit.

"We should…" he said, shaking his head, his eyes filled with piety.

Arun was walking behind him. "Yes… tomorrow, when we get back."

It might once have been the home of an actual family. But the scrub and tall weeds now covered the yard.

Arun glanced up to see a gaping window, its shutter knocked down by the wind. Another half shutter banged against the cracked wooden frame. A shrivelled tulsi plant stood by the front steps, dead. Behind it stood another hovel, muted in anguish. Graffiti had disfigured the walls of the smaller house. Sounds of laughter and prayer bells, strangled by silent wails of decay, pain and betrayed friendships.

The despair pierced Mahendra's heart. His stiff fingers curled around the Draganov sniper rifle. *"Aur kitto gairo jaano hai*[61]*?"* His cry more a statement than a question.

He absently stepped into cow dung, soiling his toe.

"Bloody Kashmiriyat," said Sudhir swearing. "Reduced to this?"

He kept his emotions hidden, but his eyes and jaw were a dead giveaway. Arun's raw anger pulsated below his twitching muscles.

Once a proud village living in harmony, Chandigam clung to its name as the only witness to its ancient diversity. Colluding for the Pandits to be driven away, Chandigam had consigned its soul to a perverse Jihad.

* * *

They'd covered some of this territory earlier. The ridgelines were familiar. They knew the woods and the cardinal directions. The folds of

---

[61] *Marwari- "How far deep do we have to go from here?"*

the ground and the dangers that lurked in them were unfamiliar. The sheer size of the area and the depth of the forests made it impossible to know every inch.

By very early morning, around 4:30 am, after a ten-hour climb, they reached a junction. Divided into three columns, Bhushan and Sudhir were in the centre and west column. Arun led the third.

"Happy, you scout east from here," said Sudhir, "We will flush the bastards and send them down to you. Detailed as a sniper, Mahendra was in Arun's troop."

Arun would take his column and wait lower down on the slope. He would deal with the terrorists running down. They would pincer the terrorists in from three sides.

Balkul Gully was a mountain pass, rising a sheer 1000 metres from the Lolab valley. It sat stride the sharp ridgeline that encircled Lolab in a possessive vice. You could climb up from the Lolab valley and walk down towards Sopore and Wullar Lake on the other side via the Gully.

"Bye," Arun's toothy smile sparkled in the starlight. "Tonight seems lucky." With a wave of his hand, he turned away.

"And if we are not?" Sudhir teased after him. "I can always look forward to the drink, Happy."

Arun stopped mid-stride and turned his neck. His blazing eyes reflected his attitude. The tone was friendly, but laced with steel, "No pressure, no diamonds."

Sudhir gaped at him.

Beaming like the full moon, Arun trotted out with his squad. The woods soon swallowed them.

There was something about the way he said it. It struck Sudhir.

* * *

The two columns reached the treeless Balkul Gully. The beautiful, starry night was fast fading. The clouds retreated, revealing the dark blue sky.

Bhushan and Sudhir stole a moment to take in the views before they parted.

Turning south, they could see the lights of Baramulla and beyond that, the hazy twinkle of Gulmarg below the ice-capped Pir Panjal.

Sudhir nudged Bhushan. The magnificence took their breath away. A valley of lights sparkled along a slender plain. The sharp, pulled back dark ridges on either side stressed the richness of the glitzy baubles. The glimmer felt like a flood of emeralds.

"Normal people won't see anything like this," remarked Bhushan, introspecting.

"Remember, normal people don't climb BalkulGully at night." A wry smile curled the corners of Sudhir's mouth.

Bhushan smacked his forehead. "Aren't we normal?"

Sudhir studied Bhushan with a level gaze. He then turned his face to look at the dark valley below. "Are we?" It was more an affirmation than question.

"That's Srinagar," said Bhushan, pointing north-east and further beyond Pulwama. They happily traced NH44, the lifeline of Kashmir, aided by the twinkling lights. It twisted like a jewelled snake across the valley.

"This beauty can fool anyone," said Sudhir, with an edge to his voice.

Bhushan nodded. The tranquil glitter of the surface masked the intense violence that lurked beneath.

Sitting on his haunches, Sudhir scooped up water from a small spring. Before he could touch the water to his lips … the sound of crickets was drowned by gunfire.

"Fuck, what's that?" yelled Bhushan.

Blood drained from Sudhir's face. The water trickled out through his astonished fingers.

Sounds of automatic fire. A muted sound of grenade bursting followed by a quiet spell … again shattered by long intense firing.

"Happy?" screamed Sudhir, his hackles up.

* * *

Arun took the lead from the junction. Following him was Hav. Baburam Maila. Next to them walked Mahendra. The rest of Baburam's squad trailed behind. Another squad, led by Hav. Prakash covered the rear.

The men walked through dense scrub, unmindful of the thorn-pricks. Streaks of gentle light dissipated the protection of the night veil. A rustle in the trees smothered the sound of their feet.

Their night vision adjusted to the growing daylight and the dangers it brought. They walked deliberately, pausing every few steps to take in their surroundings as foliage brushed their faces with cold dew.

Standing within a depression, Arun's eyes followed the slope upwards until they rested upon a massive tree trunk that extended across. It blocked his view of what lay beyond.

The forest had paused in an uncanny deathly silence. Arun closed his fist, signalling the men to wait. Baburam followed him two steps behind. Mahendra continued behind Baburam. The grass under their feet, wet with dew, squelched.

Arun braced himself against the rough bark as he climbed over the fallen tree. He froze. His back tensed as a chill ran through him; the breath stuck in his lungs.

Looking down, he saw a man making tea on an open fire. To his right, Arun sensed the presence before he saw the second terrorist. Without taking his eyes off the first, from the corner of his vision, he saw the weapon glint. Stunned, the man's looked at Arun. He opened his mouth to scream; the face a grotesque mask.

Arun fired. Shooting the man before he could even aim his weapon, cutting down the scream in his throat. He turned his foresight on the first man. The man scampered, falling into the fire. Arun shot him through the cloud of the grey ashes, breaking his shoulder.

In an instant reply, rapid fire pinned Arun down. It came from beyond. From a cave. The dark cave mouth loomed over the bushes.

Searing pain shot through Arun's collar bone in the right shoulder. It jolted his breathing. Arun front rolled, reducing his target area, making it difficult for them to aim at him. Getting into a fire position again, he killed another terrorist. Every jostle sent ripples of pain through his shoulder, back and neck.

Biting his tongue to keep the pain at bay, Arun crawled ahead. The team drew heavy rocket and gunfire from the terrorists, holed up in the cave.

Mahendra and Baburam criss-crossed through the firing, aiming at the flashes. Arun lobbed a hand grenade into the cave mouth. The explosion echoed, showering debris and dust. Unmindful of his pain, he charged through the dust.

A man shot at him. Grabbing the man in a hand-to-hand combat, Arun killed him with his knife. Pain tore through him with every movement. Ignoring the pain in his chest, or the blood seeping from his right shoulder, he tried to make sense. Trying to think straight, he assessed the situation. The pain ebbed and flowed like a wave. He knew he just had to control his mind.

He got into another hand-to-hand fight, knifing the man through his stomach, ripping him open. Blood sprouted in a fountain from the gaping belly, anointing him and his hair-raising bravery.

Arun stumbled. His knees buckled. He gradually slumped on the cave floor. It hurt so bad, he could hardly recognise the raw cave walls that moved in and out of focus all around him. Baburam and Mahendra pulled him aside, feverishly administering first aid.

Inspired by his bravery, the troops attacked the militants, vowing vengeance. A few militants jumped out and ran. A part of the squad combed the jungles behind the escaping militants, seeking retribution.

Breath ragged; Sudhir sprinted down. Bhushan followed close.

"Happy… Happy!" A harsh half-stifled yell rose from Sudhir's throat. "Keep up… speak!"

The flesh wound still oozed blood and the entire right side of Arun's body wore a purplish-red smear. The voices didn't make sense. He heard little and cared less, as his mind slipped in and out of consciousness and pain.

Sudhir's distant voice, "Happy…stay, keep up…" The light faded from his eyes until they were dark and empty.

They evacuated Arun in haste. Airlifted to Srinagar, he battled for seven days. A bullet had punctured his lung. More grievous than the other gun-shot wounds, it proved fatal.

* * *

He had come back with more than just a story.

Sudhir gulped a drink, closeted in his spartan room, tormented by Arun's prophetic words. A drink he wouldn't forget. The rum helped him to drift to sleep but not stay there. He woke up at 3:30 a.m. and lay awake, thinking disjointedly about life and death, until dawn.

"They will pay, Happy," he swore, grinding his teeth.

He remembered another night. Happy and he had laid under the stars on a mountaintop during their nocturnal wanderings. Looking up at the stars, Happy had quoted, "Dream big, and dare to fail." Sudhir had stared at his toothy smile.

That's how he wanted to remember his friend. His soul brother.

* * *

A Dangerous Game of Naqal[62]

1996 proved to be a pivotal year for Kashmir. Insurgency had reached a sluggish stalemate. In March, the Hazratbal incident brought the world's attention back to Kashmir. The security forces killed 22 militants of the

---

[62] *Persian word- imitation*

JKLF, including the leader Shabir Siddiqui, at the holy Hazratbal shrine.

Pakistan used its influence with the Labour party in UK to call for UN intervention in Kashmir. Six Labour MPs tabled the motion in the British parliament against Indian security forces and another 20 signed it. In May, Kashmir resonated with soft thuds that marked ballot papers. The general elections for the 11th Lok Sabha, after a gap of five years, signalled a complex change in the political status of Kashmir.

In September, despite the boycott by the All Party Hurriyat Conference, political winds swept away the stinging cold triggered by terrorism. An unprecedented 55 percent turnout by the ordinary Kashmiri populace was a rejection of ISI's pipe dream. Kashmir passionately demanded an end to the violence and irrationality that had tormented it for decades.

Misfortune, however, continued to linger over Kashmir that year. In August, extreme weather caused the death of 242 pilgrims during the Amarnath Yatra. November's heavy rain and snowfall caused landslides at Pir Panjal. Jammu-Srinagar highway shut down, flights to Srinagar stood cancelled.

* * *

Vinod
January 1996

In January, Sudhir sir got posted as ADC to the Northern Army Commander, Gen. Surinder Singh. While he was there, he had to escort Col. Jasrotia to receive a medal on behalf of his son, our brave Capt. Arun Jasrotia.

"I felt guilty about being alive," he told me later. Brotherhood is painful sometimes. The guilt clings to you, eating away like cancer. Silently.

The ADC assignment was temporary. In February that year, Sudhir sir proceeded for the junior command course in Mhow, where he got an

Alpha Instructor, AI grading. This was an enormous achievement and recognition. But true to form, he wore it lightly.

"You must have studied very hard, sir?" I asked him in rapt wonder. I too wanted to qualify as an officer.

He shrugged and smiled. "I do my bit…keeping a purpose is important. Your focus determines your reality."

He patted my shoulder. "Let me know if you require help."

His words seemed to lead me close, in hopes I'd provide my own answers. That was Sudhir sir.

* * * *

Vinod
Pseudo Ops
June 1996

After the course, in June, he was back with a vengeance. And he loved it.

We were sporting long hair, shaggy beards, Pathani suits, round twisted *pakol* caps with a *tabeez* strung on a black chord. We wore rough cotton *poots* and coarse *phirans*, two cloth pieces worn over one another.

Sudhir sir and our crack team of daredevils had not only adopted the clothing, but had also embraced the language, mannerisms and food of the militants, blending in with chilling authenticity. We even smelled authentic. Our phirans and poots carried the typical tangy Bakharwal smell that comes from being near animals and sharing roof and shelter with them. Our nails were sodden with dirt from the dhoks, high in the mountains.

That was creative. Intelligence trickled in spurts.

* * *

Vinod
Deera ki Gully, Pir Panjal
July 1996

The squad had spent ten days at the freezing wind-swept Deera ki Gully. Carefully attired and equipped, we had eradicated any tell-tale signs of our Indian Army background.

Occupying the rough, vermin-infested dhoks, we kept to ourselves, avoiding contact with the locals. To an untrained eye, we looked like a Tanzeem which had drifted into the isolated mountain gully with a plan.

Across the Pir Panjal were ancient trade routes, connected by passes locally known as gullys. Breaking into squads, we scoured the valleys and gullys and encountered, not militants, but something unexpected.

Walking through a Gully once, my eyes flickered past Sudhir sir. "My God… see that?"

The team glanced to see dozens of sculptures; riders on horseback, ominously gazing back at them. I had goosebumps. "Look…all the riders have the same face."

"The Horsemen of the Pir Panjal."[63]

"Who knows of this?"

"Only the locals."

"Carved by?"

Sudhir shrugged his shoulders. "No one knows. It'sa mystery. Perhaps the Huns."

Terrorism and accessibility had hampered research. Even today, the mystery of their origin remains unsolved.

* * *

---

[63] *At the gullys, these sculptures probably marked milestones or resting places for horses and men. The armed horsemen showing great detail carried different weapons, like an army on a campaign. They varied in size with up-to even three men astride a horse. Their features suggested a Hun or Central Asian origin.*

Sudhir sir gave the map a quick look.

"Tomorrow we will head in deeper." We listened without blinking."Towards Sat Sar."[64]He continued to brief the squad. Sudhir knew the area well and identified another five lakes nestled to the southeast. Word was that a Tanzeem was lurking around.

Briefing over, we cleaned our weapons. We inspected our breechblocks and the coiled springs and stared down the glistening barrels. We took apart the parts and checked for fouling, caused by the lead fumes. During a critical situation, a jammed weapon meant certain death.

We were walking into the devil's den to shake hands with him. It required extreme courage and a touch of madness. The weapon would be a part of our body. An extension of our limbs, it would keep us alive.

It was like God. It was God.

---

[64] *Sat Sar means seven lakes. Tucked away in the Girjan Valley at 11,500 feet are seven oval shaped alpine lakes. Bhag Sar is the biggest and the most beautiful.*

Deera Ki Gully, Rupri Gully, Girjan Gully, Pir Panjal

Walking along the ridgeline, for hours, we avoided lower ground. Below us was the Girjin valley. Thunder greeted our descent in the valley as the night set in. We plodded through the rain, wet to our bones.

Climbing a small grass bank, I stopped to catch my breath. It was a sight to behold. A crackling streak lit up the sky, illuminating the valley below. I could see the shimmering waters of the Bhag Sar. And across that a dhok, its chimney smoking.

While the men sat hidden behind the bank, Sudhir sir, a JCO and I approached the dhok. We heard voices. A man and a young boy. Flinging open the rough door, Sudhir sir stepped in. "*Asalaam walei kum.*"

Bewildered, the man dropped his broth and fell over. The young boy cowered, whimpering. They were not expecting someone on a dark rainy night. This sudden entry could only be of a djinn or a spirit.

"We thought you are a djinn." A furtive smile played on the man's cracked lips.

The father-son duo was out looking for their lost goats.

Sudhir sir peeped into the blackened pot.

"What's that?"

"*Markhor.*"[65] The man's eyes flickered over us. We looked dangerous. I could see the fear in his eyes.

Sharing a meal of the rough maze bread and curry, we sought to gain their confidence. I shared a chocolate with the boy.

Sudhir sir noticed the father peek at the wrapper. The twitch could have almost gone unnoticed, as he read the 'Made in Pakistan.'

Sudhir sir finally popped the question.

"…Our brothers?" he coughed. " We lost… contact."

The man's hand froze midway to his open mouth. His eyes clouded.

"…Indian dogs," the JCO sneered. His glowering eyes conveyed the loathing.

---

[65] *The largest wild goat in the world and perhaps the most elusive animal. Found in Pir Panjal around the lakes, its numbers have dwindled because of hunting and no efforts at conservation.*

"We… have to cross…" Sudhir sir fixed his gaze on the bobbing throat. "Soon."

The steel plate shook as the man kept it down and gulped down water.

He studied Sudhir sir's phiran and his weapon. He stared at our faces. He breathed in, held the air, and let it out. The silence in the room was palpable.

He nodded, looking at the walls, somewhere above their heads.

"Rupri Gully," he muttered, tight-lipped.

Sudhir sir tried to conceal his excitement. Rupri Gully was barely a kilometre from where we sat.

"How many?" The JCO kept his voice detached and controlled.

The man shrugged his shoulders. "I don't know… can't say. Maybe 20 or 30."

"Allah be thanked." The JCO spoke in chaste Pashto, raising his palms in prayer. "Will you take us?"

The man lowered his head, avoiding eye contact. His fear betrayed by his hunched shoulders. Either way, they could get killed. "Okay," he croaked. "But… we won't stay."

"Yes. Just introductions, then you're free." The team didn't want to endanger the duo's lives.

The matter settled, we waited for a few hours. First light was just two hours away.

* * *

Vinod

Rupri Gully

The gully looked ghostly in the predawn light, or maybe it was just the stress of the moment. Each man had muttered a silent prayer. Could we pull it off?

What if? The 'what if' seemed more plausible.

Bashir-ud-din the guide, walked ahead. Sudhir sir, the JCO, two more men and I, Vinod, strode close behind. The rest of the team trailed behind at a distance, avoiding a tactical formation. Their loose body language cloaked their soldierly postures.

On alert, we were all on an edge. Tuned like taut guitar strings.

A rough dhok appeared in view. We sensed watchful eyes studying every move. Without hesitating and not missing a step, the lead party rambled up. Short of the dhok, Bashir stopped.

* * *

The Afghani militants felt a sense of unease settle over them. Keeping the Koran aside, Karim observed the suspicious movement through his binoculars. An Afghan war veteran, he spoke quietly to his men scanning the rugged terrain. "Something doesn't feel right."

The others exchanged wary glances, their senses on high alert. They had grown adept at identifying threats, but this was different. There was an unsettling feeling of intrusion, as if a new player had entered the game.

Nasir, a seasoned fighter, tightened his grip on his weapon. "Keep your eyes peeled. We can't afford surprises."

The suspicion grew into an uneasy tension as they contemplated the implications. An unknown group operating in their territory was a potential threat, and the Afghans were not ones to take such matters lightly.

This was an affront to their authority, a challenge to their dominance in this unforgiving land.

One of the militants Rashid muttered, "Someone else on our turf? We need to..."

Karim silenced him midsentence with a look. Rashid gulped.

"I take the calls here. We'll find out who these motherfuckers are. Else, we kill the bastards."

The Afghani militants knew that in this harsh and unpredictable landscape. survival often hinged on swift and ruthless action, with no room for hesitation.

Karim glanced at Nasir, ordering him to follow.

* * *

Vinod

We saw two men emerge out of the narrow doorway. Sporting long hair, scraggy beards, Pashtun caps, combat jackets above their grey pathani suits and expensive trekking shoes, these were obviously not foot soldiers. Brandishing assault rifles, they were every bit menacing as they looked.

Recognising Bashir, they allowed him to approach closer. They spoke briefly, the conversation was inaudible.

Sudhir sir and our party waited at the foot of the slope. The rest of the men waited in the bushes further down.

The duo walked down, with Bashir a few steps behind them. The man striding resolutely ahead had deep grey, fiery eyes. They shook hands and exchanged pleasantries.

The JCO spoke in Pashtu. "Let's join hands and fuck the Indian dogs."

Those penetrating grey eyes were never still. They flickered over us and swept past towards the group behind. He exuded authority. And an underlying savagery.

"Never heard … you are from here?"

"These sons of swine, our enemy is …"

The grey eyes flashed for just a moment.

"Our tanzeem's … why must we fight alone? It's the same shaitan."

The fellow next to him was apparently his subordinate. His dark eyes studied us with a predator's unwavering attention. His casually held weapon pointed at us, finger on the trigger, ready for swift action. I caught him peeking sideways at the group behind us.

"The mother fucking Ikhwani[66] fight with the Rashtriya Rifles.

---

[66] *Ikhwani-surrendered militants.They become the centrepiece of the counterinsurgency operations. Used initially as intelligence sources by the Rashtriya Riflesto flush out*

Betray the Jihad…" The JCO's words trailed off as he saw a muscle twitch.

"And you…you are not Ikhwani?" The words were as bracing as a slap in the face. The grey eyes bored into the JCO.

The JCO clenched his jaw. His mouth set in a hard line. "*Inna lillahi wa inna ilayhi raji'un.*"[67]

Sudhir sir chose his words cautiously. "To fight against the infidels is Jihad; but to fight against your evil self is greater Jihad."

His forehead furrowed as his brows snapped together. An uncertain silence held the party. We all held our breath. Finally, a lopsided grin sneaked across his gaunt face and the grey eyes gleamed.

"Come… let's eat together and discuss further."

The invitation had a practiced feel, as though he had said it many times before. It didn't sound right.

* * *

"*Mashaallah… jazakallahkhyran,*"[68] said the JCO. "We will follow you."

The man twirled and rambled back up the slope escorted by his subordinate. We walked back to the main group.

The dhok was a trap, experience told us that. We noticed weapons pointed at us from the rocks above. The militants had us pinned, should there be a firefight.

In the tense moments that followed, the Afghan militants seemed to sense a moment of hesitation in our team. It was a split-second pause, a subtle shift in our movements, but it was enough to ring an alarm that something was amiss.

Suddenly in response to this vulnerability, a volley of gunfire rained down on us. Bullets tore up through the air, impacting the rocky cover around us, sending showers of debris into the air.

---

militants, they were now being used as 'prowlers.' They take part in encounters against their old colleagues.

[67] *To Allah we belong, and to Him we shall return*

[68] *Allah has willed it. May Allah reward you with good.*

Our training kicked in, Sudhir sir barked urgent orders, "Return fire! Keep them at bay." He knew any further hesitation would prove fatal.

The rocky terrain echoed with sounds of battle as both sides fought with determination. Amid the violent firefight, the team was acutely aware of the paramount importance of hiding our original identities. We fought not only to defend ourselves, but also to preserve the secrecy of our purpose. Any slip could jeopardize not only our lives, but the entire operation.

Sudhir sir's voice conveyed this urgency to the team. "Keep your faces covered, stay low."

In this high-stake covert operation where every bullet fired and every move made had consequences, hiding our identities was imperative. It was also a testament to our commitment and the sacrifice we were willing to make to ensure its success.

The firefight eventually subsided. We retreated cautiously. As we regrouped and assessed the situation, Sudhir sir's voice held a note of determination. "We survived this one, but we will be more careful next time."

The experience had taught us that in the world of covert operations, every moment held a potential for discovery and every action had to be executed with caution. It was a lesson learnt.

Our identities were intact. We had walked into the devil's lair and walked out unscathed.

We had been identified as a rival gang. That was a major victory.

* * *

Fortune favours the brave. This time it smiled on us.

We intercepted a message from two lost militants. The duo had got separated after a firefight with the Rashtriya Rifles. Probably injured, their tanzeem too was searching for them. They were in our area.

Sudhir sir slapped his knee when he heard the news. His eyes glinted. This was the opportunity we were waiting for. Infused by Sudhir sir's verve, we searched the gullys and scanned the frequencies on the radio set. The urgency was to connect with them, before their own tanzeem found them.

On the third day, we established contact with the duo on the radio set. They were in a dhok in the mountains to our north. Speaking to them, reassuring them, we gained their confidence. One of them was injured.

We reached the dhok by early evening. There was no sign of life. They had abandoned the dhok and switched off the radio set, most likely suspicious. Something had spooked them.

We spread out and searched the area. Mahendra was with me that day. We turned a corner and…

Mahendra nudged me. We could see shoes protruding from the bushes. Taking up positions against a boulder, I hurled a rock and a volley of fire rained on us. We both fired back into the bushes, speculatively. The white shoes were still there.

We saw one militant, scamper and run towards a nallah. Sudhir sir heard the firing. He came tearing behind us and saw the militant running away.

Before we could react, Sudhir sir chased the militant. I could see Sudhir sir's back, as he ran further into the nallah. I ran after him, leaving Mahendra to deal with the dead militant.

The militant slinked into a small, constricted cave, obscured by ferns.

Well knowing what Sudhir could do, I yelled for Sudhir sir to stop. You think he would listen?

Bowing his head, Sudhir sir dived in, getting on his knees to move further.

A few steps behind Sudhir sir, I could see what was happening.

In the hazy darkness, Sudhir sir saw the whimpering militant raise his weapon.

Sudhir sir's weapon was still by his knee in the dirt.

Un-deterred he growled out, "*Rakh … rakh hatiyar.*"[69]

Taken aback, the aghast militant licked his lips, his eyeballs popping. He dithered, fumbling.

Sudhir's eyes burned with fury. His face turned crimson.

"Rakh hathiyar," he growled again.

The militant went white. His weapon wavered. He cowered against the cave wall.

Sudhir sir leaped up and holding the barrel, yanked the weapon from his loose grip. The militant fell in a heap at his feet, muttering.

I was at the mouth of the cave. Eyes wide, I saw Sudhir sir drag the militant out of the cave by his scruff.

"Get his weapon … it's inside," he ordered hoarsely.

I shook my head. The man never ceased to amaze. I wished I was half as brave as him … and half as mad.

---

[69] *Drop your weapon.*

The Islamic Caliphate

Kashmir main rahna hai,
Allah-hu-Akbar kahna hoga

The sound of chatter filled Sudhir's ears as he walked down the once bustling street of saffron shops and dry fruit sellers. The air was crisp and chilly, causing him to pull his jacket closer around him. The pavement beneath his feet felt unyielding and hard; small wet stones jutted out, scraping against his shoes.

The street smelled of burnt wood, smoke and kebabs. As Sudhir rounded the corner, a wistful smell of freshly baked bread drifted towards him from the quaint bakery. His watering mouth made him realise he hadn't lost his childhood memories. It brought a smile.

Sudhir saw a familiar figure walking up through the crowds towards him. "It's been a while, Sudhir." Aslam warmly shook hands. "You look more Kashmiri now."

"I do, don't I?" Smiling, Sudhir stroked his beard.

"I see progress." Sudhir looked past the glass window of an internet cafe.

"Fresh problems."

Sudhir furrowed his brow in confusion as Aslam motioned him to follow. Aslam led him to a small tea shop. The cramped space made it impossible to avoid touching knees with the person across from him. The table was sticky, the chairs worn and creaky.

"Online radicalisation … from the internet."

Aslam looked around. He leaned close before muttering.

"These kids rushing to encounter sites. For safe passage to holed up militants … all subverted, fooled."

Sudhir looked at Aslam with newfound interest. Aslam spat out. "Poor wretched kids."

Gulping the hot tea, they stepped out to continue the conversation.

Taking in the sensory chaos of hanging wires and narrow lanes, Sudhir couldn't help but feel a sense of nostalgia wash over him. This was Srinagar, he had to remind himself, not Palampur.

"The Wahabis, Tablighees and Jamaatis are competing in establishing madrasas," Aslam continued. "They seduce kids from poor families."

"This … this Islamisation is all imported?"

Aslam nodded. "The text of Islamic studies is being radicalised. No need to go across to Azad Kashmir now. Everything is available here."

"POK!" Sudhir corrected.

Aslam nodded. "Yes. POK."

"So, what kind of influence?"

"Sunni? Maududi? Who knows?"

"But surely," Sudhir interrupted, "people can see through. Stop it."

Ignoring Sudhir, he continued.

"Exhibitionist Islam. Our Kashmiri rituals and Sufism; killed by Arabic culture."

He stopped and spread his arms wide. "An entire generation of semi-literate zombies who identify more with Islam than with Kashmir."

"Why can't you stop it?" An irritated Sudhir was abhorred by their lack of intent. Aslam ignored him again. Instead, he took Sudhir to the 'martyrs'' graveyard in the Eidgah area of downtown Srinagar. "Come. See before you question. Okay?" He glared at Sudhir.

"Check this out." Aslam walked to two tombstones. One of a local separatist politician seeking Azadi from India and the other of his own murderer. A Hizbul Mujahideen militant, fighting Kashmir's accession to Pakistan. Both buried next to each other.

Sudhir's mouth hung open in amazement as he stared in fascinated dismay.

"Yes, that's how fucked we are. A confused lot. We don't know fuck about what's happening."

Taken aback, Sudhir's eyes widened when he heard what Aslam implied.

"Now black shrouds have replaced Pakistani green flags as cerements to wrap martyred terrorists on their funerals."

Sudhir's irritation grew as he heard Aslam use the word 'martyred' instead of 'slain' or 'killed'. A minor detail, but it irked him.

Although Sudhir recognised the complexity of the situation in Kashmir, he believed that it was crucial to reveal the truth.

"Jihad in Kashmir is no longer about ISI, Pakistan or Azadi," muttered Aslam under his breath. The words tasted bitter on his tongue. "It's about the Caliphate."

Sudhir's face was frozen in shock.

Aslam's face turned crimson. "You asked why can't we stop this? Who will stop this? You?" He screamed at Sudhir accusatively. A stupefied Sudhir was too stunned to speak.

"Our politicians failed us. New Delhi failed us." Aslam breathily forced out his words.

Sudhir had never seen Aslam so angry, so distraught. He chose to remain silent.

"The anguish we endure rips our soul!" Aslam's voice trembled with emotion. "Our homes are smouldering ruins, our children's innocence twisted, and the very essence of our culture fading into obscurity. To Delhi we are merely sympathisers, and the militants think us as informers."

Sudhir allowed his silence to speak. Aslam's words hung in the air like a shroud. "And we can't do fuck about it."

His blazing argument born of deep frustration ignited like a spark in the dry chinar leaves.

"Don't just talk. Be earnest. Either do something drastic or lose Kashmir forever."

"Remove article 370?" Sudhir asked suggestively, finding his voice.

Grinding his teeth, Aslam just picked a rock and hurled it with all the might of his pent-up despair.

Aslam's rage drove Sudhir to stare at grave after grave, goading him to find the answers himself.

* * *

Vinod
Lalpora, Lolab
October 1997

By September, Sudhir sir had built his own network. Dressed to kill, we now operated with confidence in these pseudo-operations.

The Lolab valley had again become the focus of the militants. Acting on yet another input, Sudhir sir launched our squad. This time from the village of Drugmulla. The intelligence update cited Lalpora village on the eastern periphery of the Lolab bowl.

We walked through the afternoon and by evening, were close to the village. Our source had described the house: a double storied wooden house, close to the village, with three sides open. Ideal to keep a watch on any movement of the Army towards the village. Hugging a thick forest on one side, it would allow a quick escape, if needed. They had chosen it well.

Hidden in the trees, seventy-five metres away, we observed the house. Standing next to Sudhir sir, I stood scanning the open grounds for activity. Smoke rose through the chimney. There were people inside.

I nudged Sudhir sir. We could see a long-haired man through an open window. The evening light was fast fading. Soon it would be dark. A loss of surprise would spook the militants, triggering them to flee.

On impulse, I studied Sudhir sir.

Eyes narrowed to pinpricks, his gaze was steady, intent. Multiple possibilities raced through his head. Nodding, he finally decided. "Get them ready."

I signalled the team.

"We have to get close." Sudhir sir's voice was steady, "Cover the exits and the windows."

"The PIKA?" I asked.

Sudhir showed a boulder. "Open fire only if they run out." He jerked his head towards the jungle. The firer understood and using a fold in the ground, he half crawled towards his location.

We cocked our weapons. Holding them under our phirans, we walked out, casually, our body language easygoing. Only the fixed look in our kohl-lined eyes could have given us away. They gleamed with menace.

Sudhir sir led the way. I walked next to him. Steady steps and the distance narrowed down. The smoke rose happily. We could not see the man at the window.

My heart pounded so hard, I was sure everyone in the house could hear it. Even my nostrils had become super active. I could smell maze, sweet grass, budding flowers, turned earth and … danger.

I held my breath and was about to exhale when … the door was flung open, the wood groaning in protest.

Sudhir sir's fingers brushed my wrist. The touch calmed my jumping nerves.

A girl stepped out in a huff. She was having an argument with someone inside. She banged the door. That's when she noticed us.

Sudhir sir smiled with all the innocence he could muster.

"Salaam waleikum," he breathed.

Her darting eyes studied him. She looked back at the door. Hesitant, she wanted to run, but stayed. She wanted to speak, but didn't say anything.

"We came to meet our brothers." Sizing her up, Sudhir sir grinned again.

"There's no one here, only my father…" her voice trailed off.

"He's unwell," she said, too rapidly. We could detect fear in her voice, and anger. But also, curiosity which was what Sudhir sir wanted. The men fanned out with calculated precision, calmly positioning themselves around the house, their steady hands poised for threats, their footsteps betraying their trained expertise.

"We've come from far," Sudhir sir said, gesturing towards the mountains. "Our brothers…"

"But there's no one," she insisted, breathing too fast.

With a loud creak, the window opened wide. The long-haired man in a grey Pashtun cap climbed out of the window. He stood on a narrow ledge, his weapon trained on us. He eyed us suspiciously. Muffled by the sound of the wind, he could discern bits of the conversation.

The girl craned her neck and they exchanged a look. Sudhir sir watched as she tilted her head, the motion so slight, we almost missed it.

I was watching the man. I saw the man's upper lip curl. And I saw the expression change before I saw the AK-47 move. Body already coiled with nervous energy, my muscles jerked with velocity. I pushed Sudhir sir to the ground.

Dirt kicked up around us and a hole burnt through my phiran Reaching for our hidden weapons, we fired back through instinct, without aim. Bullets thudded into the wooden window. Hit in the chest and face, the man tumbled head down, following the cap, which tumbled before him.

The girl ran screaming.

The house exploded from the inside. Fire burst out through its lower windows. Sudhir sir and I dived for cover, flattening ourselves in a wet ditch, filled with cow dung.

Sudhir sir inhaled deeply as the smell triggered a recessed memory from childhood. His home had smelt like that. He would help his mother apply it on the floor, like most of rural India. He opened his eyes and grinned. I couldn't help but laugh. I too took a deep breath.

On signal, the PIKA opened fire. Using the diversion Sudhir sir and I ran to the door.

Kicking the door, I lobbed a grenade and Sudhir sir burst into the room, weapon blazing. The burst hit a man leaning against a wall, aiming his weapon at us.

The man slumped to the floor in a pool of blood, leaving red streaks on the cow-dung plaster. His rifle clattered on the wooden floor.

Sudhir sir was already looking into the corridor beyond.

Breathing hard, I casually glanced at the dead militant. The hair on my nape bridled. The dead Afghan's hand clutched a grenade.

"Sir!"I yelled."Grenade!"

We both jumped out of the room, pulling the door shut. Just in time. The boom rattled the hinges and the rusted handle came off. I felt a muscle catch in my hamstrings. But there was no time for that.

Sudhir sir stepped in again. I limped in behind him.

Squinting through the stinging smoke and acrid smell of gunpowder, our eyes flickered past the walls pock-marked by shrapnel. We scanned the dark corners with our weapons.

The squad had moved in now. Two men cautiously climbed the creaking, rickety steps. Noticing a smaller room next to the open kitchen, Sudhir sir peered inside. The cheerless dark room smelt of mould. The floor, strewn with mattresses and blankets, appeared out of place.

Sudhir sir followed another commando inside. They looked around, puzzled. Nothing. And yet he could smell the malodour of dank wood and compacted humanity. Sometimes, he wished he didn't have a heightened sense of smell. But this time was different.

Sudhir sir stepped back, inching for the door, unease ticking inside him.

He glanced left and his hair went stiff. There, in the shadowy darkness, he stared down at the cold steel barrel of a weapon, pointed at him. He could detect the finger curled around the trigger. He looked into a pair of dark, smouldering eyes burning into him.

The man tugged at the trigger.

Sudhir sir's rifle was pointing ahead. He swung the barrel, for what seemed like an eternity. Body coiling for the expected burst of automatic fire, he fired. The wooden panels splintered. He continued to fire, till he was sure no life threatened him.

Hidden in a small alcove, the wooden panels concealed a hideout. It could hold two or three men. Hammering with our weapon butts, we smashed through the wood to pull out the dead man.

The putrid stench of the cramped space clung to our skin. A commando noticed a loose plank.

"Fuck… look at this!" he hollered, prying open the trapdoor with his knife. It led down to a series of steps and a tunnel. Switching on their torches, two men stepped in. Standing at the trapdoor, the squad heard the muffled sound of fire. It echoed through the closed walls.

Apprehensive of what had happened, we yelled out the names of our comrades. Our own voices echoed back and then an unnerving silence.

"I am going down," I said. Bubbles of anxiety erupted at the pit of my stomach.

Sudhir sir held me back with a stern, "Wait."

We heard scratching and shuffling. Pointing our weapons towards the dark steps, we waited, holding our breath, as seconds ticked past agonisingly slowly.

And then two soot blackened faces emerged. Their grinning white teeth sparkled in the torchlights aimed at them. Behind them, they dragged another dead militant. Intrigued, Sudhir sir finally inspected the weapon that had come close to shooting him. He couldn't resist the temptation. It had clogged.

"Didn't I tell you?" he boasted to the squad. A broad smile covering his face. "There's no bullet for me yet."

I looked heavenwards, praying for it to be true.

* * *

Wadi-e-Lolab

A Tale of Debt
August 1996

Biting into the last soggy biscuit, he crinkled his nose, washing it down with a gulp of stale water. Kheem Singh sneered, "What did you expect? English biscuits served by a *gori* madam, Anchal?"

The woods darkened, bringing into accent the lingering sweet smell of wildflowers and the chirping of crickets.

"That's enough to keep me warm," said Anchal, smirking. Comfortably sleeping in their warm beds, few realised the sacrifices of these men.

Reeking like the sodden undergrowth, the damp seemed to squeeze in through the waterproof jackets they wore.

Cold, hungry, bone-tired, they had been out in the mountains for 48 hours. Pushing himself and the team to the limits of endurance, Sudhir had combed the dense forests of the Gagal ridge. Behind, towering to a sheer 10,000 feet, the imposing Khobalmargh Top dwarfed man and rock menacingly. It quickly melted into the dark clouds.

Smoke from fires made the tin roofs of Sorigam and Voora shimmer like mirages, beckoning them. Dotted with rice fields, the oval, picturesque Lolab was barely five kilometres wide. Surrounded by thick pine and deodar forests, its heart-stopping beauty had seduced travellers for decades.

Disturbed by Muktiyar's fidgeting, a bush swayed. Mukhtiar extended his stiffened limbs. His stiff fingers felt numb. The team had taken up their position for hours. The forest fell silent. No life in sight. No hostile life.

A streak of lightning lit up the breath-taking Lolab valley below, as a sharp clap shook the ground. Soon, small streaks of lightning crackled across the sky, emphasising the majestic pines that encircled the basin. A rain drop fell on his cheek. Sudhir, with a swipe of his hand, looked up as the stars disappeared. The crescent moon had vanished. A storm would break any moment.

They still had a couple of hours before the vehicles picked them up, headed for the base. Peering at the gaunt faces and hollow eyes, he made a quick decision.

Walking through the bushes, he tapped Mukhtiar on the shoulder.

"Okay let's go down," said Sudhir, his words sounding toneless and flat. "We'll rest in Gagal." It had turned out to be yet another futile hunt. It was time to close the operation.

A small, quaint village, Gagal was situated deep in the belly of Lolab valley. The dense forests obscured their view of the village completely. The smell of tantalising kitchen fires, nevertheless, seduced their hunger as it drifted upward through the air.

Emerging through the black veil that covered the forests, their dark figures approached the village cautiously.

On reaching the outskirts, Mukhtiar identified a house on the periphery. A flash lit up the house. A modest wooden two storied structure with a small balcony running on the top. Sudhir nodded. The storm finally broke in a loud crash, as squashing feet rushed inside, pursued by the heavy drops.

Unlacing his shoes, Sudhir peeled off his clammy socks, letting his damp feet breathe, heartily sipping the piping hot salted tea that was offered. "This is heaven," he grinned, wriggling his toes as the crackling flames tickled his feet. Allowing his mind to slacken, sleep finally closed his heavy eyelids as the fatigue of the last two days took control. Propped against his backpack, he fell into an exhausted stupor. Howling winds swept through the valley, gusts with icy fingers pinched the skin through the wall cracks.

Abruptly, his eyes opened. An unusual chatter of Kashmiri voices.

Eyes flashing, he instinctively reached for his weapon, threatened by the odd sound. With the spectre of danger invariably present, his mind was subconsciously always on alert. They had trained it thus.

For survival.

"It's a hundred times more powerful," he invariably joked. He was not wrong. The subconscious was indeed scientifically validated to be more potent than the conscious.

The chattering was coming from the next room. A hesitant boy was dragged in. A young woman shuffled in behind him. Avoiding eye contact, she gave him a once-over.

"What happened?' enquired Sudhir, eyes boring into the distraught boy sceptically.

Wearing a phiran frayed at the edges, tear streaks had stained his apple cheeks. A toe peeped out through the mud-stained broken shoes.

Pursing her lips, the women lisped, "Janab..." she hesitated, "his Abba is very sick." The boy was wringing his fingers, looking down. "And they have no money..." her voice trailed off.

Ever watchful, Sudhir lifted an eyebrow. "Why is he walking in the rain?"

"Collecting money from every house," said the woman, her mouth twitching.

Softening his gaze, Sudhir asked gently, "What's your name, boy?"

"Amir... Amir," hiccuped the boy, wiping his nose on his sleeves.

"How much do you want?"

"Just a hundred rupees, janab," said Amir, wheezing.

"Where is the doctor?" asked Mukhtiar. Pitiably, the village hardly had any infrastructure. Dropping his shoulders, Amir looked up at the woman, unsure. "Kupwara... Kupwara, janab," replied the women.

"But that's nearly seven kilometres away. How will you?"

"I don't know," howled the boy, sitting down on the floor, holding his head. "Abba will die without a doctor." Tears ran down his cheeks marking the floor. "Abba... Abba," he sobbed.

A loud lightning raked the room, sounding ominously close.

"How will they go on a night like this?" stuttered the woman, biting her lip, looking heavenwards. Infrequent, the bus services were unreliable even by day.

Help from the villagers was impossible in the night. With militants and security forces prowling outside, the darkness terrified the villagers.

The boy pressed himself against the floor, whimpering, shutting his eyes.

The pitiful sight of the boy, yearning for his father, stirred something deep within Sudhir. "Amir," said Sudhir, hauling him up, "We will give you a lift." Disbelief clouded Amir's watery eyes. Stunned, he gaped at Sudhir. "Don't worry, we are heading that way, too." He patted the boy on his back.

On instructions, Mukhtiar pressed money into Amir's hand. Dumbstruck, his eyes widened. They held a kaleidoscope of conflicting emotions, this time laced with grateful tears. Sudhir gently chided, "There, there, no need for tears."

The sound of approaching vehicles alerted them. Mukhtiar nominated two soldiers.

"Now, take these two men to your house. They will carry your Abba to the vehicle."

A bumpy ride and one hour later, they dropped the father-son duo with a local doctor in Kupwara. "Treat him well," instructed Sudhir, fixing his gaze on the doctor. The doctor nodded.

"Don't worry, Amir," he said, tousling Amir's dishevelled hair. "Abba will be alright."

Slipping his boyish palm into Sudhir's bold hand, Amir whispered softly, "Janab, how will I return your money?"

"Oh, forget it," said Sudhir, realising the struggle that had gone into those words. He pinched Amir's cheek lovingly, as Amir held back his tears.

As an afterthought, he pulled the boy aside and kneeled before him. "If you have any information about militants," he said, "That's where I stay," pointing at some dilapidated army barracks down the road. "My name is Maj. Sudhir Walia."

Sneaking a glance at the barracks, Amir shrugged, digging a hole with his toe.

"You'll remember that, won't you?"

Nodding, Amir grinned, revealing a gap where a front tooth had chipped.

Forgetting the incident, life settled back to routine. Eat, sleep, operations and a persistent hope of leave.

* * * *

Vinod
The Trimukha Operations
September 1996

Maj. Bhushan let out a gasp at the sight of the horizon stretching before him. The gold and red hues seeming to go on forever. Customarily a man of action, he had scant moments for such trifles.

Nature went on, undeterred by the fear that filled the Lolab, its brilliance revealed in the glint of morning dew and the vibrant tints of the trees.

"*Harud,*" said the singsong voice. Taken aback, he spun around and saw the kind-faced women, dropping a bundle of hay to the mooing cow. "*Harud,*" she repeated, pointing at the trees, her eyes crinkling in a gentle smile. It was the Kashmiri word for autumn.

Smoking his hookah, her husband sat on a log. His skullcap, yellowed at the edges from sweat, sat firmly on his head. The chequered phiran covered a kangri inside.

"*Ae Wadi-e-Lolab,*" the old man sighed wistfully as he adjusted his cracked glasses, revealing a charming gap between his two front teeth.

"It's all ruined now." He spat out in disgust.

"Lolab's history intertwines with the *Mahabharat*," he said. "The Kalaroos caves take you to Russia."

"That's hearsay," chuckled Maj. Bhushan. "Has a Russian ever emerged from there?"

As the team readied to climb, Maj. Bhushan, the team commander, and the old man shared a moment of brief camaraderie, their faces lit up by the late afternoon sun. Their son, a soldier too, was serving in the BSF[70]. 'That's why,' thought Bhushan sir, realising the reason for the friendliness.

Acting on an intelligence tip, the vehicles had dropped them off at the BSF camp on the outskirts of Lalpora, a village in the Lolab valley. From here, they had to hunt out the terrorists in the impregnable forests above.

Senior to Sudhir sir, Maj. Bhushan had done a stint in the Engineers regiment, before joining 9 Para. Slim, dark and rock solid, he carried his reputation lightly on his square muscled shoulders.

"We are ready, sir," Sudhir interrupted his conversation. Checking his weapon, Maj. Bhushan cocked it, flicking the safety catch, "Okay, let's go." He nodded at the old man and led us into the undergrowth.

Despite the quickly darkening evening, we persevered, pushing through the tall undergrowth, feeling the sharp hawthorn brush against our skin.

Scratched and pierced, we slaved upwards painfully, eventually finding ourselves in the thick, resinous deodar forests.

The air had gone sharply cold. We could feel our laboured breath as we climbed the steep, draining climb. A sudden rain now caught us off guard. It became heavy and icy against our skin. Without pause, the sound of its persistence bounced off the leaves.

A meadow soon came into view. Keeping a safe distance from the

---

[70] *Border Security Force*

Gujjar dhoks in the distance, we continued on our trail, clinging to the tree lines.

Maj. Bhushan squinted through his rain-blurred vision to get a glimpse of the dark patch ahead. We were tired. "Let's wait out the rain," he said, the rainwater dripping off his nose and chin. He sat down under a massive branch. We had been walking for nearly nine hours. The squad welcomed the brief break.

"Here," said Sudhir sir, opening his palm. Bending closer, Maj. Bhushan saw some whitish yellow cubes. He wrinkled his nose at the strong peculiar smell. Unflinchingly, Sudhir sir crammed one in his mouth, beaming as he crunched at it.

"*Kalari*[71]," said Sudhir sir, in response to Maj. Bhushan's curious look.

"Emergency ration of the militants.

Maj. Bhushan's jaw dropped. "Chew like them… think like them," said Sudhir sir, eyes lighting up.

"You mystify me, Sudhir."

"They won't expect us in this weather, sir," he said. "Let's press on."

Maj. Bhushan took a deep breath and tried feebly to gain some time again. Unwavering, Sudhir sir held his ground. "This rain will hide us. It's our advantage."

Kindled by his exuberance, the team pursued their search.

I found a goat track. With Puran Gunjal at my shoulder, we treaded the path cautiously, feeling the ground beneath our feet. As we rounded the corner, a chill ran down our spines. Right up ahead, we spotted the corner of a mattress poking through the dense undergrowth.

The squad instinctively went to the ground. We observed, taking in the night's darkness, listening to the soft chirping of nearby insects. The rain continued to patter down. After what seemed an interminable wait, we slowly inched ahead.

Perfectly selected, this was a lookout position with a full view of

---

[71] *Traditionally ripened, it is made from goat or cow's milk. Kalari is Himalayan cheese prepared by separating solid milk by churning and adding matha, sour milk.*

the track we had walked down on. The rain had forced the militant to abandon the location. Luck was with us. We were close, extremely close to them.

The meandering track led us downwards. We had gone some fifty steps, when in front loomed a cave. Sitting at the mouth, the silhouette of a sentry was visible. As the team spread out, the militant heard us and a barrage of bullets whizzed through the air, thudding into the trees above.

Sudhir sir dived behind a rock. Keeping his foresight steady, he got the man with a clean shot. A thunderous firefight had now started. Fire from a machine gun, sprayed the vegetation, ricocheting off the rocks. Maj. Bhushan inched forward, lobbing a grenade in. He followed it up with rapid fire, downing two more militants.

Puran Gunjal noticed three militants escaping and gave chase along with Kashmir Singh. The militants ran, taking turns to fire back at the pursuers, the sound of the bullets reverberating in their wake. The militants quickly disappeared into the black night and dense undergrowth.

The firefight at the cave continued. Sudhir sir ordered for the rocket launcher to be fired. The shaped charge of the 84 mm Carl Gustav swooshed in, exploding loudly. The concussion stunned the militants in the closed confines of the cave. One militant was blown to smithereens as the projectile hit him.

Taking advantage of the chaos, Maj. Bhushan closed in and shot a militant at point blank range. A militant, hiding behind a rock, jumped up, grappling Maj. Bhushan. In the scuffle, Maj. Bhushan threw him down over the edge, to his death, barely preventing his own fall, clinging on to some bushes.

Eventually, we had killed eight militants and captured a rich haul of weapons and equipment.

Beyond the mouth, the cave was dark. It could only be accessed by crawling through its long, constricted belly. Hidden from view, the militants had stocked it with provisions.

Ammunition, radio batteries and other essentials littered the cave, signs that they had used it as a hideout for some time. We stumbled upon a treasure trove of intriguing personal photographs in which the militants posed as fancy outlaws.

* * *

Redeeming the Debt
October 1996

He had grown used to the beauty of Lolab, no longer feeling the same amazement. He only yearned for a warm bath to soothe his muscles, a warm meal to satiate his hunger and a warm bed to lull him to sleep.

A few months later, Sudhir had returned after another long walk in the treacherous mountains, in what had become a routine. Relaxing in his room, he had written his first letter to the girl in Delhi.

Kheem Singh walked in. "Sir, there's a boy at the gate."

"Tell Mukhtiar to meet him."

"He's insisting on meeting you."

"What?" asked a puzzled Sudhir.

"He knows you," said Kheem Singh. "Says it's important."

Sudhir scratched his head, confused, trying to recollect any boy he had encountered.

"Says he is Amir."

Sudhir sighed, "Okay, send him in," still trying to make sense of the situation.

Sudhir surveyed the little boy in the grey phiran, noting his rosy cheeks, yet still unable to place him. Sudden recognition jolted him, when the boy said, "Janab…my father…you gave me money a few months ago."

"Oh, yes." Sudhir beamed, "How's he?"

"Janab, you helped...." Amir sighed with relief, thanking Allah for sparing him.

"And you're returning the money?" Sudhir teased him. "Are you?"

"No, janab," Amir blinked. "You asked me to come if I had any…"

A half smile touched Sudhir's lips. He looked on, puckering his forehead.

"I want to share..." Amir whispered, a flush spreading over his face.

Pulse pounding with excitement, Sudhir pulled up a chair, inviting Amir to take a seat. Licking his lips, Sudhir leaned forward, eyes flashing, "Where, when, how many?"

Colour drained from Amir's face. Dropping his eyes, Amir bit his lip. Sudhir waited patiently, wondering what the struggle was about. He offered Amir water.

Sudhir noticed Amir's hand shaking as he held the glass. Gulping the water a little too quickly, Amir choked. Coughing and gagging, the water spewed out of his mouth.

"Now… now." Sudhir gently thumped his back. "Don't worry. No one will know."

Amir was trying to fight back his tears.

"And if you are feeling guilty, forget it. You are just ridding the country of vermin," said Sudhir, his teeth showing. "Maybe when you grow up, you can join the Army."

Amir shook his head. His eyes welled up. Eyes darting, they settled on Sudhir. Pleading, a tiny drop escaped and ran down his cheek.

He whispered. "In...in my house. One man."

Sudhir continued to stare at him, jaw set.

"If… come before dark." Sudhir noticed the boy's hands shivering. "You can…," his words trailed off.

Sudhir didn't press Amir further. He had shown immense courage for his age, coming all the way from his village to the army post.

Crossing the room to a map hanging on the wall, Sudhir ran his eyes over it, more out of habit than necessity. He already knew the area and could operate blindfolded, if required.

He called for Mukhtiar. "Get the boys ready."

Mukhtiar nodded. Minimal orders were needed. A fighting patrol was ready within minutes.

"From here to Ziarat by vehicles," said Sudhir, addressing the men. "I'll get off with ten men."

Ziarat Peer Baba was a prominent shrine in the Lolab valley.

Looking over at Puran Gunjal, he commanded him to go to Sorigam and to keep in touch on the radio in case he needed help.

Gunjal nodded.

"I will skirt the village till we reach the house. Keep your movements smooth and quick. Any doubts or questions?"

Every man knew his job. They had repeated it countless times. It was etched in their minds.

The drive up the hilly road was pleasant, with valleys on one side and hills on the other till it reached the dense pine forests. The team hardly had time to enjoy the view. They were busy checking their weapons and radio sets. Engrossed in thought, Sudhir went over the plan and the operation.

Dropping off, the ten men set a punishing pace through the forests. At the peak of their physical conditioning, they could outlast most trained armies in a battle of endurance. A compass, fixed with the degrees, helped them maintain a steady course in the dense woods. The tireless trot brought them within half a kilometre of the village.

The men spread out in the paddy fields, encircling the village. This was when surprise could be lost. These were crucial moments. A few tense moments later, the team was in place, surrounding the house.

The house was small compared to the others. Its size a measure of the family's meagre resources.

Sudhir thought of the militant, demanding food and money from the family, as usual. Summoning a local, they dispatched him into the house with a message. "Surrender."

The answer was prompt – a volley of gunfire. No surrender.

Pausing briefly for the family in the house to exit, the firefight began. Not to jeopardise their support system, most times the militants did not use the locals as human shields. They faced death alone especially if they were local militants. The troop set their sights on the house and showered it with bullets. The trapped man ran room to room, firing back.

A well-timed grenade through the window finished the fight swiftly. His death got him the hoors and jannat. It got Sudhir and his troop another kill.

"One less to fight for Jihad-e-Kashmir," muttered Sudhir with a lopsided grin.

As they removed the militant's bloody body from the house, an anguished wail arose from the village. The wail sent a shiver down his spine. It always did. The dead man was a local.

Acknowledging the fight that the man had put up, Sudhir glanced at the corpse with respect. Taking one last look, he tried to capture every detail in his mind for his debrief later, drawing in the sight of destruction. The onlookers shuffled back to their houses. That's when he noticed them, standing under the shadows of a walnut tree. Amir stood next to an old man, holding his hand. Sudhir furtively glanced around to make sure nobody was around before he approached them.

"Your father, Amir?" said Sudhir. "Looks fine. Well done, boy. That was a man's work. It takes courage to do what you did."

Crumpling a few hundred rupees in a ball, Sudhir extended his hand toward Amir. "Inam for what you did."

Amir stood frozen, unmoving, eyes widened in shock. The silence was palpable.

"Here," insisted Sudhir, extending his arm further. "And if you drop in tomorrow, I'll buy you a tape recorder from the canteen."

"Shukria, janab," said Amir, his voice breaking. Tears welled up in his eyes, "I didn't do it for the money." Tears ran down his cheeks.

Sudhir's eyes darted to the father. Clutching Amir's hand for support, the father, too, was weeping unashamedly.

"You saved my Abba's life," said Amir, wiping his tears.

The father spoke up. "In return, we gave you something you hold precious as a soldier. Another life."

A muscle in Sudhir's jaw twitched. Something was amiss.

"You owe us nothing. What price can you pay us, Huzoor?" The father sounded brittle.

"He was my…" Amir gulped his words, then forced them out again, "my elder brother, my only brother."

Sudhir felt the hair on his nape bristle. His head spun around.

"Remember us in your prayers," the father said, "*Khudha hafiz.*"

Blood drained from his face. The battle-hardened soldier just stood rooted, clenching his jaw. The sound of that childish voice was to torment Sudhir for a long time. With their hands clasped in grief, the old man and the boy turned and trudged up the hill. Unmoving, Sudhir just watched them go.

* * *

Stars and Stripes

Fort Huachuca, United States Army
February 1997

They had met in the first-floor service lounge, reserved for service personnel at the Tucson International Airport in Arizona. Sudhir's small palm disappeared in his huge grip,

"Capt. Abam from Ghana, *chale*[72]."

Abam's smile was as big as the grip. Sudhir connected instantly with the gentle giant. "Like a duck to water," Abam would joke later.

---

[72] *Chale- Friend*

"Ti's only scorpions and rattlesnakes here, man?" the Ghanaian captain protested, staring out of the Greyhound bus, his American dream evaporating faster than a Mexican bandito's smoke signal.

Just short of the Mexican border, the arid, remote landscape of Cochise County, Arizona, was home to the Army Intelligence Centre of Excellence or the USAICoE. Better known as Fort Huachuca. It trained officers and men of the US Army in intelligence. Sudhir turned to read the Fort's motto, 'From Sabers to Satellites,' prominently displayed, as the bus crossed the gates.

Sudhir was here to enrol for an advanced intelligence course.

* * *

The instructional course opened with an address by the commandant of the Fort Huachuca. He stated three priorities they should have as an officer: "Mission, people and yourself."

The general exhorted them to remember "To whom much is given, much is expected."

* * *

It was a sweltering day in the Arizona desert.

Inside the fortified walls of the Int school, the team of international students poured over the encrypted messages. Each cipher revealed a chilling clue, leading them down a dark and treacherous path. They uncovered hints of a secret meeting, a timeline for attack and a list of potential targets.

"Hi, I am Sharon Mizrahi," said the blue eyes and blond ponytail. The voice fruity, Sudhir noticed. He peered past the looks; observing her uniform, the beret tucked casually under the epaulettes.

He had been teamed up with her.

Initially reluctant, biased by her gender and good looks, Sudhir had grudgingly grown to respect her. He had never rubbed shoulders professionally with a woman, that too with combat experience, and a brilliant Int analyst. It was an awakening.

The terrorism plot with layers of deception and misdirection was designed to confound even the sharpest mind. Sharon delved deeper into the enigma.

In the analysis, a breakthrough came, a seemingly innocuous phrase, "Crimson Serpent. "It was the clue that led them to uncoil the meticulously crafted coils of the serpent spread across a fictitious rouge state in the Central Asian republics.

A pulse-pounding simulation ensued, a battle of wits. They finally destroyed the headquarters, the head of the Serpent, through precision guided munitions. The exercise had made them think on their feet, make split second decisions and operate under extreme pressure.

Leaving the Crimson Serpent behind, Sudhir wiped the sweat from his brow. "It's tested our limits," observed Sudhir.

"And stretched us," Sharon added.

Sudhir leaned in, looking conspiratorial. "The last time I stretched, I got a catch in my neck."

"Says the man from the land of yoga!" winked Sharon.

"Well, that plot could only be tackled by intelligence and quick thinking." Sounding appealing, Sudhir ignored her teasing.

"And it is not about strength and combat skills, Major." Sharon looked him over. "That must have come as a shock to you?"

"It's also about adaptability," quipped Sudhir ignoring her taunts

"Like you adapted to me?" Sharon teased him.

"That was me strategizing and seizing the moment," Sudhir refused to give in.

"I was never a moment, Major," said the quick-witted Sharon. "I am a lifetime."

They both burst out laughing.

Sudhir, with his Kashmir experience in hand, had performed

brilliantly, much to the appreciation of the instructors and envy of his fellow officers.

Sharon and Sudhir exchanged stories and experiences bridging the gap between their cultures and backgrounds.

She showed him her 'Om' tattoo. "Rishikesh," she said with a nostalgic smile.

"We have been to Himachal," she said with a twinkle in his eye, "Parvati Valley."

"We?" Sudhir asked.

"My boyfriend. Husband now. Same batch."

"He's an int officer too?"

"No, Special Forces. Now in a Kibbutz, farming. Caring for our son, saving our marriage." She winked. "While I save the world."

Their conversations delved into the complexities of their regions; Palestine and Kashmir, both marked by conflict and a longing for peace. Sharon's mention of the Intifada in Palestine struck a chord with Sudhir, who had witnessed the turmoil in Kashmir firsthand.

India's goodwill and its status came as a pleasant surprise to Sudhir, and he made friends easily.

"Indian teachers have taught me since school," remarked the Ethiopian Officer from Mekele, a border town in North Ethiopia. "Even our textbooks are from New Delhi. Nai Sarak, I think."

Indian academicians always had an old association with Ethiopia, especially Mekele.

The officers from Singapore and Nepal had completed their pre-commission military training from Dehradun. The Malaysian officer had done his weapons training from the Infantry School in Mhow, India. The British officer's great-grandfather had died in India in the 1857 mutiny. The Zimbabwean officer had served with Indian troops in a United Nations mission. The Jordanian officer had served under an Indian Force Commander in another UN mission. He loved Indian film actresses and music. The Namibian officer's mother had been treated at the Tata Cancer research Hospital in Mumbai. The list went on.

* * *

But apparently all wasn't well.

The Horned Toadbar in Sierra Vista, a one-horse town close to Fort Huachuca, was a popular watering hole for the officers. At the bar sat two students.

"They bloody seem to stop at nothing," said the Canadian.

Sudhir and the Canadian from the Royal Mounted Police were both vying for the first position. The Irish Canadian didn't stomach the competition lightly and Sudhir had just pipped him to the post one time too many.

He let out a harsh breath. "We will soon probably have a turbaned defence minister in Canada."

"A Singh?" gaffed the Britisher, "That's funny."

The Canadian scrutinised the Britisher with reservation. "You might have an Indian Prime minister one day. Now that would be funny."

"The English would never accept it," said the Brit, losing his smile. He clucked his tongue. "We are too conservative for that."

* * *

They had been out on a run. She beat him to the barracks. Laughing, as he grudgingly puffed up, she tapped his shoulder. "Any more hang-ups, Major?"

Having a keen sense of Sudhir's old reservations, Sharon had rubbed in the idea that women could be equal compatriots in uniform. Sudhir shook his head sheepishly.

Wanting to escape, he changed the subject. "And how to do you deal with the PLA[73]?"

Sharon laughed. Knowing his shenanigans, she played along.

---

[73] Palestine Liberation Army

"Anticipating the PLA response keeps us alive in Israel. We depend on accurate profiling of people routinely." Sharon studied Sudhir's poised demeanour, sensing the underlying intensity. "The PLA is notorious for human bombing."

Sudhir met Sharon's gaze, his eyes reflecting his unorthodox approach. He wiped his sweat. "Indeed," he said with a hint of his characteristic charm. "Profiling earns you precious seconds of life-saving time. I too am attending a short course on profiling before I go back to India. "

"And your response?" Sharon asked her voice lilting, "personally, in a close situation."

Sudhir's response was measured, a testament to his unwavering confidence.

"My superior training already gives me an edge while fear slows the militant down." His tone walked the line between confidence and chance. "And I have calculated the risks. His chance shot in my hand or leg, against mine through his head."

The exchange highlighted the intricate dance between skill, strategy and the willingness to embrace calculated risks that defined the roles of Special Forces officers.

* * *

The final exercise was a real-life scenario in a world plagued by the spectre of global terrorism. Sudhir and Sharon found themselves engaged in an incessant battle against a web of extremist organisations spanning continents.

The scenario build up was a series of devastating terrorist attacks that ripple across major cities worldwide. Each attack carried a chilling message, a symbol from the terror network to re-shape the world order.

They were entrusted with a mission to track down the masterminds and dismantle the global terrorist network.

The journey took them from the bustling streets of New York to the ancient alleys of Marrakech, as they followed a trail of cryptic clues. They discovered a deeper, more sinister conspiracy. The terrorists were not just targeting cities, but were unleashing events that would shake the foundations of global security.

From laboratories in Syria, to biological attacks in Germany, the trail led them through Iran, into the golden triangle on the Pakistan-Iran border, and the drug routes through Baluchistan and Khyber Pakhtoonwala.

They had to uncover the conspiracy, analyse the intelligence, use cyber inputs and strategize to adopt a response to the terror that had a final showdown in the mountains of Afghanistan.

The participants quickly realised that they had to piece together a mosaic of information and transcend borders, that demanded brilliant teamwork and a multi-faceted approach.

The Canadian, lacking combat exposure, struggled to get his analytics right. His theoretical knowledge a poor substitute. Detecting his dilemma, Sudhir offered help. Sceptical, the Canadian hesitantly allowed Sudhir to clean up the rough edges in his analysis.

In a dramatic culmination, the participants crafted a strategy to intercept the simulated operation encountering hostile combatants and executed a precision attack to thwart the organisation's motives.

During the debrief that followed, it became evident that the exercise had not only tested their skills, but also highlighted the significance of international intelligence and cooperation.

Sudhir's superior insurgency experience, through years in Kashmir, helped him outshine everyone and he emerged first on the course. Sharon had backed him all the way.

"Sharon, this course has been unlike anything I've ever experienced."

She screwed her eyes, "And the friends you made?"

He laughed, nodding his head. "Yes, that's a takeaway too."

He would now have to present a paper at the Pentagon. "That's a huge honour, man," beamed Abam, thumping Sudhir on his back.

Pentagon served as the headquarters of the US Department of Defence covering the three military services – Army, Navy and Air Force.

* * *

The moon hung low on the horizon, casting a faint silvery glow over the rugged terrain surrounding Fort Huachuca.

They were out celebrating; the end of the exhaustive 16-week course and Sudhir's achievements, at the Horned Toad. Shorn of her uniform, in jeans and a casual white shirt she looked prettier, her face framed by her crinkly curls which she tossed with good effect. They downed their third Tequila shots at the bar.

"Enough! No more," Sudhir protested. "I have a bloody presentation to give tomorrow morning."

Sharon mocked him with her mascara lined eyes.

"So, Sudhir, in the light of your recent learnings," she batted her eyes coquettishly, cocking her head. It was a flawlessly executed ambush. "Do you think women can be accepted in combat roles?"

"Of course, why not?" He shot back, a little too tipsy to see it coming.

"In the all-male Indian Army too, Major?" Her honeyed tone shot him point blank.

Sudhir gulped downed another tequila, swiping his mouth slowly. He knew when he was beaten.

* * *

Standing on the podium, Sudhir gazed at the faces of the officers from eighty nationalities who were part of his course. In the front row sat his instructors and officers from the Pentagon.

Sudhir spoke with a quiet intensity. The presentation was flawless.

As Sudhir walked off the stage on shaky legs, a figure stood at the bottom of the steps.

"Congratulations, Colonel," said the Canadian saluting him, addressing by a nickname Sudhir had acquired on the course. "You owe us a drink, mate." They shook hands warmly.

* * *

Once he was back in India, Sudhir went through a series of postings till he finally landed in the prestigious Indian Military Academy in Dehradun as an instructor. He met up with his course mate Capt. Harinder Walia, also posted as instructor at IMA.

"Congratulations mate... you are on your way up." Harinder boxed him on the chest.

Sudhir made a face, shaking his head.

"Honestly, you know this int course in the US. It's a fucking big career move!"

Sudhir shrugged. He wore the achievement lightly. "Que sera...sera."

Not happy with the instructional posting either, he confided in Harinder, frustration evident in his voice. "I am a field soldier, Harinder. This regimented peace time posting makes me restless."

"But it's...a feather in your cap. This instructional tenure," said Harinder, trying to knock some worldly sense into him.

"I am not cut out for this spit and polish. Give me the chaos and unpredictability of a fight."

"What don't you like about this posting?"

"This drill square life. It's not for me. I don't know what I am doing here."

"You've lived on the edge for so long Sudhir, that everything else looks lame."

Sudhir shrugged again. "I guess it's altered my DNA forever. That's the price we pay."

"Oh that feeling, when you don't even know what the fuck you're feeling," whispered Harinder rolling his eyes.

Luckily, Sudhir found an escape from the IMA. The Army Chief selected him as an ADC.

* * *

The Last Tango

Haphruda - Seek and Destroy
Kupwara, North Kashmir
August 1999

The year was chaotic for Kashmir. After dominating Kashmir for years, equating secession to Jihad, the Hizbul Mujahideen was losing control. Terrorist groups with extreme ideologies, like JeM and LeT, were weakening its power.

Counter-insurgency operations by the security forces had gained momentum. Many local Kashmiri militants died in encounters or got apprehended. Once considered glamorous, young men were now reluctant to join a futile Jihad.

The ISI's recruitment base in Kashmir valley started drying up. Coerced recruitment continued for some time. The ISI then placed its reliance on foreign mercenaries.

The ISI rhetoric that Islam was in danger in Kashmir bought over mercenaries. Hired mercenaries from POK, Pakistan, Afghanistan, Saudi Arabia, Iraq, Egypt, Libya and Algeria came into Kashmir.

ISI tempted criminals in Pakistani jails to join the Jihad for a shortened sentence. Lured with reprieve of their sentences if they completed an ISI ordained duty, foreign mercenaries ran up from 15% in 1994 to 40% by the end of 1998.

The people initially accepted the guest militants. Fighting for an obscure Jihad, detached from the aspirations of the people, the mercenaries subsequently resorted to rape, loot and murder. Some even kept harems.

The locals soon got disillusioned by the domineering ways of the foreign mercenaries with whom they did not identify. The security forces started receiving actionable intelligence – whereabouts, numbers, groups, leaders and timings.

The mercenaries did not receive the promised support from the people, contrary to what ISI had mentioned. Food and shelter were scarce and the constant flight from the security forces was tiresome and most inconvenient.

They also found the Indian Army a force to reckon with. Realisation struck that a mercenary's life span in Kashmir was a mere four to six months. The tide turned, and the security forces slew 320 foreign mercenaries in violent encounters in 1998.

***

Stationed in Kupwara after the Kargil war, 9 Para (SF) camped next to the 28 Inf Div HQ, known as the Vajra Divison. The tactical headquarters of 9 Para, along with A, B and C teams, were all barracked together.

True to its nature, the unit took advantage of the brief respite after the Kargil war. They gave personnel who had been away from home for eight months much needed leave. And yet, they established an intelligence network.

Continuing its alert after the Kargil war, the Army was still high on tempo. Search and destroy missions were being launched every day.

***

"Hello, Manju, hello?" Speaking into the handset, Kheem Singh's voice carried a distinct note of concern. The booth gave him a little privacy, a rare luxury in the life he lived. Blustery gusts infiltrated through the cracks, rattling windowpanes, muffling his voice. Life as a soldier in Kupwara offered slight relief.

"Hello… hello?" said Manju. She could barely hear him. The booth operator noticed her eyes go moist as she brushed away an annoying tear. Just past twenty, she was a few years younger than her 27-year-old husband.

Her friends had snickered at his photograph that came with the marriage proposal. His boyish looks, the cherubic smiling face with the thin wispy moustache made him look very young. Marriage hadn't changed his looks.

"The doctor… what did he say?"

"Check up again next week." She looked down at her young son. "He is okay now."

Panchpakria, their small village, did not have any mobile connectivity, leave alone a medical setup. She had travelled two hours, troubled by the smell of diesel fumes on the rickety bus, as she made her way to the Army establishment in Banbasa in Uttrakhand.

"Your application? Any update?"

Manju had applied for a primary teacher's job in the Uttarakhand education department.

"Nothing," she murmured, her words laced with disappointment. She pushed a brown lock behind her ear.

"Why?"

"Why? Without money?" A moment of silence. At a loss of words, she could hear him breathing. "This is civil… not the Army," she grumbled.

"They gave me leave, Manju." He was hoping to make her happy.

"Really? Are you sure?" she said in a huff, not giving in easily. She missed him.

"Yes, Manju," furrowing his forehead, he shook his head.

"You seem to be the only one. Kargil is over now. You have a family, too. A son."

"I will be home soon."

"The broken tiles, the tractor work… I can't." She brushed away another tear. "How come only you don't get leave?"

"Manju, I will be there. Sudhir sir himself told me."

"He's not even married, how will he understand?" she grumbled. Her longing and suffering directed its ire towards the only authority she knew.

"You idolise him so much...you think he has all the answers?"

"He doesn't?" The badly timed joke went awry.

"Go, marry him then!" She banged the phone down.

Nk. Nawal Kishore, a fellow Kumaoni, couldn't contain his laughter on seeing Kheem's crestfallen face. "I never thought I'd see the day a black belt in karate turning into a mouse!"

From Himachal, Paratrooper Raveendra Singh sniggered," My father, a retired subedar, can't face my mother's fury even today."

His experienced colleague, Hav. Birendra Singh thumped Kheem Singh on the shoulder. "Don't worry bro, welcome to the married club." Birendra belonged to Sambha, a border town short of Jammu. Everyone just called him Sambha.

* * *

Kupwara, North Kashmir
26th August, 1999

The sentry manning the machine gun at the 28 Inf Div HQ grimaced and turned up his nose. The pungent odour of unwashed bodies and saturated sweat was uncomfortable.

He shot a look over the top of his LMG's foresight as they sauntered past on the way to their camp. The sentry's companion, a wide-eyed young soldier, watched the bare-headed, bandana-clad man with fascination. The heavy walk could not conceal the lithe muscles resisting underneath. He knew they could explode like a coiled spring.

Their eyes met. The embarrassed sentry fumbled and saluted. Sudhir, who smiled and waved back. They were returning from Balkul Gully after yet another operation.

"Every hunt cannot be successful," said Mahendra, boxing Kheem Singh in his shoulders. "We will get our kills the next time over."

Kheem Singh pulled a face. His tired eyes, sunk in their sockets with the four days of physical exertion, still flickered with excitement. He would soon be home.

* * *

Four days earlier…

"We have to go to Balkul Gully," spoke Sudhir, his eyes dark with memories.

Mahendra's skin prickled. Balkul Gully always reminded him of Arun Jasrotia.

"Is it definite?" asked Mahendra, eyes narrowing to slits, enhancing the crow's feet, acquired from squinting into too many suns.

Sudhir's glance was as conspiratorial as a wink.

"Yes… I know, sir," said Mahendra, grinning. "We need to dig them out like worms." Intelligence was never a hundred percent. They had to act on the bits that came through.

The team, with minimal gear, made their way once again to Chandigam in Lolab, a place marked with loss and pain.

Orion, the hunter, was visible in the night sky. A close associate, the star constellation had been their guide during countless night movements. It had witnessed the glint of raw courage in its starlight and beheld their brave exploits.

Navigating by the stars in the Sword of Orion to head south, they walked along a gurgling stream. Like predators out for a kill, they crossed the small Chandigam dam. After a brief rest, they refilled their flasks in the stream.

Taking a gulp, he wiped his mouth with his burly hand. A mischievous spark sparkled in his eyes. "The villagers rumour this water is nectar of the gods," said Mukhtiar. "It's an aphrodisiac."

"No wonder these villagers need *mehaman* militants to fight us," said

Mahendra, "They are just too bloody busy." He made an obscene motion with his fist.

"Don't accuse the gullible villagers. They are just following their urges." Mukhtiar winked. "The culprit is this potent water that flows down from Zaloora. That's what's causing the mischief."

"If you two scientists have finished your findings, can we move?" said Sudhir making a face. The scowl ping-ponged between Mahendra and Mukhtiar, wracking into a smile.

Led by Sudhir and Mahendra as scouts, the team climbed the steep inclines enveloped by dense deodar trees. Orion's belt kept guiding them south through the tree canopy. Short of early morning, they broke through the forest to reach the bald ridge line.

Silhouetted against the night sky, the dark shape of the Zaloora Top blocked out the stars. Mahendra looked up towards the top. Sudhir nodded. After a lifetime of operations together, speech was extraneous. Balkul Gully was further south.

Following the ridge line, keeping the picturesque Zaloora Top as a reference point, they climbed towards Balkul Gully.

Sudhir and Mahendra had become so familiar with these impenetrable mountains that they could map out their paths with their eyes closed. They did not need a map.

By early morning, they were in position. They laid a perfect ambush on the probable route that the militants would take. Then they waited.

The wait extended to twenty-four hours. They shifted positions and waited for another twenty-four hours. They were running short of food. Sudhir extended the wait by another day. Their drinking water was now over. Yet, they waited. A test of their resolve and psychological strength, they battled fatigue, sore limbs, hunger and thirst.

A red-eyed Sudhir tasked Mahendra to find water. Trained in jungle survival, he brought back foul-smelling water in pitiable quantities, sourced from tree trunks. They rationed sips between themselves, keeping their parched instincts alive. They had been out for close to ninety-six hours. There was no activity. The forests were quiet.

"Okay, let's head back," said Sudhir finally. The words sounded like music to the worn men.

Mahendra glanced at Sudhir. His eyes still radiated a fierce, uncompromising energy.

Everyone looked ahead to a hot bath, some warm food and lots of sleep.

* * *

Kupwara, North Kashmir
26th August, 1999

Back in the barracks, a hot meal and bath lulled them into a drugged slumber. They had slept through the light drizzle in the afternoon. Sudhir stirred to a sky blanketed in clouds and a cool breeze, sipping the strong tea from the men's langar. His room smelt typical. It was a mix of kerosene vapours, a musty sleeping bag, the smell of gun oil and wet woollen socks. And a longing for life.

Immune to the odour, he devoured the salty *shakarparas*, savouring every bite of the chef's reverently cooked delicacy.

As the evening settled in, Mahendra accompanied Sudhir to the telephone booth in town. Eyes flickering over the profane graffiti-scribbled wall, Sudhir turned his back and dialled 176061. The code for Palampur. He counted the customary four rings, before she picked up the handset." Hello… hello, Sudhir."

"Ma…"

Mahendra moved away, giving Sudhir a little privacy. As much as the cracked window panes would allow. Sudhir's emotional tone still leaked out the cramped booth.

The small booth was a haunting reflection of the tiny size of their personal lives and the absence of normalcy that most people didn't think twice about. Normal was the abnormal of their lives.

Sudhir spoke at length with his mother. Mahendra overheard him say, "Yes Ma… soon. I promise. Just a few days more."

Mahendra felt a lump. Sudhir's concern for his mother touched a raw nerve. He rubbed his bleary eyes and looked up at the stars.

Sudhir then dialled another number. The meter flashed Delhi. "Hi, there," Mahendra heard him say, "What's up, beautiful?" Sudhir's husky voice implied longing. Mahendra chuckled. He moved further away. This conversation required more privacy.

* * *

27th August, 1999

The knife mark on a tree a little distance away from their camp was the sign Sudhir had been waiting for. Tight-lipped, he strolled down to the dead drop, a boulder next to an idyllic river bend. Back in the camp, avidly pouring over the hurriedly scribbled rumpled paper, he thumped the table, a grin breaking out. Months of efforts had borne fruit. He had his big intelligence tip.

Seated on a rough-hewn chair, Sudhir jiggled his knee, eager to meet the man. The call of the muezzin from the mosque loudspeaker echoed softly.

Face masked, the man finally sneaked in to the room keeping close to the wall, avoiding the window. Sudhir pointed with his chin, asking him to sit. Jameel sat down on his haunches a few feet away.

"How many, Jameel?" asked Sudhir, narrowing his eyes to slits, peering at the man.

Jameel's voice trembled as he replied, "Can't… can't say. Probably a few, janab."

"Be more specific." Giving him a hostile glare, Sudhir picked up his bayonet, "Or I'll slit your throat myself."

Jameel cast a glance back over his shoulder, uttering "It's a *thikana*[74], janab."

Electrified, Sudhir's ears perked up. '*A base?*' He stared at Jameel without blinking.

"In the jungle…a *gufa*. They are up to something."

"Reliable?" questioned Sudhir, his voice on an edge, clenching his fist. "Who gave you the info?"

"Met him as we did the *wuzu*[75]." He paused. "After the prayers, we spoke."

Sudhir kept a straight face, controlling his expressions.

"*Ek mukhbir,*" he said quickly, in a hushed voice, leaning in. "*Illyas Kashmiri ka…unka aslamu yassar karta tha*[76]."

He had come straight from the mosque after the Friday afternoon prayers.

His breath quickening, Sudhir pulled his chair closer to Jameel. Ilyas Kashmiri[77] and Nasrul Mansoor Langrial had worked closely in Banihal. Langrial had escaped from him once, in Kapran.

"Name of the *mukhbir*[78]?" asked Sudhir, curling his lip, placing his palms on the table. Sudhir noticed Jameel's kohl-lined eyes dart towards the door.

"Abu…" muttered Jameel reluctantly, the words hardly audible.

"What?" said Sudhir glaring, anger creeping into his voice, hissing through his teeth.

"Haji…Haji Abu Bakr, janab," said Jameel finally resigning, slumping his shoulders.

---

[74] *Hideout*

[75] *Ablutions before prayers*

[76] *He was Illays Kashmiri's man. He used to organize weapons for Kashmiri's group*

[77] *Six months later, in February 2000, Ilyas Kashmiri would take back the severed head of an Indian solider, Bhausaheb Maruti Talekar from the Maratha Light Infantry and present it to Pervez Musharraf. Pakistan would flash the pictures in many national newspapers.*

[78] *Mukhbir – Informant*

"Why did he tell you?" asked Sudhir, in a voice that could cut glass, unconvinced. Experience had taught him to smell a trap, look for pieces that did not fit.

"One of the Harkat Mujahid forcibly married his 13 year-old daughter."

Sudhir shook his head, he spat on the floor, "Bloody animals don't even spare their own." His voice was full of disdain.

"Tanzeem?" Sudhir questioned, sliding across a few crumpled currency notes. Nails caked with dirt, Jameel grabbed the notes. They disappeared in the deep folds of the phiran.

"Probably Hizbul Mujahideen," he spat out. "Mostly *mehaman mujahid*[79], probably Afghani." He whispered. Was it a mere coincidence that Habibullah from the Kapran Camp was also in this group?

"And the location?" asked Sudhir, eyes smouldering with excitement.

"My cousin, janab, from Cheer Kot knows," said Jameel, pushing his *kufi,* the prayer cap back, scratching his head. Sudhir noticed the tanned reddish-brown line below his skull cap. Cheer Kot was a small village deep inside the forests of Haphruda.

Spread over twenty villages, Haphruda in Kupwara district was about 130 kilometres north of Srinagar. It was a vast hilly area covered with thick pine forests. Frequently used as a base because of its dense forest cover, it was also the stronghold of the Hizbul Mujahideen and the guests from across.

"Okay, he will come with us," ordered Sudhir nonchalantly.

The man protested, "Janab, they will kill him."

"I will kill him myself if the info is false," warned Sudhir raising a finger. Face flushed with passion; he couldn't wait to get started.

"Don't worry, we will release him after he points out the location," assured a paratrooper, standing close by.

"Show me where?" spat out Sudhir, throwing a chalk at him.

---

[79] *Mujahid Guest militants*

The man drew out a rough sketch on the dirt floor. "What's that?" asked Sudhir, bending forward, hands on his thigh.

"Tumina and this is Cheer Kot." These two villages formed a triangle with Haphruda, which was further up north.

He pushed a forefinger into the mud. The discoloured, broken nail stopped at the likely location of the hideout. Jameel looked into Sudhir's eyes without uttering a word.

Sudhir stared at the furrow in the mud floor in deep silence. Bending forward, he held Jameel by his hair, jerking his head back. The warm stink from his breath washed over Sudhir. The naked blade of the bayonet bit into Jameel's throat, near his jugular.

Sudhir curled his lips. Jameel felt icy dread wash over him as he looked into Sudhir's scornful eyes. In the room's stillness, their breathing was the only sound that was heard. The message was loud and clear.

Abruptly releasing him, Sudhir snapped his fingers. "Lock him till we get back," he instructed.

Two paratroopers lifted the hapless man and took him out. Pulling out a map, he spread it on the table. Using the bayonet, he traced the route via Batpora, Warsun and up till Chowkibal. The serpentine route meandered through dense jungles up to the 9000 feet Sadhana Pass, on the Shamshabari ridge, some 30 kilometres away from Kupwara.

"From here on, we walk," he said, poking the Sadhana Pass on the map with the blade. The two young officers, Lt. Prince Jose and Lt. A.S. Dabas nodded.

Finally, tracing out Tumina and Cheer Kot, Sudhir studied the deep gullys in between. His gaze moved to a probable location between the ridge lines.

Drawing in a sharp breath, he gripped the bayonet and struck it with fury, embedding the blade tip into the wood through the map. "This is where we seek and we destroy," he said gruffly.

Hair bristling on their napes, the two officers glanced at the vibrating blade. It showed the power of his intent. It also undeniably defined their attitude.

There was no room for weakness.

* * *

The troops would have no backup for ammunition, medicines and food. Their only reliance was self-sufficiency. While their training catered to it, they had to tackle other issues.

The Haphruda forest area was notorious for poor communication. The erratic weather coupled with the steep, rocky ridgelines and dense jungles caused radio signals to be blocked out. Radio batteries would need to be conserved with ruthless efficiency. The entire operation would have to be planned with a low predictability of reliable contact with the base in Kupwara.

Detailed orders had to be given. Ambiguity had to be factored in, coordination emphasised, timings predicted and preordained. The unknown had to be understood, codes rehearsed, battle worthiness checked… and the gods appeased.

The night and morning went by in quick preparations. The late afternoon sun broke through the cloudy sky.

"You didn't detail me with Sudhir sir?" Eyebrows bunched up, Mahendra asked the JCO, planning the detailing.

"I detailed Kheem Singh this time," said the JCO. "You are in the other operation. They were short of men."

Mahendra protested.

"It's okay, Mahendra," Sudhir thumped him on his broad back. "Next time. Let Kheem be with me now."

Mahendra wasn't happy.

With a soul-igniting war cry, bundled up in vehicles, they set off.

* * *

Sadhana Top, Kashmir
28th August, 1999

As the sun dipped towards the horizon, the party finally reached the secluded drop-off point on the meandering road. The trucks cut their speed and the soldiers slipped off quickly, blending in with the shadows of the jungle in a matter of seconds.

The vehicles rumbled along the road. Their engines buzzed, the headlights illuminating the darkness. To anyone watching, the team's destination was further away.

The adhoc team, led by Sudhir, had two officers and about seventy-odd paratroopers organised in three troops. Lt. Jose and Lt. Dabas led a troop of twenty paratroopers each. Sudhir himself led the third troop.

They slithered down a steep goat track to reach the *nallah* below, climbing down from the drop off location on the ridge. From this point on, they embarked on a zigzag course to access the expected site.

Mapping their journey through the deodar jungles, aided by stars and compass bearings, they walked over three ridgelines. Their camouflaged faces, covered in green and brown paint, helped them blend seamlessly into the foliage. Wrapped with scrim garnish, a jute mesh, even their weapons were camouflaged.

Near invisible if they stood still, their bodies were as much a part of the trees as the other nocturnal creatures that prowled for prey. Conserving their energy, they stopped to take brief rests. They sipped sparingly, rationing water.

On the long walk, the moon was visible through the clouds, its soft glow guiding them. As the night grew darker, the moon disappeared, leaving them to an eerie silence and their uncertain fate. The merry crickets now became their chirpy companions.

Jameel's cousin, the spotter, followed alongside Sudhir's party. Sandwiched between two burly escorts, he walked in silence, the crunch of leaves echoing through the stillness of the night. Attired in a phiran, he wore a dark hood that blocked out his face. It had slits just narrow enough for his eyes to peek through.

"Even your mother cannot recognise you," sniggered Sudhir, eyeing him.

August in North Kashmir was cold. The temperature plummeted, the night air falling to an icy eight degrees. The eight hours of walking left them chilled, yet sweaty, their tunics clinging to their backs. As they crossed a clearing in the woods, a faint breeze would brush against their sweat-covered skin. The weight of the rucksacks pulled on their shoulders.

Soon, the sky lightened, signalling the coming of daybreak. They heard the rustlings of the jungle awakening and the flapping of feathered wings above. Sudhir could smell the spotter's fear as they approached the final ridge line. He glanced at the spotter and received an almost imperceptible nod in response.

* * * *

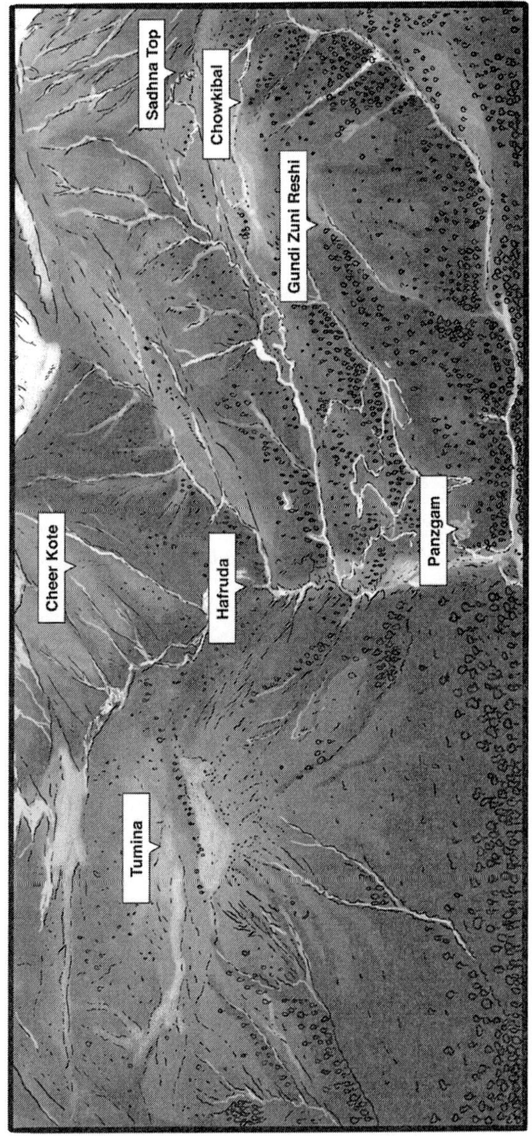

Haphruda, Kupwara - The Final Encounter

The Firefight, Haphruda
29th August, 1999

Spreading out, they moved cautiously. Deliberately.

The scouts walking ahead saw something out of the ordinary. They both kneeled down and signalled the team behind. Sudhir trudged up the incline, the scent of wildflowers following him as he surveyed the landscape below. Two large, charred logs wedged between massive boulders. The mustiness of the damp wood hung in the air as he surveyed the makeshift shelter.

They summoned the spotter to the forefront. He pointed to the area, his voice barely audible in the hushed atmosphere, "That's an old hideout."

Averting his gaze to Sudhir's inquiring look, he added, "Rashtriya Rifles burned it…raided it last year."

Sudhir questioned him. "And the hideout? Where?"

The thick vegetation reduced visibility to a few metres.

"I don't know exactly…it's close. Somewhere there," he pointed ahead.

Sudhir murmured, "Take him back." He shot the paratrooper a knowing look. The paratrooper nodded, his body tensing as he comprehended Sudhir's silent command. If the spotter attempted to flee, he had to kill him. The fate of the operation would rest on the Paratroopers' swift reaction. They couldn't afford a loss of surprise.

He instructed a troop to move ahead and search the area. On receiving confirmation about the area being clear, the rest of the team moved up. Sudhir commanded the troop to spread out and form into groups of three, blocking off all the potential escape routes. He positioned the stops to eliminate any terrorists escaping from the hideout during the raid. Mukhtiar was part of this troop. The team left their rucksacks behind.

Sudhir led the other two troops along a circuitous route further down. He now deployed another troop under Lt. Jose in nallahs, along goat tracks, river bends and outcrops, forming a cordon of stops around the area.

Once satisfied that the probable hideout area had been ringed with stops on every escape route, Sudhir started the search with Sambha's squad. Hav. K. P. Singh's reserve squad followed them.

The squad scoured the dense jungles. The first rays broke through, yet they had not come close to engaging with the hidden militants. As they neared the perimeter of the forest, they heard the river. Not noticing anything unusual, they faced the forest and loosened their limbs by its banks.

Sambha walked to the river's edge to gargle his mouth, scooping up the water with his palms. He glanced at his rippling reflection, tinged by the morning sun. Naval Kishore squinted at Kheem Singh, "Do you think…the motherfucker?" He handed over the water bottle to Kheem Singh.

"Deceived us?" butted in Raveendra, wiping his face on a bandana around his neck.

Kheem Singh curled his lips, "I'll wring his bloody neck, if..."

"Alpha1…Alpha1!"

The frantic cry from Sambha cut off his words. Sudhir ran down to the water's edge. What he saw made his nape bristle.

White toothpaste foam lurked menacingly near the shoreline. Wide-eyed Sudhir's gaze met Sambha's as a momentary silence hung in the air.

They were at the lair's mouth. Close. Very close.

Despite their exhaustion, the squad fanned out again and resumed the search. Kneeling, scanning, observing. Sniffing. One foot at a time.

They formed a tight group, walking in a diamond formation. Kheem Singh and Sudhir led the squad through the dense forest, peering ahead, unmindful of the strain in their arms, as they looked down their barrels. Sambha and Naval Kishore walked on the flanks, fingers on the trigger, ensuring they did not get ambushed from either side. Raveendra and another paratrooper brought up the rear. Scanning the bushes, they pointed their foresights on anything suspicious.

Kheem Singh stiffened mid-stride, his back muscles constricting, an unmistakable sign which Sudhir saw. He quickly stepped aside, feeling the rough bark scrape against his shoulder. He shielded himself and followed Kheem Singh's gaze.

A kneeling Kheem Singh signalled.

A blue plastic water-proof sheet stood in stark contrast to the green foliage. Its alien presence ringing alarm bells, even though the foliage had tried to cover it.

The sheet billowed in the wind; the edges tucked under the enormous deodar logs laid across a hollow, creating a makeshift shelter. They looked at each other, the silence between them thick with unspoken understanding.

Not taking his eyes off, Kheem Singh stood up, aiming his cocked weapon toward the shelter less than 25 metres away. He listened intently for any giveaway sounds. Barely conscious of the sweet, earthy aroma of the early morning as he darted past the tree, slithering ahead to the next one.

Sudhir simultaneously changed his position, inching closer, aligning his foresight on the shelter for a better shot.

* * *

The sharp crack of the twig woke up the yawning sentry.

Positioned on a mound next to the hideout, the 25-year-old Khyber Pakhtunkhwa resident looked through the bushes. His eyes bulged out as he saw a soldier emerge from a tree.

And next to him another one. Without even looking, the militant knew the man wielded authority. His confidence, and the way the first soldier looked at him, evidently identified him as a senior.

Too stunned to move, the sentry just watched wide eyed. The only sound was his ragged breathing. He had no time to alert his sleeping comrades. He gulped, steadied his breath, regained control and taking aim, pressed the trigger.

* * *

The sound of automatic fire pierced the silence. A hail of bullets shredded the leaves, thudding into the bark.

From the corner of his eye, Sudhir observed Kheem Singh stumble.

Distracted by the blue sheet, they had both missed the lookout man. It was a fatal mistake. It would prove very costly.

Having first advantage, the militants' accurate fire came down on Sudhir. A shot slammed him against the tree stump. Sharp pain stabbed his shoulder; as though a hot poker was pressed against his skin.

Cursing himself under his breath, "Bhenchod..." Sudhir whispered, "Fuck...fuck." Swinging his weapon, he fired three shots in quick succession. It was too late.

His jaw felt like a mule had kicked it. He absorbed the shock, swallowing the pain, then kicked his way slowly back to the surface. He realised he had been shot in the jaw too. The momentary respite allowed Kheem Singh to struggle up. He fired back, disregarding the pain in his chest. He tried to focus through his blurring vision, his body reacting through muscle memory, honed through intensive training. The sentry shifted his fire back to Kheem Singh, shooting him again in the chest.

The brave soldier fell on his knee, firing back, finally slumping in the soft mud, his face hidden in the green ferns.

The well-trained militant again shifted his aim and fired at an exposed Sudhir. The bullet went through him somewhere. A searing pain shot through his back.

Steeling his jaw, Sudhir leaned against a tree. He steadied his breathing, his vision and his aim. Fixing the militant in his foresight,

Sudhir gently squeezed the trigger.

The militant fell dead shot through his head.

* * *

Alerted by the sudden firing, pandemonium reigned inside the dugout. All hell broke loose. Four or five terrorists took up positions in the hideout's mouth, firing back with ferocity. Some terrorists emerged from the rear, firing wildly as they ran out.

Sudhir shot one more terrorist through his head as he sprang up

Red rivulets from Sudhir's jaw ran down his throat. Pain was just an illusory sensation that his mind could shut down if it needed to, he told himself.

The squad had closed in, taking up positions around.

"Shoot the bastards!" yelled Sudhir. "Nawal… go right." His words were not coherent. He wondered why?

The firing was intense. Both sides continued to fire unabated. After ten minutes of engagement, one more terrorist fell dead.

Sambha got close enough to see Sudhir. He could see splashes of red on Sudhir's jaw.

"Get back, Alpha 1," he protested, concerned. "Get—"

The firing drowned out his words.

Acrid smoke stung their throats. Their eardrums hurt from the deafening sound. His back propped against the tree; Sudhir changed his magazine. "Sambha, cover the rear… fire the PIKA!"

Glancing over his shoulder, he fired another burst, "I am okay… don't let them…." He fired a long burst. "…bloody escape."

The red patch from his wound on the shoulder grew bigger. Soon his tunic was wet. It stained the bark of the tree red.

"Allah hu Akbar!" screamed an Afghani terrorist, raising his arm to lob a grenade. Sudhir shot him through his arm, the second shot went through the militant's chest. The grenade rolled over and exploded, showering mud and debris. The concussion hurt their ears.

He was drawing fire. He needed to get into a better firing position. Regardless of his injuries, Sudhir shifted, changing his position. He was close enough to see the whites of their eyes now.

"Alpha1, I'm coming!" screamed Sambha through the commotion, "Wait… don't move!"

* * *

"Raveendra, watch your flank!" yelled Sudhir. "I am okay." He nodded at Sambha.

Two terrorists were trying to make a run for it. Raveendra fired in rapid succession. He shot one dead.

Shot through his leg, the second terrorist jumped behind a rock. "*Kusmodar*[80]!" screamed the terrorist, "*Go khor*[81]," firing back. Another terrorist joined him, "*Kerim da basta khanadanet*[82]," he cursed, firing at Raveendra.

The volley ripped off the bark from the trees, exposing the tender sapwood and cambium below. Raveendra felt the ground shake as a burst came close, kicking up the pebbles near his feet. Air fanned his face as three shots whizzed past, narrowly missing his head. They thumped into the tree behind him.

Raveendra, pinned by the volley of bullets from the two gunmen, ducked low, unable to move.

"I'll slit your throats, motherfuckers!" he replied above the din.

He could barely make out the man hidden by the bushes. Aiming low, Sudhir fired speculatively, shooting the man in his stomach.

Automatic fire crackled through the dying Afghan's barrel. The bullets ricocheted randomly, sparking off the rocks. He fell on his face, spilling blood and saliva, dead before he hit the ground.

---

[80] *Kusmodar – Mother fucker*
[81] *Go khor – Shit eater*
[82] *Kerim da basta khanadanet – I'll fuck your whole family*

"Sambha," ordered Sudhir, "Get KP ahead…cover the rear…" His speech was slurring.

The firing lasted a good thirty minutes more. Finally, as the firing stopped, K.P. Singh's squad moved ahead and searched the area.

They counted nine bodies. Sudhir had shot four.

Swiftly, with practised efficiency, Sambha organised the squad. While the rest of the paratroopers continued the search, two paratroopers applied a field dressing on Sudhir's shoulder wound. His jaw was in terrible shape.

Sudhir doggedly persisted in giving directions. His voice reverberated through the radio sets, "Running to you…stay vigilant!"

Not just pain-tolerant, or pain-resistant, Sudhir appeared pain-defiant.

The running terrorists ran into the stops headlong, in ones and twos. Well-positioned, the stops shot them down easily. By evening, the tactical headquarters would receive intercepts of over twenty militants killed. It would set a record of sorts.

Lt. Dabas and a few soldiers carried Sudhir between them. Still conscious, but in pain now, Sudhir cursed. Chortling despite himself, "Don't kill me. Motherfuckers…be gentle." Love and years of kinship, all muddled up.

Mukhtiar ran up with his medical satchel. He examined Sudhir's jaw. Alarmed, he and Sambha exchanged a glance. The bullet had hit Sudhir below his nostril and exited through his jaw below the right ear. With a sense of unease consuming him, Mukhtiar anxiously tended to Sudhir, his hands trembling, avoiding eye contact.

Suspecting more injury, Mukhtiar wanted to examine further. Gentle hands turned him over. He didn't so much regain consciousness as he began sensing pain. Sudhir cursed, "Bhenchod…kill me first!"

Mukhtiar tried to distract Sudhir from his pain. "Sir, you are a hero. Our hero."

"Ya, but I do my own…st… stunts," slurred Sudhir, covering his pain with a grimace. His tongue had grown heavy.

The bullet had exited through the shoulder, smashing the bone.

Mukhtiar's hands were red as he tore away the tunic to examine Sudhir. Sambha saw Mukhtiar's face drained of colour. He looked down at the ugly gaping wound in the back. Mukhtiar padded it with field dressings. It would hold for now.

Blood still oozed out like a rivulet. Mukhtiar found the gunshot wound in the stomach. The third one. The bullet had exited the back. "We need to evacuate him quickly." Mukhtiar's voice was hoarse.

"Finish the search," hissed Sudhir, baring his red teeth. Sambha nodded. "Yes, sir." He was going to disobey that order.

Mukhtiar warned, "He has lost too much… blood."

"Kheem Singh?" asked a delirious Sudhir. "He needs help, too." Mukhtiar pressed Sudhir's outstretched hand, shaking his head.

"No!" he screamed through his pain, "NO!" Holding Mukhtiar's wrist Sudhir screamed at the sky. "Fucking… bloody shit." Mukhtiar felt Sudhir's fingers bite into his skin.

As buddies, they had been through innumerable near-death situations. Now Kheem Singh was no more. But he lived.

Guilt was the most painful companion of death.

His head hurt too much. His body hurt too much. Everything hurt too much. There were bruises and cuts and scrapes and maybe some breaks. He kept his eyes closed, not because he didn't want to see where he was, but he thought it would hurt too much to open them.

Oblivious to the growing crimson patch on his thigh, Mukhtiar held Sudhir, adjusting the saline bottle.

"Mukhtiar…" Sudhir choked, spitting out blood. He clutched Mukhtiar's sleeve, tugging hard, eyes screaming in anguish. "I don't want to…" His voice trailed off, the conclusion inescapable.

"Never, Sahabji!" lied Mukhtiar. Guilt flooded his flashing eyes. He gripped Sudhir, the fingers biting into Sudhir's shoulder.

"You have a gift…nothing can touch you," he lied. The breathy explosion of words sounded hollow, even to himself.

The memory of that tug had burned into Muktiyar's skin, marking his spirit. He could never erase it. Mukhtiar looked down at the man, who had mocked death all his life. His clammy hands trembled as they soothed the brave warrior in his lap. "You will live…forever, sir," he whispered hoarsely.

They prepared a stretcher to carry Sudhir.

As the bearers lifted the stretcher, Mukhtiar silently squeezed Sudhir's arm, swallowing through his choked throat. Standing motionless, the burly Sikh warrior finally wept unashamedly. "Until death, it is all life," he muttered through his tears, remembering an old quote.

* * *

The Tactical Headquarters in Kupwara made the frantic call for the helicopter evacuation. They shifted Sudhir into the helicopter from the truck near the village.

The men heard the helicopter as it took off. It rose like an ominous black bird above the treetops, carrying away their spirits, embodied in a man they revered. Each of them would have gladly stood in the line of fire and shielded Sudhir.

The sound of rotors whirled in the background; inside, the smell of metal and fuel filled the cabin. Fingers stained red, Sudhir scribbled a letter to his mother, smudging the paper with his fingerprints, as he felt his last breaths slipping away. Sudhir searched for the scratch on his wrist. It had healed, sadly. His ragged breath turned into a sigh.

He closed his eyes. A lullaby rang through his head twenty-six years after it had been last sung. A tear escaped, spilling on the shuddering metal floor, in last gratitude to his mother.

He died en route.

* * *

They had to follow legal procedures and report the encounter. The littered bodies identified and handed over to the local police station. An FIR had to be written and details submitted.

It was impossible to extricate the militant bodies through the thickly forested ridge lines and carry them to the police station.

"Improvise," growled an irritated Sambha when a paratrooper asked him.

The J&K police inspector at the Drugmulla Police Station in the Lolab valley jumped out of his skin when he looked up to see a weary paratrooper drag in a rucksack full of heads. It left a trail of red droplets on his floor. "Here, write your bloody FIR," groaned the weary paratrooper, dropping the rucksack on his table.

* * *

Vinod
Sunderbani, Jammu

I was at home on leave. I switched on the evening BBC radio bulletin, pouring a glass of water.

The news reader started, "This morning in Haphruda in Jammu & Kashmir, in a fierce encounter with foreign militants, Maj. Sudhir Walia …."

Choking, on the water, I coughed painfully. My head swam. The day he died, neither Mahendra nor I were with him. Such is fate.

BBC had picked up the details of the encounter and broadcast in their evening bulletin. Indian channels true to form, lagged. By the time I called up the unit, the tragedy had already been confirmed.

I lost my hero that day. In fact, I lost my verve.

* * *

THE AFTERGLOW

Exactly a month after Kargil, Gen. Ved Malik and his wife were returning from a visit to a martyr's bereaved family. In the car, he received a phone call informing him that Sudhir had died on the way to the hospital in Srinagar.

On 29th August1999, the nation lost a gallant soldier. For the Chief of Army Staff, the loss was personal. He went down in glory as he had sworn he would.

* * *

Rajeswari Devi never opened the letter. She could never muster up the nerve. It continues to lie sadly next to his picture, illuminated in the afterglow of a flickering flame of an earthen lamp. It holds something precious.

Worthy of the last moments of his brave life. A last farewell of a warrior to an anguished mother.

* * *

Raj Path
26th January, 2000

The winter morning was freezing. Not very different from the morning in the Haphruda forests.

A frail man in a Himachali cap walked up the four steps to the presidential dais on the Raj Path, heralded by the fluttering flags. Some suggested it could be the breath of warriors. His chest heaved as he heard the citation being read out. Sub. Maj. Rulia Ram stood straight and proud, his face a mask of stoic determination. But his eyes gave him away. And a single tear threatened to spoil his composure.

With unwavering hands, the father received the Ashok Chakra from the President of India. This was the highest peace time military honour, awarded to his warrior son. The hands were wrinkled, but his grit was unshaken.

The president, symbolising a grateful nation, stood in solemn silence. His head bowed in reverence, he absorbed the magnanimity of the sacrifice made.

*** * * ***

An eerie green glow settled in the dimmed lights of the cabin. Closing his eyes, the retired general settled back, as the aircraft cruised at 33000 feet above sea level. Sensing a presence by his knee, he opened his eyes to see the air hostess kneeling before him, fighting back tears.

She gulped. "Sudhir and me…" Her voice trailed off, eyes welling up.

"I know… I understand." Taken aback, he tried to get a grip, trying to deal with it like a soldier.

"Why?" She fought back her despair, before sorrow choked her throat again.

"He was..." He fumbled; his voice gravelly. "He was brave." Finally finding his voice, "Some men are destined for glory. How could he ignore his destiny?"

"No." She sighed and shook her head. She bit her lip, tears on a brink. "No… it wasn't to be like this." The reality stonewalled by her grief. "He had always promised no bullet could touch him."

She forced out the words. "He lied to me!"

His moist eyes flashed in anger. Gen. Malik kept a hand on her head.

"He got his glory…you, a hero. The family, the pride. And me?" The regret in her voice accusive in its ire. "Can't even mourn…" Her gaze bore into the general, fiery in suppressed agony.

"You have a life waiting, beta."

Her wet eyes looked up in a frown. She stared at him, astonished. Breathing in sharply, she held her anger at bay. They would never understand.

"He would have wanted you to..."

"It's only about him?" She shot back. "Should I bury the shattered pieces too?"

She whispered. "That's all I have."

Her eyes clouded with pain, pleading. "Please, let me keep something? My last few memories? Leave me something."

"I didn't say. I mean… Of course, child!" He shrugged his shoulders. It was impossible. Death took away so much.

She sniffled, faking a smile, her eyes holding on to the memories.

Seeing her walk away with pride, the ex-chief realised he was holding his breath.

Courage walked in different ways.

✳ ✳ ✳ ✳

AFTERWORD

They awarded Capt. Arun Jasrotia the Ashok Chakra for his outstanding courage, devotion to duty and supreme sacrifice. The Punjab government also conferred on him the 'Nishan-e-Khalsa' award in 1999. The then US Ambassador to India, Frank G. Wisner wrote a letter to Lt. Col. Prabhat Singh Jasrotia, Arun's father.

…I admired you as you took the award in his memory. I met your son when I visited the Special Forces unit in Dehradun in June 1995 and I was most impressed by his professionalism.

* * *

Mahendra retired as a Subedar Major and Honorary Captain. Having cheated death once, a quirk of fate drew the braveheart back to Haphruda on 3rd September 2015. Hauntingly, the encounter took place just metres away from where Sudhir and Kheem Singh had died. He had helped pull out two of his injured colleagues, before a bullet injured his spine, leaving him paralysed waist down. Decorated with a Keerti Chakra and Sena Medal, he remains confined to a wheelchair.

Once a proud warrior, the man carries his heroism lightly. The muscular frame has sagged a little, but his eyes still breathe fire. "They died once. I die every day in this wheelchair."

* * *

Mukhtiar, too, retired as Subedar Major and Honorary Captain. He carries a Shaurya Chakra on his proud chest.

Maj. Prince Jose suffered a stroke later because of the injury in Kargil. He left the Army after suffering a disability.

Puran Mal Gunjal retired as Honorary Captain to his remote mountain village in Uttrakhand.

Vinod realised his dream. He got commissioned as an officer in another prestigious infantry unit– the Third Grenadiers. He has since retired as Major and spends time in his village. His back still hurts from the fall during the Kargil War before the attack on Zulu Top.

* * *

Neither age nor injury has, however, diminished their memories. Their eyes still sparkle with fierce pride when they remember him. They still recollect the legend, the man they called Rambo.

'How can a man die better, than fighting fearful odds,
But for the ashes of his fathers and the temples of his gods.'

* * *

Worthy of honour, there are countless others, who have also served with Sudhir, equally heroic and courageous. For reasons of brevity and to simplify the story line, I had to pick a few names. A task I am not envious of.

For who am I to disregard their valour or sacrifice? Each of them is worthy of being exalted, acclaimed and anointed. Each of these unknown soldiers is worthy of being honoured as a hero.

'Men apart, Every man an Emperor.'

—*Field Marshal Bernard Montgomery*

BIBLIOGRAPHY

1. Singh, T. Khurshchev.HuJI in India: An Asssement Strategic Analysis. *www.tandfonline.com.* [Online] Mar 19, 2009. https://www.tandfonline.com/doi/abs/10.1080/09700160802518510?journalCode=rsan20.

2. *Terror Outfits Active Outside J&K', Times of India,* Mumbai: January 2, 2008.

3. Puri, Lt. Gen. Mohinder. *Kargil; Turning The Tide.*

4. Peer, Bashir. *Curfew Night.*

5. Joshi , Manoj. *The Lost Rebellion.*

6. Herald, Kashmir. *Harkat ul Jihadi Islami.* : A kashmiri-pandit.org publication, Oct 2002. Vols. Vol 2, No5.

7. Kulkarni, Lt. Gen Ramesh, KarpeAnjali. *Siachen,1987.* New Delhi: Harper Collins Publishers India.

8. Pandita, Rahul. *The Lover Boy of Bahawalpur: How the Pulwama Case was Cracked.* New Delhi, 22 June, 2021.

9. Assad, Bashir. *K FILE.* New Delhi : Renu Kaul Verma Vitasta Publishing Pvt Ltd, 2019.

10. Abdullah, Sheikh. *Flames of Chinar.* New Delhi: Penguin Books India Pvt Ltd., 1993.

11. Adkin, Mark & Yousaf,Mohammad. *The Bear Trap.* Lahore:Jang Publishers, 1992.

12. Ahmad, Shamshad. *Dreams Unfulfilled.* Lahore: Jahangir Books.

13. Ali, Lt Col Syed Ishfaq. *Fangs Of Ice (Story of Siachen).* Rawalpindi: Pak American Commercial Pvt. Ltd, 1991.

14. Akbar, M.J. *India: the Seige Within:Challenges to a Nations Unity.* New Delhi : Roli Books Pvt. Ltd.Lotus Collection, 2003.

15. Report, Associated Press. *India Launches Major Offensive in Kargil.* New Delhi: The News, 17 May, 1999.

16. Aziz, Sartaj. *Between Dreams and Realities: Some Milestones in Pakistan's History.* Karachi: University Press, 2011.

17. Bammi, Lt. Gen Y.M. *Kargil 1999: The Impregnable Conqured.* Dehradun: Natraj Publishers, 2002.

18. Bose, Sumantra. *Kashmir: Roots of Conflict,Paths to Peace.* New Delhi: Vistaar Publications, 2003.

19. Chandra, Ramesh. *United States Views Kargil with Serious Concern.* New Delhi: *The Times Of India,* 1 June, 1999.

20. Deshpande, Urmila. *Kashmir Blues.* New Delhi: Tranquebar Press, 2010.

21. Edited by Ira Pande. *A Tangled Web.* Harper Collins Publishers, 2011.

22. Report, The Kargil review Comittee. *From Surprise to Reckoning.* New Delhi: Sage Publications, 1999.

23. Krishnan, Murali. Battle Reports: Cold facts. *Outlook.* 21 Jun 1999.

24. Malik, General V.P. *From Surprise to Victory.* New Delhi: Harper Collins Publishers, 2007.

25. Raghavan, Lt. Gen V.R. Review Article on Siachen: Conflict without End. *Frontline.* Vol. 19, 23.

26. Jose, Prince. My-Story. *The Logical Indian.* [Online] Jul 25, 2020. [Cited: Oct 10, 2022.] https://thelogicalindian.com/my-story/ kargil-vijay-diwas- 22556.

27. Life, Kashmir. Charar After Mast Gul. *Kashmir Life.* [Online] May 17, 2016. https://kashmirlife.net/charar-after-mast-gul- issue- 09-vol-08-105467/.

28. Malik, Gen VP. Vartalap. *Gen VP Malik speaks about Maj Sudhir Walia. Desh,* July 26, 2020.

29. Chinna, Mann Aman Singh. Article/India. *Indian Express.* [Online] Indian Express, Jul 26, 2018. https://indianexpress.com/article/india/ kargil-war-eight-sikh-played-a-pivotal- role-in-the-capture-of-tiger-hill- says-brigadier-mps-bajwa-5276535/.

30. Talks, Ruchi Singh. Inside story Of Kargil. Brig MPS Bajwa. [Online] 2019. https://www.youtube.com/watch?v=wgIs6Md3LE0.

31. Zehra, Nasim. From Kargil to The Coup: Events That Shook Pakistan. Lahore: Sang-e-Meel, Oct 2018.

32. Harkat-ul-Jihadi al-Islami. Centre for International Security and cooperation. [Online] Stanford University. [Cited: Sep 10, 2021.] https://cisac.fsi.stanford.edu/mappingmilitants/profiles/ harkat-ul- jihadi-al-islami#text_block_17815